Governing Ch

MCGILL-QUEEN'S STUDIES IN THE HISTORY OF RELIGION

Volumes in this series have been supported by the Jackman Foundation of Toronto.

SERIES TWO   In memory of George Rawlyk
Donald Harman Akenson, Editor

1 Marguerite Bourgeoys and Montreal, 1640–1665
   Patricia Simpson

2 Aspects of the Canadian Evangelical Experience
   Edited by G.A. Rawlyk

3 Infinity, Faith, and Time
   Christian Humanism and Renaissance Literature
   John Spencer Hill

4 The Contribution of Presbyterianism to the Maritime Provinces of Canada
   Charles H.H. Scobie and G.A. Rawlyk, editors

5 Labour, Love, and Prayer
   Female Piety in Ulster Religious Literature, 1850–1914
   Andrea Ebel Brozyna

6 The Waning of the Green
   Catholics, the Irish, and Identity in Toronto, 1887–1922
   Mark G. McGowan

7 Religion and Nationality in Western Ukraine
   The Greek Catholic Church and the Ruthenian National Movement in Galicia, 1867–1900
   John-Paul Himka

8 Good Citizens
   British Missionaries and Imperial States, 1870–1918
   James G. Greenlee and Charles M. Johnston, editors

9 The Theology of the Oral Torah
   Revealing the Justice of God
   Jacob Neusner

10 Gentle Eminence
   A Life of George Bernard Cardinal Flahiff
   P. Wallace Platt

11 Culture, Religion, and Demographic Behaviour
   Catholics and Lutherans in Alsace, 1750–1870
   Kevin McQuillan

12 Between Damnation and Starvation
   Priests and Merchants in Newfoundland Politics, 1745–1855
   John P. Greene

13 Martin Luther, German Saviour
   German Evangelical Theological Factions and the Interpretation of Luther, 1917–1933
   James M. Stayer

14 Modernity and the Dilemma of North American Anglican Identities, 1880–1950
   William Katerberg

15 The Methodist Church on the Prairies, 1896–1914
   George Emery

16 Christian Attitudes towards the State of Israel, 1948–2000
   Paul Charles Merkley

17 A Social History of the Cloister
   Daily Life in the Teaching Monasteries of the Old Regime
   Elizabeth Rapley

18 Households of Faith
   Family, Religion, and Community in Canada, 1760–1969
   Nancy Christie, editor

19 Blood Ground
 Colonialism, Missions, and the
 Contest for Christianity inn the
 Cape Colony and Britain,
 1799-1853
 Elizabeth Elbourne

20 A History of Canadian Catholics
 Gallicanism, Romanism,
 and Canadianism
 Terence J. Fay

21 Archbishop Stagni's Reports on the
 Ontario Bilingual Schools
 Question, 1915
 *Translated and Edited
 by John Zucchi*

22 The Founding Moment
 Church, Society, and the
 Construction of Trinity College
 William Westfall

23 The Holocaust, Israel, and
 Canadian Protestant Churches
 Haim Genizi

24 Governing Charities
 Church and State in Toronto's
 Catholic Archdiocese,
 1850–1950
 Paula Maurutto

SERIES ONE
G.A. Rawlyk, Editor

1 Small Differences
 Irish Catholics and Irish Protestants,
 1815–1922
 An International Perspective
 Donald Harman Akenson

2 Two Worlds
 The Protestant Culture of
 Nineteenth-Century Ontario
 William Westfall

3 An Evangelical Mind
 Nathanael Burwash and the
 Methodist Tradition in Canada,
 1839–1918
 Marguerite Van Die

4 The Dévotes
 Women and Church in
 Seventeenth-Century France
 Elizabeth Rapley

5 The Evangelical Century
 College and Creed in English
 Canada from the Great Revival to
 the Great Depression
 Michael Gauvreau

6 The German Peasants' War and
 Anabaptist Community of Goods
 James M. Stayer

7 A World Mission
 Canadian Protestantism and the
 Quest for an New International
 Order, 1918–1939
 Robert Wright

8 Serving the Present Age
 Revivalism, Progressivism, and the
 Methodist Tradition in Canada
 Phyllis D. Airhart

9 A Sensitive Independence
 Canadian Methodist Women
 Missionaries in Canada and
 the Orient, 1881–1925
 Rosemary R. Gagan

10 God's Peoples
 Covenant and Land in South Africa,
 Israel, and Ulster
 Donald Harman Akenson

11 Creed and Culture
 The Place of English-Speaking
 Catholics in Canadian Society,
 1750–1930
 *Terrence Murphy and Gerald Stortz,
 editors*

12 Piety and Nationalism
 Lay Voluntary Associations and the
 Creation of an Irish-Catholic
 Community in Toronto, 1850–1895
 Brian P. Clarke

13 Amazing Grace
   Studies in Evangelicalism in
   Australia, Britain, Canada, and the
   United States
   *George Rawlyk and Mark A. Noll,
   editors*

14 Children of Peace
   W. John McIntyre

15 A Solitary Pillar
   Montreal's Anglican Church and
   the Quiet Revolution
   John Marshall

16 Padres in No Man's Land
   Canadian Chaplains and
   the Great War
   Duff Crerar

17 Christian Ethics and Political
   Economy in North America
   A Critical Analysis of U.S. and
   Canadian Approaches
   P. Travis Kroeker

18 Pilgrims in Lotus Land
   Conservative Protestantism in
   British Columbia, 1917–1981
   Robert K. Burkinshaw

19 Through Sunshine and Shadow
   The Woman's Christian Temperance
   Union, Evangelicalism, and Reform
   in Ontario, 1874–1930
   Sharon Cook

20 Church, College, and Clergy
   A History of Theological Education
   at Knox College, Toronto,
   1844–1994
   Brian J. Fraser

21 The Lord's Dominion
   The History of Canadian Methodism
   Neil Semple

22 A Full-Orbed Christianity
   The Protestant Churches and Social
   Welfare in Canada, 1900–1940
   *Nancy Christie and
   Michael Gauvreau*

23 Evangelism and Apostasy
   The Evolution and Impact of
   Evangelicals in Modern Mexico
   Kurt Bowen

24 The Chignecto Covenanters
   A Regional History of Reformed
   Presbyterianism in New Brunswick
   and Nova Scotia, 1827 to 1905
   Eldon Hay

25 Methodists and Women's Education
   in Ontario, 1836–1925
   Johanna M. Selles

26 Puritanism and Historical
   Controversy
   William Lamont

Governing Charities

Church and State in Toronto's Catholic Archdiocese, 1850–1950

PAULA MAURUTTO

McGill-Queen's University Press
Montreal & Kingston · London · Ithaca

© McGill-Queen's University Press 2003
ISBN 0-7735-2534-3 (cloth)
ISBN 0-7735-2535-1 (paper)

Legal deposit second quarter 2003
Bibliothèque nationale du Québec

Printed in Canada on acid-free paper that is 100% ancient forest free (100% post-consumer recycled), processed chlorine free.

This book has been published with the help of a grant from the Humanities and Social Sciences Federation of Canada, using funds provided by the Social Sciences and Humanities Research Council of Canada.

McGill-Queen's University Press acknowledges the support of the Canada Council for the Arts for our publishing program. We also acknowledge the financial support of the Government of Canada through the Book Publishing Industry Development Program (BPIDP) for our publishing activities.

National Library of Canada Cataloguing in Publication

Maurutto, Paula, 1966–
   Governing charities: church and state in Toronto's Catholic archdiocese, 1850s–1950s / Paula Maurutto.
   (McGill-Queen's studies in the history of religion. Series two; 24)
   Includes bibliographical references and index.
   ISBN 0-7735-2534-3 (bound).–ISBN 0-7735-2535-1 (pbk.)
   1. Catholic Church–Ontario–Toronto–Charities–History.
   I. Title. II. Series.
BX1424.T6M38 2003   361.7'5'08822   C2002-904586-X

This book was typeset by Dynagram Inc. in 10/13 Sabon.

For Daniel and my mother, Anna, with love
Questo libro e dedicato a mia mamma, Anna, e a Daniel

Contents

Acknowledgments xiii

Introduction 3

1 The Origins of a Catholic Benevolent Enterprise, 1850s–1890s 15

2 Market Mechanisms and Charity Governance 30

3 From Catholic Charity to Catholic Welfare: The Impact of Social Work 45

4 Social Casework during the Depression 66

5 Private Policing and Surveillance of Catholics, 1920–1960 82

6 The Role of Catholic Private Agencies in Community Corrections, 1890–1940 103

Conclusion 125

Appendices

1 Catholics in the Toronto Region, 1841–1960 131

2 Catholic Charities in the Archdiocese of Toronto, 1849–1930s 133

3 Provincial and Municipal Grants to the Protestant House of Industry and the Catholic House of Providence in the City of Toronto for the Years 1870–1880   136

4 Provincial and Municipal Grants to Protestant and Catholic Orphanages in the City of Toronto for the Years 1870–1880   137

5 Catholic Welfare Bureau Year-End Report on Charitable Work with Single Unemployed Men, 1933–1939   138

6 Monthly Report of the Family Welfare Division, Catholic Welfare Bureau, on Charitable Work with Families on Poor Relief, 1932–1933   139

7 Casework Assessment Form Used by the Family Welfare Division, Catholic Welfare Bureau, with Poor Relief Applicants   140

Notes   143

Index   181

Tables

2.1 Provincial grants to Toronto charities, 1874–1875 35

4.1 Social problems outlined in the Catholic Welfare Bureau 1935 annual report for family agency 79

6.1 Number of juveniles in Catholic industrial schools, 1930–1935 109

Acknowledgments

The assistance of many people made this book possible. Mariana Valverde was the first to encourage me to pursue the topic, and I benefited enormously from her theoretical insights, extensive criticism, confidence in my abilities, and friendship. Her scholarship has shaped this book and my intellectual development in significant ways. Gordon Darroch introduced me to historical sociology and taught me much about grounding insights in empirical study. I learned much about research and writing from Lorna Erwin, who was a constant source of intellectual and personal support. I am indebted to her and to Penni Stewart for providing office space and a feminist working environment. I would also like to thank Susan Houston, Roberto Perin, and in particular, James Struthers, who provided thoughtful critiques of my work.

Most of the book's research was conducted at the Archives of the Roman Catholic Archdiocese of Toronto, where I received expert assistance from Marc Lerman, Suzanne Lout, and Linda Wicks. At the Archives of Ontario, I benefited from the able help of Daniel H. Bryant and Leon Warmski. As well, I wish to recognize the capable assistance of George Wharton, of the Toronto Archives and Records Centre, and Sister Mary Jane Trimble, of the Sisters of St Joseph Archives.

Funding for this project was provided by the Social Sciences and Humanities Research Council of Canada, the Ontario Graduate Scholarship program, and the Mariano Elia Chair Scholarship in Italian Studies, York University.

Members of my dissertation writing group were especially helpful and encouraging. For their insights and support, I thank Mariana Valverde, Lucy Luccisano, Kelly Hannah-Moffat, Carol Ann O'Brien, Jacinth Samuels, Janice Hill, Lealle Ruhl, and Annette Bickford. Thanks also to Ruth Urbach for her support. I would also like to thank the anonymous reviewers at McGill-Queen's University Press for their invaluable advice and criticism. Thanks also to Elizabeth Hulse for her careful editing and to Cheryl Lemmens, who compiled the index.

I received a tremendous amount of support from my sister and her family: Agnese, Domenico, Stefania, and Nando DeFrancesco. I am indebted to my lifelong friend Lucy Luccisano for her daily phone calls, which made the writing process endurable. She spent endless hours over numerous espressos helping me refine ideas.

My mother, in many ways that she may not recognize, provided the stability, support, and inspiration needed to complete this work. She, along with my late father, Nino, taught me much about the Catholic Church.

Daniel Robinson was my best critic. His passion for history helped to minimize historical errors. I thank him for his continuous emotional and intellectual support, which ensured the completion of my work. He more than anyone will take pleasure in the publication of this book. Jacob and Cailan, our sons, brought us endless love, laughter, and joy.

Governing Charities

Introduction

In Canada, as in many other countries, the retrenchment of the welfare state in recent years is said to have generated a rebirth of the charity sector. As governments dismantle Canada's social security system, they are calling for a return to the alleged historic roots of voluntarism. Voluntarism is being promoted as the solution to the excesses of the welfare state, a solution in keeping with the new consensus about balanced budgets and low tax rates. In much of this discourse about the fiscal and ethical virtues of voluntarism, it is assumed that charities and the state are quite distinct. This view is accurate neither historically nor in the contemporary context. Because of the conventional belief in the separateness of the two spheres, however, little research has been devoted to their interconnection.

Increasingly, governments are claiming responsibility for stimulating the growth of voluntarism. In a 1983 address to the Progressive Conservative Party, Brian Mulroney claimed that social programs would be reformed by "encouraging the voluntary sector to participate more in the implementation of social programmes. Volunteer work is the most efficient method of work in Canada."[1] In Ontario in 1995, a week after cutting welfare benefits by 22 per cent, Premier Mike Harris announced in the throne speech the future appointment of a parliamentary assistant to the premier who would promote voluntarism in Ontario.[2] And in December 2001 the Liberal prime minister, Jean Chrétien, announced a landmark "accord" between his government and the voluntary sector that would "strengthen" relations between the two and further the "capacity" of the voluntary sector.[3] Governments not only are looking to charities to pick up the slack as they continue to slash social programs, but are directly involved in the promotion of the voluntary sector.[4]

That there are more than 77,000 registered charities in Canada is one illustration of the federal government's commitment to licensing charity operations.[5] Ontario's workfare program is another, more concrete example of how governments have entered into partnerships with the charity sector. Workfare, still in the pilot-project phase, requires welfare recipients to take on jobs with local communities in order to receive their benefits. Such projects are thought to be beneficial to all involved parties: the state claims that this approach will reduce welfare provisions; the work of charities is supposedly stimulated with new, however reluctant, volunteers; and welfare recipients are said to be empowered with self-esteem as they work for benefits and acquire new skills (even though these skills may be untransferable to the paid labour market). Moreover, as homelessness increases in response to declining welfare benefits and more stringent eligibility criteria, municipalities are supporting the expansion of homeless shelters. Toronto's Out of the Cold program, founded in 1987 by Sister Susan Moran and consisting of forty-three temporary shelters for the homeless in churches and synagogues throughout the city, is heavily subsidized by the municipality. In 1997 the City of Toronto donated $150,000 to open another shelter, St Mary's Home, also run by Sister Moran. As well, the city agreed to fund the home with per diem grants from its emergency housing office.

The shift away from government-sponsored social welfare programs is emblematic of a return to a more laissez-faire market orientation. Governments are said to have in the past played a far too interventionist role in social welfare, building large expensive, centralized, bureaucratic structures that have stifled personal initiative and community responsibility, while fuelling a soaring debt crisis. The Canadian debt crisis is portrayed as a product of mismanaged social programs that have "thrown money" at problems and failed to respond properly to the needs of clients. Little is said about the impact of personal and corporate tax reductions on debt growth. On the other hand, private provisions are increasingly perceived as more efficient because, as governments claim, they can respond to social service "consumers" (formerly referred to as "clients") more quickly and effectively than large bureaucracies. Their loose structures enable them to more easily modify their services to cater to the needs of their communities. Government services are being blamed for slowing down the growth and development of the charity sector and, in the process, increasing dependency and inefficiency. According to Jacquelyn T. Scott, neo-conservative governments are justifying their reduction in programs as "a morally responsible action because it motivates people to become altruistic."[6]

What is not talked about in neo-conservative discourses on the changing role of welfare and charity is the extent to which governments regulate private social programs. The rolling back of state welfare programs should not be confused with a quantitative reduction in governance. Non-profit agencies may be assuming greater responsibility for the delivery of social services previously administered by the state, but they do not operate autonomously. Instead, voluntary agencies are increasingly subjected to regulatory and accounting processes. Charities are compelled to conform to legislative requirements and to manage their agencies as quasi-businesses in competition with other organizations for scarce resources. They are also subjected to various forms of inspection, accounting, and auditing practices that make their internal operations more visible to state bureaucracies. The discursive dichotomy between welfare and charity reflects a neo-conservative practice in which the state disperses, extends, and obscures the channels by which it continues to regulate the charity sector. Thus we need to examine more closely the claims made by governments as they advocate a less interventionist state.

More specifically, we need to question the construction of the charity sector as a private sphere of civil society. Most discussions and studies of social services represent welfare as the domain of the state and charities as the preserve of private bodies. Little is known or said about how charities have historically relied on substantial public subsidies. Claims that we are returning to a pre-welfare "era of voluntarism" ignore the extent to which governments were involved in the regulation and funding of local charities. Neo-conservative governments, and thinkers and writers outside government, are promoting the view that welfare states stifle the growth of charities. Yet charities flourished under the welfare state, and they did so with large amounts of public subsidies. Many of the studies on "the welfare state" or "the voluntary sector" have ignored the interrelation between the public and the private in governing social services, and in the process they have made less visible the complexity and contradictions residing in social service delivery.

The objective of this book is to provide a historical overview of the linkages between the state and voluntary agencies in the governing of both charities and their clients. More specifically, it examines the interrelation between Toronto's Roman Catholic archdiocese and provincial and municipal governments in order to illuminate the historical development of partnerships and joint ventures in Ontario's welfare history. This historical review serves to underscore how contemporary restructuring practices are not new phenomena arising in response to the retrenchment of the welfare state. They have historical roots dating back to the 1850s. The principal foci of this study are the following: the ways in which Catholic charities in the Roman Catholic Archdiocese of Toronto have acted as distributary agents of the state; the ties between such non-profit agencies and the state in the regulation of recipients' private lives; and the techniques and programs developed to govern the Catholic voluntary sector. Some of these practices date back to the 1850s, when Catholic charities were first established, but the major part of this study concerns the period from 1900 to 1940, when the foundations for the later ties between public and private agents were laid.

In tracing these connections between the Catholic Church in Toronto and the provincial and municipal governments, the book calls into question received accounts of Canadian social services. Much of the historical writing on the welfare state suggests that welfarism represented a fundamental rupture with earlier, voluntary forms of social service delivery.[7] Nineteenth-century Ontario is described as lacking a conception of public welfare, a society in which the poor were largely left to the benevolence of religious charities. Consider here Stephen Speisman's claim that, "prior to 1900, the very religious character of Toronto mitigated against the assumption of social welfare responsibilities by the city government."[8] On a closer examination, however, it becomes clear that, since the late 1820s, governments, in cooperation with benevolent organizations, have been involved in regulating voluntary agencies.[9] Rainer Baehre traces the development of public subsidies back to 1828, when the provincial treasury began providing small grants to support the Emigrant Temporary Asylum.[10] These initial grants heralded a new era in social welfare practice, in which assistance to the needy increasingly took the form of partial state support for organized institutions. By 1837, public funds were regularly channelled through Toronto's House of Industry, a Protestant poorhouse. Although these grants were administered and dispersed by House of Industry volunteers and were perceived by recipients as charity, they were nonetheless in part government money. Lynne Marks argues that in many small Ontario communities, charities were almost non-existent during the late nineteenth century.[11] In Ingersoll, Cobourg, Mount Forest, and Belleville, municipal councils, for the most part, provided the bulk, if not all, the poor relief budget. This public money, however, continued to be administered by local women's associations, which decided how to distribute the funds to the deserving poor. In other small communities, local municipal councils secured and distributed the funds themselves, as there were few voluntary organizations in existence. According to Jane Lewis, the historical perception of charity as independent from state processes functioned as a "superior instrument" of the state, "in that the poor could never claim relief as a right."[12] In other words, the belief that charities operated independently from the state served as a political tool that concealed the extent of state intervention.

This study also disputes the characterization of the welfare state as an evolutionary progression from a pre-1920 "golden age" when the churches dominated the voluntary sector to a modern, scientific, and secular welfare state. As welfare bureaucracies began to expand during the 1930s and 1940s, they did so by building stronger links with private voluntary agencies, not by disabling them. Far from being shunted aside, the private agencies, such as Catholic charities, became increasingly entrenched within the expanding welfare state system. The Catholic and Jewish Children's Aid Societies, for example, continued to operate during the welfare state era and were eligible for public subsidies equivalent to those granted to the non-denominational Children's Aid Society. And during the height of the Depression, the Catholic Welfare Bureau was one of the main relief-granting agencies in the city. Since the 1930s, municipal governments have assumed increasing responsibility and control over welfare provisions, but they have also developed extensive cooperative ventures and partnerships with the nonprofit sector, which itself has undergone expansion and growth.

Welfarism in this work is envisioned not simply as the growth of an interventionist state but, rather, as a new way of governing social problems. It is understood as having emerged in response to a range of social problems, including ill health, declining birth rates, delinquency, anti-social behaviour, and problem families. Although not new problems, with the rise of the social sciences – in particular, psychology, psychiatry, criminology, sociology, and social work – these issues began to be conceptualized, problematized, and regulated in new ways. Increasingly, national growth was tied to the well-being of society and the minimization of social risk through universal social programs and social scientific expertise. In the words of Nikolas Rose and Peter Miller, "the key innovations of welfarism lay in the attempts to link the fiscal, calculative and bureaucratic capacities of the apparatus of the state to the government of social life."[13] Such a perspective eschews a dichotomous or evolutionary analysis and explores the multiple players and strategies included in welfarism. It rejects the assumption that social welfare is the domain of the state.

The term "governance" is used to characterize the governing of charities, from their inception in the 1830s through to the contemporary era, as the product of multiple interactions and interdependencies. This focus is not to deny the importance of either voluntary or state actors in the governance of welfare. Rather, the intent is to unravel how the administration of charities involved a number of calculations and strategies that were the outcome of a complex negotiated exchange between numerous actors. This loosely Foucaultian approach, while not used everywhere or to the exclusion of other perspectives or methodologies, has been highly influential in focusing my attention on the *techniques* of governance – not only on the techniques used by charities to govern the poor but on the much less studied techniques used by government and semi-governmental bodies to regulate the work of charities.[14]

Much welfare history has generated explanations based on, and presupposing, an often idealist notion of "changing ideologies." For instance, the welfare state is sometimes said to be directly related to the rise of new notions of social citizenship. Reacting to this focus on ideology/discourse, Marxist writers have often described the goals and ideals of various government programs as "mere rhetoric," as an ideological cover for the "real interests" of the ruling classes. The loosely Foucaultian perspectives that are being developed by those calling themselves "historians of the present" break through the dichotomy of ideology versus interests, discourse versus material reality, by focusing analytic attention on neither discourses nor interests, but rather, on an important realm generally left unstudied (or studied only by empiricist historians of administrative law) – what is called here "techniques of governance." The focus on administration techniques is designed to highlight the "effects" of administration, that is, how it became possible to regulate charities in Ontario. Such tools as standardized yearly reports, inspections in person, audits, case records, and urban mapping are essential technological innovations that, while not "determining" particular social policies, can nevertheless shed much light on shifts in policy and programming.

Insofar as government bodies demanded the implementation of some of these techniques among the charities subject to inspection and funding, governments exercised a great deal of control under the apparently neutral and non-directive banner of "administration." A focus on techniques reveals how the governing of the charity sector was made possible through the invention, modification, and deployment of apparatuses and devices that shaped practices and the understanding of problems so as to achieve certain ends. Paying due attention to the realm of administrative detail – which is often neglected by those pursuing the analysis of either high politics or economic interests – reveals how what will here be called "the mixed social economy" was made technically possible. Without very specific reporting, inspection, and auditing techniques, there could not have been a smooth articulation of public powers and philanthropic resources. It is this articulation that forms the main topic of this book.

This study pays particular attention to the emergence of social work as a mechanism for governing social problems through techniques of assessment and treatment. According to the Foucaultian governmentality literature, governing problem populations or individuals necessitates that they be constructed into definable categories from which knowledge can be formed. As Rose argues, by "rendering subjectivity calculable it makes persons amenable to having things done to them."[15] The application of social casework, for example, enabled social problems to be measured, calculated, and compared in terms of norms and abnormalities. It turned social problems into categories that could be analyzed, diagnosed, and monitored over time. The information afforded by case records was used to diagnose, reform, and improve individuals through education and rehabilitation. It was through the production of such techniques as casework that individuals were made amenable to intervention by both private agencies and the state.

The professionalization of social services is often interpreted as having thwarted the role of voluntary organizations. The rise of social science, and the corresponding professionalization of psychologists, psychiatrists, and social workers, is said to have precipitated the collapse of religious-based charities.[16] Although, by the 1920s, volunteers were increasingly being replaced with the graduates of university social work departments, this development was not coterminous with the displacement of denominational services. The Catholic Church, for instance, embraced social scientific methodologies and began to train and hire its own professional staff. Catholic charities restructured themselves to incorporate the new scientific methods of social casework. Even within Protestant denominations, as the work of Nancy Christie and Michael Gauvreau demonstrates, religious reformers were at the forefront of social scientific advancements. Christie and Gauvreau argue that, "unlike the fate of progressive reform in the United States, which after World War I became increasingly divorced from Christian endeavour, in Canada the increasing specialization in the social sciences, the creation of such new professions as social work, and the growing dependence of government upon expert scientific knowledge – the hall-mark of modern social policy creation – occurred under the governance of the Protestant Churches."[17] They further add that it was "under the banner of evangelicalism" that the modern profession of social work was founded.[18]

Most studies of religion and social welfare history, including that by Christie and Gauvreau, focus primarily on Protestant organizations. The contributions of Catholic and Jewish charities have been largely ignored by historians and sociologists. Collectively, Canadian social welfare history has reproduced the hegemonic dominance of the Protestant churches. Even within Catholic history, relatively little research has focused on benevolent institutions.[19] Yet the making of the voluntary sector, at least in Ontario, hinged on the active participation of numerous denominational social services. Furthermore, the existing analyses make little effort to describe the connections between non-Catholic organizations and the various levels of government.[20] However, a closer examination of the daily operations of religious-based charities reveals the extent to which they were linked to state processes.

Few historical studies explore the interplay between non-profit agencies and the public sector. Notable exceptions include work by Mariana Valverde, Margaret Little, and Lynne Marks.[21] These studies, like my own work, draw on Valverde's concepts of the governance of the "mixed social economy" and moral regulation. The mixed social economy offers an analytic framework for deconstructing the dichotomies between public and private and between state and civil society by highlighting the "complex web of relationships" involved in the operation of the charity sector. It sheds light on how the state supports voluntary action through subsidies, information, and legal sanctions. It also reveals how new policy directions did not always originate with the state but, rather, were often encouraged and lobbied for by non-profit agencies. As Valverde notes, "studying the regulation of charities has shown that at least in the social service sector, and possibly in other spheres as well, there is not one public/private split but many, depending on whether we are discussing financing, service delivery, or inspection and regulation. Each of these private/public distinctions is subject to major shifts in the relative weight of each pole."[22] The concept of the mixed social economy, in conjunction with the focus on techniques of governance, entails advancing beyond the study of who governs in order to investigate how governing was made possible through the production of techniques that were promoted, modified, and deployed by various actors.

Explorations of the mixed social economy have tended to focus on its emergence in the Victorian or pre-welfare-state era, as in the work of Valverde, Little, and Marks, or on the development of contemporary partnerships, as in the work of Josephine Rekart.[23] James Struthers, however, explores how these relationships arose in private nursing care during the heyday of the welfare state.[24] In the face of inadequate social welfare programs for the aged, private for-profit agencies gained incorporation into Ontario's health care sector.

While Valverde and others mostly confine their analyses of the mixed social economy to the charity sector, the concept is used here in the last two chapters to examine the interplay between the Catholic Church, professional experts, and the state in the areas of policing, national security, and the criminal justice system.[25] Policing and law enforcement are redefined as phenomena that operated beyond the exclusive domain of the state. For example, in the 1930s the Catholic Archdiocese of Toronto hired its own spies to root out, infiltrate, and report on communist activity in the city. The archdiocese also operated industrial schools for the rehabilitation of juvenile delinquents and ran parole and probationary services with the aid of the state. This analysis seeks to develop a broader notion of national security and policing by examining the interplay between public and private institutions in the surveillance of families and the regulation of juvenile delinquents.

A focus on the governance of the mixed social economy also eschews a reductionist analysis in which regulation is coextensive with state control or the interests of a particular dominant group. Hence regulation is not reduced to one set of relations, be they class, as in the Marxist perspective; patriarchy, as posited by many brands of feminism; or social control, as presented by socialization theorists. Even some works that adopted a Foucaultian perspective maintain a state-centred focus, such as Philip Corrigan and Derek Sayer on British state formation and Bruce Curtis on nineteenth-century Canadian education.[26] This monofocal analysis ignores the complexity in which regulation is exercised through multiple and contradictory sites.

Catholic-run agencies can not be understood simply as coopted by the state. They had their own agendas, and their governing priorities more often reflected directives from Rome than from Ottawa. The working relationship between the church and municipal and provincial governments came about because these institutions viewed their collaboration as mutually beneficial. Immigration, poverty, vice, and crime were seen as social problems in need of moral reform by both public and private authorities. Miller and Rose use Collon and Latour's idea of "*interessement*" to illustrate how networks are established "not because of legal or institutional ties or dependencies but because they have come to construe their problems in allied ways and their fate as in some way bound up with one another."[27] Both the church and the state saw their interdependence as crucial to achieving their respective goals.

This analysis is not intended as a detailed historical account of the development of Catholic benevolent work. Nor does it deal much with Catholic intellectual history. The objective is to highlight significant trends, techniques, and devices that affected the development and organization of Catholic charities. As well, it documents the influential role played by the Catholic Church in shaping social welfare provisions in Toronto. Given the emphasis on the interrelation between voluntary institutions and the state, the analysis is limited primarily to charitable works that received government funding. Hence the important voluntary work performed by organizations such as the St Vincent de Paul Society and the Catholic Women's League, among others, does not figure prominently in the discussion, despite these organizations' significant contributions to the relief of the poor. They were primarily organized at the parish, rather than a city-wide, level, and they did not receive public grants. Moreover, they were far more involved in promoting devotional, rather than philanthropic, aims. As there is no extensive literature that deals with the history of Catholic charities, the book relies heavily on secondary sources to contextualize more than a hundred years of Catholic charity in Toronto.

This study comprises six chapters. Chapter 1 charts the origins of the mixed social economy in English Canada since the 1830s, and it traces the emergence of a Catholic voluntary infrastructure in Toronto from the 1850s to the 1930s. As no full-length history of Catholic charities in English Canada exists, this chapter analyzes in detail the early development of Toronto's Catholic voluntary structure. Chapter 2 examines early administrative techniques that formed the basis of a "business" ethos among benevolent organizations. Accounting systems, bookkeeping, annual reports, standardized forms, and the rise of inspectors served to make independent charities more accountable to the directives of both state bodies and the central hierarchy of the Catholic Archdiocese of Toronto. In chapter 3 I document the role of Toronto's Catholic Church in the areas of social reform and social work during the interwar period. Far from being displaced by secularizing trends, the church, by cooperating with other denominational institutions, was an active participant in the promotion of an expanded state welfare system and the burgeoning social work profession. Chapter 4 examines the role of the Catholic Welfare Bureau in Toronto's public relief structure during the Depression. As governments directed more attention to the pressing problem of poverty during the 1930s, they looked to private charities to assist them in both monitoring and providing relief to the growing destitute population. During this period, the Catholic Welfare Bureau emerged as one of the city's main relief-granting agencies.

The final two chapters highlight the involvement of the Catholic Church in law enforcement, the criminal justice system, and the maintenance of national security. Chapter 5 explores the private policing and surveillance tactics adopted by the church to prevent the spread of communism, particularly within its congregation. Catholic "spies" and informants kept the church abreast of "subversive" manoeuvrings in ethnic communities, in religious organizations, and on university campuses. Organizations such as the Catholic Welfare Bureau and the Catholic Friendship House worked to curb the spread of communism among ethnic congregations, the unemployed, and the destitute. Chapter 6 analyzes the Catholic archdiocese's role in the sentencing, institutionalization, and after-care of juvenile offenders. Responsibility for disciplining delinquent youth devolved almost exclusively on privately run institutions such as the Catholic industrial schools and the parole and probationary services of the Catholic Big Brothers and Catholic Big Sisters.

The study concludes with a discussion of the relevance of this historical study to neo-conservative welfare trends. The agility with which conservative governments have cut welfare services has much to do with the long-standing presence of charities. Private charities such as those of the Catholic Church did not disappear during the heyday of state welfarism. Rather, they flourished under considerable government support and financing. Since the mid-1970s, successive neo-liberal and neo-conservative governments have been able to off-load public programs by tapping into this pre-existing voluntary sector, whose infrastructure has quickly expanded to meet the challenge. Thus the partnerships and joint ventures that characterize contemporary social service delivery in Canada are not new phenomena; their roots date back to the mixed social economy of the mid-1800s.

1 The Origins of a Catholic Benevolent Enterprise, 1850s-1890s

The 1850s marked the rise of a Catholic charity infrastructure in Toronto. Previously, benevolent aid had been distributed by local parish communities, but a city-wide charity organization did not emerge until the influx of thousands of destitute Catholics, many of whom had escaped the Irish potato famine. As the number of Catholic poor in the city expanded, the church responded by establishing its own centralized benevolent institutions. From their inception, these institutions rarely operated independently from government assistance. In fact, their viability depended on government financing and legislative support.

This chapter provides a historical examination of the development of Catholic charities within the wider socio-political and economic context of nineteenth-century Toronto. First, I review the impetus for the formation of charities in Upper Canada during the late 1820s. I then focus more directly on the rise of Catholic charities in Toronto during the 1850s. Attention is paid to the predominant ultramontane world view of this period and the political and religious tensions between Catholic and Protestants that promoted the formation of a separate and distinct Catholic charity infrastructure. Finally, I explore the beginnings of cooperative social reform efforts between Catholics and Protestants. As religious tensions began to subside by the 1880s, Protestants and Catholics came to share a mutual interest in promoting social reform and increased government intervention in social welfare. Yet their visions of benevolent work continued to be marked by striking differences. While Protestants adopted a more philanthropic approach in which social aid hinged on the moral reform of individual character, Catholics largely maintained a commitment to a charity-based model.

THE DEVELOPMENT OF PUBLIC SOCIAL WELFARE, 1820S–1840S

Public social welfare in Canada dates back to the late 1820s. In 1828 the Emigrant Temporary Asylum for the relief of the poor received its first monetary instalment from the government of Upper Canada,[1] and by 1839 the receiver general was allocating annual public grants to Toronto's House of Industry, a Protestant-run poorhouse. This early public involvement in social welfare was in part a response to changing public perceptions, which by the early 1830s linked poverty to health risks; it also reflected a growing preoccupation with the merits of laissez-faire liberalism. Cholera epidemics in 1832 and 1834 drew attention to "the perils" of poverty. Concerns for the health of the indigent were brought to the foreground as poorer districts of the city were perceived to be infested enclaves from which disease would spread to more affluent neighbourhoods. Added to this concern, the growth of a permanent class of paupers following the depression of 1837 challenged the perception of poverty as a temporary condition that could be overcome in "the land of opportunity." This burgeoning shift in public opinion stimulated a growing demand for a public response to social distress. New social reform movements began denouncing the imprisonment of the homeless in city gaols, and they called for the erection of houses of refuge to care for the destitute. As these movements gained momentum, public responsibility for social welfare was redefined. Governments and charitable organizations would henceforth be increasingly called upon to play a greater regulatory role in social questions.[2]

This trend was not specific to Upper Canada; similar developments had emerged in Britain and the United States. The 1820s saw the emergence of what Jacques Donzelot refers to as the beginning of "the social" and what Mary Poovey describes as the "making of a social body."[3] According to Donzelot and Poovey, the 1820s sparked a new mode of governing such social problems as morality, health, poverty, and crime. Social governance, or the specific concern with "the social," arose in response to the failure of laissez-faire liberalism to address the pressing urban issues of poverty and crime. The social sphere consisted of a set of problems which, although related to both the economic and the political spheres, did not fall squarely in either category. According to Poovey, "in the 1830s, the statistical societies founded throughout Great Britain repeated and elaborated this categorization by separating 'social' topics like education and crime from economic subjects like imports and exports."[4] This new sphere, or mode of governing citizens, relied on the intervention of public and private powers. Indeed, Donzelot argues that what was specifically novel about governing through the social was that it opened up the private sphere of the family to government regulation.

Donzelot is careful to note that this type of intervention did not simply introduce a new way of repressing families. Rather, they actively participated in these new modes of governing the social. The regulation of the social through moral reform and the encouragement of hygienic norms and methods of saving would not have functioned successfully without the active involvement and cooperation of families. In the case of Catholic charities in Toronto, the Irish poor participated in charitable endeavours not simply because of financial need but because they came to view a charity infrastructure as crucial to the maintenance of their cultural heritage and their kin groups.

In Canadian social welfare literature, few studies have documented the rise of the social as a new site of regulation. Typically, the rejection of the English Poor Law by Upper Canada in 1792 is cited as evidence of the state's reluctance to intervene in matters relating to poverty. Yet as Rainer Baehre and Richard Splane illustrate, governments and public opinion were not opposed to the principle of public support; what they rejected was the use of property taxation to support poorhouses.[5] Moreover, while initially governments may have lacked the authority to draw on property taxes, by the mid-1830s the province had licensed municipalities to draw on such taxes for the specific use of poor relief. The 1837 House of Industry Act was the first piece of legislation that allowed municipalities to collect taxes on rateable property for the sole purpose of erecting houses of refuge. A succession of acts in 1846, 1849, 1853, and 1866 strengthened the power of municipalities to extract taxable income in support of local charities. The Municipal Institutions Act of 1866 enabled taxes to be appropriated from general revenues.[6] Although most of these measures had little effect, since few were routinely enforced, nevertheless they reveal a growing involvement by provincial and municipal governments in questions of poor relief.[7]

Indeed, Ontario's charity sector has always been a distinctively public and private venture. According to Richard Splane, the history of social welfare in Ontario before Confederation can best be described as "a sharing of responsibility between public and private bodies that was to become an enduring characteristic of social welfare organization in Ontario."[8] The prevailing pattern was one of joint ventures and collaborative endeavours between the public and private realms. Governments and voluntary agencies were increasingly drawn into partnerships as they sought to govern social problems. The case of the Catholic Church is an illustrative example.

CREATING A CATHOLIC CHARITY INFRASTRUCTURE, 1840s–1860s

A city-wide Catholic charity infrastructure in Toronto did not emerge until the 1850s. Prior to this, benevolent aid was limited to disbursements by local parishes. In 1841 Toronto's Catholic population was a mere 2,400, and the church lacked the institutional infrastructure necessary for the support of Catholic charities. By the 1850s the situation had changed drastically. A series of events provided the impetus for the development of a charity system. These included the elevation of the Toronto Catholic Church to diocesan status in 1841; the influx of Irish immigrants following the potato famine of the 1840s; conflicts with the Protestant Orange Order; and the appointment in 1850 of Bishop Armand-François-Marie de Charbonnel.

Initially, the Catholic Church had lacked a central power base to facilitate the coordination of a city-wide relief operation. It was only in 1841 that the church in Toronto was organized into a diocese (it became an archdiocese in 1870). Previously it had consisted of individual parishes under the See of Kingston, whose ecclesiastical administration lay in Quebec City. With the appointment of Michael Power as the first bishop of Toronto in 1842 (a post he held until his death in 1847), the episcopal authority of the church in the city was strengthened. The bishop gained centralized control over the Catholic community, including such areas as financial resources and service provisions. Prior to Power's arrival, charitable fundraising efforts were limited to individual parishes, which rarely generated sufficient funds for an organized benevolent infrastructure. But the prestige and reverence embodied in the bishop attracted a broad range of support. In effect, the appointment of a bishop enabled a transformation from social action defined largely by individual efforts to a coordinated organizational infrastructure, a change that proved pivotal to the church's ability to respond adequately to the social welfare needs of the growing Irish immigrant population.[9]

In the short span of ten years the Catholic population of Toronto more than tripled, growing from 2,400 in 1841 to 7,940 in 1851[10] (see appendix 1). This increase was spurred primarily by Irish immigrants fleeing the potato famine of the 1840s.[11] Most of them were poor immigrants who settled in urban slums occasionally beset by cholera or typhoid. The growing threat of disease and the sheer number of impoverished families were unprecedented challenges for the Catholic Church. By the 1870s, Catholics comprised 50 per cent of those receiving poor relief in the city, though they made up only 21 per cent of the population.[12] The need for an organizational Catholic response was great, especially since the financial resources of small parishes were limited.[13]

Together with this concern for the welfare of the poor, the Catholic Church was motivated by fears that Catholic immigrants would turn to the voluntary efforts of Protestant churches if Catholic services were unavailable. Religious charities, whether they were Catholic or Protestant, were not limited to providing aid to the poor. Their agendas also encompassed moral reform, religious conversion, and assimilation. Existing social services, such as the Widows and Orphans Fund and the House of Industry, were increasingly used as a means to convert the Irish poor to Protestantism.[14] The Widows and Orphans Fund, for example, regularly placed Catholic orphans in Protestant homes. And according to Murray Nicolson, the Protestant leadership of these institutions ensured that "it remained their decision as to whom, or under what conditions aid would be given, or what religious instruction would be allowed. As a consequence public institutions became involved in proselytism, more readily assisting those who accepted conversion for aid."[15] The Catholic Church had unsuccessfully campaigned to ensure that Catholic orphans would only be placed in Catholic families, and this failure intensified the church's concerns over the potential depletion of its congregation.[16]

Expanding the Catholic base was of fundamental importance to a diocese that found itself in a minority, particularly at a time when anti-Catholicism was widely prevalent. Whereas in the 1840s Protestants and Catholics had shared relatively cordial relations, by the 1850s tensions between these groups had intensified to the point that the era was labelled "the fiery fifties."[17] The restoration of the Catholic Church in England in the 1840s launched a wave of anti-Catholic "papal aggression" that reverberated in the Canadas. In addition, the revival of French Catholic nationalism in Canada East aggravated "anti-popish" evangelical sentiment in Canada West. In Toronto, Protestantism was suffused with partisanship for the British crown, a loyalty in pronounced opposition to Irish Catholicism.[18] Brian Clarke's study of Irish Catholicism in Toronto notes that "the Orange order offered a timely and appealing vision of the United Canadas as a thoroughly British and Protestant colony. All Irish were not alike, and by differentiating themselves from Irish Catholics on the basis of religion and British loyalism, Irish Protestants reinforced the image of Catholicism as an alien threat."[19] The antagonism between the Orange and Green Irish in Toronto heightened with the appointment of Bishop Charbonnel in 1850.

Bishop Armand-François-Marie de Charbonnel (1850–60) came to power in the Diocese of Toronto brandishing a program of reforms designed to instill bureaucratic authority informed by ultramontane principles. Ultramontanism, a specifically Roman Catholic pastoral approach that gained popularity in the mid-nineteenth century, promoted the supreme authority of the pope over civil society and regional or national church autonomy. This loyalty to Rome was denounced by Protestants as "popish tyranny." Informed by Catholic social reform and romanticist ideas, ultramontanists attacked industrialization and laissez-faire economic liberalism. They associated such trends with the further proletarianization and displacement of the poor. Within ultramontane philosophy, state authority was to be subordinate to the church, particularly in the areas of education and social welfare. The role of the state was to support religious organizing through financial aid and legal recognition. Schools, hospitals, benevolent institutions, and, indeed, all cultural and social events were to be tied to religious devotion. The church was to become the centre of all community activity. Charbonnel's ultramontane approach provided the foundation for the Catholic mixed social economy in Toronto. It also triggered nativist sentiments among dominant social groups.[20]

The bishop's ultramontane approach launched him into a bitter debate with Egerton Ryerson, chief superintendent of education for Upper Canada, over the separate school question. A review of this conflict over educational funding is warranted here since the outcome had important implications for Catholic voluntary organizations. The right to public funding for Catholic separate schools and its later entrenchment in the

British North America Act provided the Catholic Church with legal privileges not shared by other non-Protestant religions. It also, in part, ensured the development of a vibrant Catholic social, cultural, and religious community in which Catholic children could opt out of the assimilationist agenda inherent in public schools. Moreover, it served as a precedent for the acceptance of public funding to other Catholic social services. Once Catholics won the right to publicly funded schools, government grants to Catholic charities became less of a contentious issue.

Prior to Charbonnel's arrival, the previous bishop, Michael Power, had collaborated with public school administrators to ensure the rights of Catholic education. Indeed, Power was elected chairman of the public Board of Education for Upper Canada. Charbonnel, in contrast, objected to the mixed schooling practices supported by his predecessor and was determined to develop a completely separate parochial school system, which, he argued, should be entitled to public funding commensurate with public schools. At issue here was whether the separate school system would share equally in the tax base at a level proportionate to the number of children attending Catholic schools. On the one hand, Ryerson, a defender of the common-school system, denounced such a proposal, claiming that it would weaken the state schools since a substantial sum of money would be lost to the separate system. Charbonnel, on the other hand, argued that public education undermined Catholic values and ultimately imposed Protestant religious dominance. Brian Clarke notes that, "with the arrival of Ultramontanism ... public support for Catholic schools was seen as [a] matter of fundamental justice in which the civil rights of Catholics, both as individuals and as a group, were at stake. Since education was ultimately concerned with the religious formation of the child, to deny Catholic schools state funding was seen by Catholics as a denial of parents' right to educate their children as their conscience dictated."[21] A series of battles throughout the 1850s and early 1860s ended with the constitutional entrenchment of separate school education in the British North America Act of 1867.[22] For the Irish Catholics, such debates were reminiscent of conflicts back in Ireland when public education was imposed as a means of furthering British imperialism. In Toronto, Irish Catholics championed the separate school cause as a question of the cultural survival and spiritual preservation of their children.[23] These same sentiments were reinforced in the separate social services debate.

Along with the establishment of separate schools, Charbonnel envisioned a widespread Catholic infrastructure for the delivery of social services. The success of his plans hinged on the voluntary labour afforded by orders of sisters and brothers who immigrated to Toronto to head up schools and benevolent programs. As religious orders maintained vows of perpetual poverty and were often paid in kind rather than through wages, they were able to provide services at relatively low costs. Initially, only the Sisters of Loretto had worked with school children since 1847, but Charbonnel soon enticed three other religious orders to move to Toronto to assist in building a Catholic social network. The Sisters of St Joseph arrived in 1851 to oversee the care of orphans, and in 1856 they opened the House of Providence, a refuge for the aged, sick, widowed, and prostitutes. In the following years, they would assume responsibility for hospital care, educational instruction, and boarding homes for unemployed youth.[24] In the same year the Christian Brothers began to provide educational services for boys, and in 1895 they opened the St John's Industrial School for boys. In 1852 the Basilian Fathers were invited to advance Catholic educational training and to establish a seminary for the education of English-speaking Catholic priests. All three orders originated in France, where religious associations had a long tradition of involvement in educational and charitable work. Thus Toronto's Catholic benevolent institutions were initially modelled after French charity structures. In contrast, Catholic social welfare services in Ottawa and Kingston were developed by religious organizations from Quebec.[25] The weak association with Lower Canada may, in part, explain the rapid transition from French to Irish control of social welfare delivery in Toronto, a development that is discussed later.

Charbonnel also worked to foster lay communities to assist in his benevolent organizing. In 1850, within a month of his appointment, he had inaugurated the St Vincent de Paul Society, a lay organization fostering male piety and charitable endeavours. The organizational structure of this society also originated in France, where, in Lyons, Charbonnel had been an honourary member. Its emphasis on lay participation proved to be a cost-efficient and effective mechanism for administering outdoor relief to the poorest segments of Toronto's neighbourhoods. Parallel associations were initiated for women, who participated in fundraising drives, distributed used clothing and other basic essentials, and visited female prison inmates and the infirm.[26] (see appendix 2).

The growth of Catholic services and religious communities soon became a contentious issue among militant Orange organizations. In

August 1857 an unsuccessful attempt was made to bomb the House of Providence, and the Catholic Orphanage Asylum was raided on several occasions.[27] Though these religious orders originated in France and not in Canada East, this French connection was viewed by some Protestants as evidence of French-Canadian efforts to extend their power into Canada West.

Charbonnel's efforts to develop Catholic social institutions sparked controversy not only among Protestants but within his own congregation as well. Irish Catholics praised him for developing institutions that promised to preserve their religious identity, but they opposed the preponderance of French clerics and religious orders. As the majority of Catholics in the city were Irish, the continued French dominance of the church became a point of contention. For Irish Catholics, the construction of a separate social network was crucial for the maintenance of their cultural distinctiveness; it became a symbol of Irish patriotism, a situation that turned many otherwise nominal Irish Catholics into devoted adherents. Moreover, as Choquette argues, "English-speaking Catholics were as prone as Protestants to ... [assume] English-language superiority and related racist doctrines."[28] Mounting French-Irish tensions in part underlay Charbonnel's decision to leave his post as bishop of Toronto in 1860. His successor, Bishop John Joseph Lynch (1860–88), an avid francophobe from Ireland, ensured that the future of the Catholic Church in Toronto would be identified with Irish cultural and religious values. The ethnic composition of priests and orders of sisters and brothers increasingly took on a Celtic-Canadian character. Elizabeth Smyth's work on the Sisters of St Joseph, for instance, documents this ethnic transition: 655 novices entered the order between 1851 and 1920, the majority of whom were Irish.[29]

The Business of Fundraising

The creation of Catholic benevolent associations raised new concerns over the need for organized fundraising to support charity expansion. Charities in the 1850s had few economic resources. For example, the scarcity of capital had forced the Sisters of St Joseph to apply to the bishop for permission to "beg" in the streets.[30] The diocese relied on generous donations from prominent, wealthy members, who at times bequeathed lands and buildings to the chancery; it was also dependent on smaller contributions from less well off parishioners. The participation of working-class members who, for instance, offered their labour and materials for the construction of new buildings was invaluable. These efforts, however, were insufficient to ensure the financial success of an expanding charity network.

The search for sources of income to maintain operations propelled the Catholic community into adopting new fundraising techniques, such as public campaigns, door collections, and the "charity sermon." On Sundays priests would promote charity giving as a way of acquiring spiritual rewards. Lay benevolent societies, such as the St Vincent de Paul Society and the Ladies Catholic Benevolent Society, began making public appeals for support. Women, who were typically discouraged from active involvement in public spaces, organized social events to raise money, such as bazaars, picnics, clothing drives, and sewing clubs. In addition, Bishop Charbonnel instigated new banking methods, including the Cathedral Loan Fund and the Toronto Savings Bank. The bank was promoted as a depository for old age, a hedge against such misfortunes as unemployment or illness, and an investment in the financial future of children. A percentage of its profits was channelled into charitable work. Many of these fundraising schemes were modelled on Catholic efforts in the United States or were taken from local Protestant fundraising drives.[31] They served to introduce new strategies for mobilizing resources that brought the laity into closer cooperation with church activities, and thereby fostered a stronger, more devoted Catholic congregation.

In addition, a range of accounting practices were adopted to monitor the flow of money. As Nicolson notes, "No longer could the Diocese be run from Bishop Power's simple bookkeeping methods."[32] Accounting procedures were needed to track interest rates on loans and the reimbursements of investments. Charbonnel's solution was to remove such financial decisions from the clergy and place them in the hands of financial specialists. Henceforth, priests were expected to submit records of bazaars, picnics, pew rents, and door collections to the chancery. One-tenth of parish revenues was transferred to support the expansion of voluntary institutions.[33] Such practices also served to bring the internal dynamics of individual parishes under the scrutiny of a centralized financial body overseen by the bishop. This change forced the clergy into even greater cooperation with the central diocese.

Ultimately, the long-term financial viability of Catholic benevolent institutions lay in the voluntary service of religious orders. As the mandate of such religious communities included a vow of poverty, their labour was provided at minimal cost.[34] Much of the work was offered gratis or in exchange for room and board. Religious orders were specific to the Catholic Church; there were no comparable Protestant orders in Ontario. Thus the operating costs of Catholic voluntary institutions were often much lower than other denominational or secular services.[35]

While the church relied heavily on private voluntary support, it also received a modicum of public aid. Community leaders, under the direction of Bishop Charbonnel, lobbied the government of Canada West for financial compensation. They reasoned that since Catholic charities were contributing to the common good by relieving social problems such as poverty, they should receive funding commensurate with that of Protestant institutions. Under growing social pressure to respond to the plight of impoverished citizens, many of whom were Irish, the government agreed to provide limited grants to Catholic charities. In 1854 the Roman Catholic Orphanage Asylum became the first Catholic institution to receive public grants in Canada West. The second such grant, beginning in 1859, was for the House of Providence. By 1866 the two institutions received $640 and $320 respectively, just under 3 per cent of the provincial total spent on charitable institutions in Canada West.[36] Ongoing religious rivalries ensured that Catholic institutions received considerably less than did Protestant-run organizations (see Appendices 3 and 4). However meagre the amount of public support, Catholic benevolent institutions had at least achieved some level of political legitimacy by the 1850s. As Brian Clarke notes, public funding secured two main goals for the church: "The first was the viability of Catholic social institutions; the second was the public recognition of the Catholic subculture that such funding would imply. English-speaking Catholics were determined to secure such recognition, even if the efforts meant all-out conflict with the Protestant majority."[37] As the provincial government was increasingly called upon to deal with social problems, its own best interests were seen to lie in funding and fuelling the expansion of Catholic charities.

CATHOLIC CHARITY VERSUS
PROTESTANT PHILANTHROPY

By the 1880s, Toronto's Catholic population had changed significantly. The hostility and institutional bigotry it had encountered in the 1850s had subsided significantly, although opposition was by no means eliminated, and Catholics increasingly became integrated in Ontario's social and economic mainstream. A disproportionate number of Irish Catholics continued to live in dire circumstances, but increasing numbers were experiencing forms of social mobility to middle-class status. Gordon Darroch and Michael Ornstein's study of the 1871 census reveals that Irish Catholics were represented in all occupational categories, although they were significantly overrepresented as labourers.[38] The upwardly mobile Catholics began to integrate into Canadian society, adopting a new Canadian identity that served to further distance them from French-speaking Catholics. Catholic priests, too, were increasingly trained and born in Canada, and they began to identify themselves more as Canadian citizens than as Irish nationalists. As Mark McGowan indicates, by the 1890s, Irish Catholic nationalist associations were giving way to North American English Catholic voluntary organizations that championed Canadian patriotism and loyalty to the church. Participation in devotional and benevolent societies fostered a new Canadian Catholic identity that resulted in the "waning of the green."[39] This shift worked to foster growing links between Catholic associations and Protestant initiatives.

While participation with Protestant groups had previously been condemned, by the 1880s the Catholic Church increasingly worked alongside Protestant social and moral-reform groups to demand social legislation. Catholics, for example, were active in the fight for safe working conditions and minimum wage levels. And despite the Quebec bishops' condemnation of the Knights of Labour in 1887, Toronto's archbishop, John Joseph Lynch, joined American bishops in lending support to the Knights.[40] According to McGowan, after "1888 the majority of bishops serving in Toronto departed from the policy of isolating Catholics from the non-Catholic world and encouraged their flock to build Canada side by side with Protestant Canadians but to retain their faith in the process."[41] Moreover, the 1891 papal encyclical *Rerum novarum* inaugurated a new approach to social issues.[42] In the encyclical the Vatican denounced the vicissitudes of laissez-faire capitalism and called for greater state intervention to protect the rights of workers. It encouraged both clergy and laity to be more outspoken on social issues and to play a more direct role in the pursuit of "social betterment." As Brian Clarke observes, *Rerum novarum* "prompted many anglophone Catholics to embrace the cause of social reform. In keeping with the Church's traditional teaching, these activists advocated a distinct Catholic understanding of social justice, but at the same time they urged Catholics to work with people from other religious traditions to bring about social reform. In this respect, they not only promoted social reform but also encouraged Catholics to participate fully in the political and social life of English-speaking Canada."[43] The encyclical provided the theological underpinning for a new Catholic commitment to public dialogue aimed at enhancing social and economic "justice." However, this new Catholic political activism was to occur through the "strengthening" of Canadian society; radical or militant action that could disrupt social stability was not what the church had in mind. As Paula Kane notes, the North American interpretation of the encyclical did not lend support to progressive forms of socialism or feminism.[44]

The Catholic approach to charity, though similarly involved in efforts to improve the city and provide spiritual uplift, differed in significant ways from Protestant philanthropic aims. The philanthropic model promoted by the Protestant churches was steeped in moral-reform projects that aimed to uplift the character of those seeking aid. It was informed by new scientific theories, such as social Darwinism, which suggested that the "defective" character of the poor could germinate and result in the degradation of society as a whole. In these accounts, poverty was in part associated with limited opportunity, but the fundamental problem was understood as a lack of moral character. In other words, the poor were deemed a pauperized class whose failure might be repaired by proper moral training.[45] The philanthropic approach that emerged in the 1880s vowed to "bring to light the moral fault" of the pauper in order to work on its elimination through training, advice, and constant supervision.[46]

The old practice of charitable assistance was denounced for fostering continued dependency; it merely provided aid with little investment in the rehabilitation of behaviour. Small amounts of aid could prove beneficial, but their distribution was to be used only as a means of building moral fibre. Philanthropists, Valverde notes, "sought to rationalize and often curtail the material aid, focusing instead on training the poor in habits of thrift, punctuality and hygiene – an economic subjectivity suited to a capitalist society."[47] It was this philosophical outlook that led to the imposition in 1886 of a labour test for all recipients of aid from the House of Industry. The test aimed to instill a proper work ethic in the pauper.

Although the philanthropic rhetoric did influence Catholic social work, and Catholic agencies increasingly adopted measures of moral reform, charitable assistance remained the foundation of Catholic benevolence. The Malthusian logic and the image of the self-made individual that informed the philanthropic vision were foreign to Catholic teachings on the poor. Catholic charity was more reminiscent of the New Testament story of the prodigal son. Despite having squandered his wealth, the prodigal son, returning home, is greeted with open arms and later a feast. Catholic social teachings centred more on notions of personal faith and discipleship, where individuals would learn by example rather than through the imposition of moral responsibility.[48] Papal encyclicals such as *Rerum novarum* continued to use the language of charity and emphasized its importance in the pursuit of social justice.[49] Rudolph Villeneuve clarifies this critical distinction between charity and philanthropy:

it [charity] has God as its object from which it envisages all things, charity is distinguished from pure philanthropy which helps man for his own sake and his own natural ends ... The motives of modern philanthropy are purely human motives. At best, they rest on a natural and laudable human sympathy, a feeling of solidarity with the other strata of society. At worst, they may rest on a calculated fear of revolt unless the underprivileged classes are given at least the bare necessities of life. Philanthropy considers man in the light of human experience, charity views him in the light of faith. Charity thus surpasses philanthropy as God surpasses man, it is of another order – one is supernatural, the other is natural; one is divine, the other is human.[50]

Arguably, accounting for the distinction between Catholic charity and Protestant philanthropy was the fact that many of the priests and nuns who ran benevolent institutions were themselves of Irish poor origins and descendants of the famine émigrés. Such a class position engendered an empathetic response to the plight of the poor that differed significantly from programs devised by middle-class Protestants.

In his study on voluntary associations, Brian Clarke argues that the Protestant nineteenth-century distinction between the deserving and the undeserving was irrelevant to Catholic benevolent workers. The objective of Catholic charity was to "save souls." In refusing aid to those deemed "undeserving," the church risked losing members of its flock, and more seriously, it risked losing them to the Protestant religions. Commenting on the St Vincent de Paul Society, Clarke also notes that, "as long as the applicants to the society were without means, relief was often granted irrespective of other consideration when children were concerned, particularly in families headed by women. In such cases, even when it was a question of flagrant intemperance, the [societies] were usually reluctant to refuse relief."[51] Despite the parents' behaviour, there was always the hope of converting the children, or at least ensuring their enrolment in separate schools. For Catholics, the potential for religious conversion outweighed concerns over moral character where charity was involved.

2 Market Mechanisms and Charity Governance

By the 1870s the Ontario government may not have been directly involved in the distribution of welfare provisions, but it was actively regulating and supporting the expansion of the charity sector. Approximately one-fifth of the provincial budget was allocated to voluntary services, including charities, hospitals, asylums, prisons, and eleemosynary institutions.[1] Initially, direct expenditures to charities constituted only a small fraction of the total spent on voluntary organizations; a mere $12,610 in 1870 was distributed among sixteen charities. By 1876 this amount had almost doubled to $21,367.26, and the number of benevolent institutions increased to twenty-seven. Over the next twenty years, this amount increased more than sixfold. By 1890 a total of $77,731.82 was apportioned to seventy-two charities.[2] As monetary commitments to charities expanded, so too did the legislature's resolve to oversee and control investments. Aid to charities was increasingly accompanied by a range of business-style management techniques. Standardized bookkeeping and other forms of accounting methods designed to trace the flow of capital were imposed on grant recipients. As well, charity inspectors were hired to monitor the internal operations of charities and to ensure compliance with government standards and reporting methods. Charities that did not strictly comply with the new requirements risked having their funding revoked. The result was an intensification of government intervention in and regulation of the charity sector.

These new bureaucratic systems enabled legislatures to "govern at a distance." Bureaucrats were able to monitor charity operations from their legislative offices as standardized reports made visible the internal operations of individual agencies. Numerical computations, made possible through the imposition of standard forms and common bookkeeping methods, offered new ways of analyzing, comparing, and acting upon voluntary organizations that transformed the very life of voluntary organizations. Henceforth charities were subject to a constant state of surveillance and regulation. Every aspect of their programs came under enumeration and scrutiny by centralized authorities.

The bureaucratic techniques of regulating charities have to date received little attention in scholarly works on the history of the charity sector. Most academic studies of benevolent agencies have focused on the internal dynamics of charities and, in particular, on the administration or regulation of those in receipt of aid. As a result, the governance of charities themselves has been largely overlooked. This lack of investigation has led to a general perception that, up until the interwar period, governments had little interest or involvement in the area of social welfare. A close examination of reporting techniques reveals otherwise.

This chapter reviews how techniques of administration brought individual charities under the scrutinizing gaze of governing bodies. First, it charts the development of the Office of the Inspector of Asylums, Prisons and Public Charities. The rise of inspectors reflected the beginnings of a bureaucratic civil service designed to bring charities under public scrutiny. This part of the chapter also assesses the importance of changing funding criteria for the future of Catholic charities. Through the replacement of government grants with per diem rates under the 1874 Charity Aid Act, Toronto's Catholic benevolent organizations received a larger share of government funding in comparison to their Protestant counterparts.

The chapter then examines the impact of a scientific management ethic on the charity sector during the early 1900s. Scientific management thought, made popular on the factory shop floor and in the economic sphere in general, soon came to pervade the charity sector. For those in charge of providing funding to the voluntary sector, concerns about the efficient management of operations took on increasing importance. New commissions and centralized agencies, such as the Social Service Commission and the Federation for Community Services, functioned to monitor and regulate the use and dispersal of charity monies. Similar concerns within the Catholic Archdiocese of Toronto prompted the creation of its own centralized structures, such as the Catholic Charities organization and the Federation of Catholic

Charities. The development of such organizations, whether publicly enforced or church-run, signalled the further expansion of a bureaucratized charity sector.

It should be emphasized that the application of bureaucratized management techniques was not always imposed on charities. Often voluntary workers themselves called for greater municipal and provincial involvement in social welfare. Social reformers and charity workers were as influential as the government and local businessmen in advancing a charity bureaucracy. Indeed, by promoting their own interests, charity workers helped to define the contours of state practices and involvement. The development of a charity bureaucracy was characterized more by a complicated web of state involvement and private benevolent initiatives than by a social control model emphasizing state control of voluntary organizations.

THE DEVELOPMENT OF CHARITY INSPECTION, 1867–1890s

As the province established its bureaucratic apparatus in the years immediately following Confederation, the use of inspectors emerged as one of the "pre-eminent instruments of regulation."[3] Politicians interested in bringing civil society under greater government control were reluctant to intervene directly in the affairs of private institutions because doing so would breach the liberal promise of non-intrusion into private life. Consequently, they licensed a new cadre of civil servants – namely, inspectors – to intervene and regulate private institutions on their behalf. Inspection authorized public servants to collect information that could then be used by governments to monitor, shape, and control private institutions. As sociologist Bruce Curtis argues, "no central state agency could govern a population about which it was ignorant; inspection provided indispensable elements of intelligence to state agencies."[4] The inspector's detachment from the formal governing party was seen as a way of ensuring responsible government while reducing partisan politics. Curtis equates their function to Foucault's panopticon, in which power – in this case, state power – is obscured by mechanisms that appear autonomous and independent yet derive their authority from the government.[5]

The use of inspectors in Canada predates Confederation; the first inspector was hired in 1843 in the field of education. However, it was not until the post-Confederation period that inspection evolved into a common tool of government regulation. By the early 1900s an "army of inspectors" had been hired to extend government authority into a wide range of areas.[6] In the field of social welfare, Ontario's first "Inspector of Asylums, Prisons and Public Charities," John Woodburn Langmuir, was appointed in 1868.[7] A second position was created in 1881, and by the turn of the century a third post became available. As well, a "Superintendent of Neglected and Dependent Children" was hired in 1893. Such inspectors were to oversee and report on all institutions in receipt of provincial money. Charities, including Catholic ones, could no longer run their institutions independently; henceforth they were subject to annual inspections and an audit of their accounts. New methods of standardized record-keeping, note-taking, and accounting procedures were imposed on grant recipients. Charities were required to maintain detailed records of the number of charges, the number of days each individual spent in the shelter, the type of food provided, and the amount of money received from donations. These collected data would then be compiled in extensive reports that were submitted to government inspectors. It was such statistical knowledge that imbued inspectors with the authority to propose policy changes and hence "exert considerable influence over the conduct" of charities.[8] A negative review by an inspector could result in the termination of government aid.

The effect of this standardized knowledge was to submit private institutions to new regulatory techniques of inscription, tabulation, and comparative analyses, which were then used to inform social policy debates. Statistical reports were said to provide "objective" data that could be used to reduce power politics and pressure from influential interest groups. Corruption, partisan politics, and political favouritism were viewed as impediments to "good government." Accounting through inspection was promoted as a means of curbing such interference. Numerical computations allowed for comparisons among and evaluations of charities, and for policies to be debated and justified according to economic calculations. Such standardized techniques of reporting did not exist prior to 1847, but, as Curtis notes, they quickly developed into the principal method of governmental regulation. According to Peter Miller, this shift occurred precisely because "the elegance of the single figure provides a legitimacy" that, on the surface, seems to lie outside political interests but in reality reflects the social relations under which it was produced. Numerical facts obtained through accounting practices always affect and structure available choices.[9]

The Charity Aid Act: A Victory for Catholics

One of the primary objectives of Inspector Langmuir when he accepted his post in 1868 was the collection of standardized statistical data from each agency under his mandate. Prior to 1870s, haphazard information had been collected on the internal operations of charities, but henceforth, detailed accounts were maintained, accumulated, and analyzed in annual reports. In his review of charity reports, Langmuir was disturbed by the lack of coordinated decision-making that characterized funding procedures. Grants, he determined, were allocated, not on the basis of work performed, but according to partisan preference, which resulted in Protestant charities faring better than Catholic benevolent agencies. For example, in 1873 Catholic voluntary agencies received only 25 per cent of the total provincial budget allocated to Toronto's charities, yet they provided services to about 45 per cent of those receiving aid.[10] Given his pragmatic business sense, Langmuir was determined to overhaul the funding criteria and introduce a more rational system in which state compensation was tied to the quality of work performed and the extent of care provided. His proposals formed the basis of the Charity Aid Act of 1874.

Under the act, lump-sum grants to benevolent organizations were replaced by a new system of per diem rates in which funding was tied to the number of individuals cared for. Under this new system, charities were divided into three general groups: hospitals, poorhouses, and orphanages and rescue homes. A different standardized per diem rate was devised for each category.[11] The act was viewed as a victory for Catholic voluntary associations because it effectively removed the discriminatory granting procedures that had privileged Protestant charities. A comparison of the funding structure for Toronto's orphanages and poorhouses before and after the act demonstrates this point[12] (see table 2.1 and appendices 3 and 4). Prior to the act, Catholic and Protestant orphanages had been awarded a fixed amount of $640. The Catholic Orphanage Asylum, however, housed approximately three times as many children than did its counterpart, the Protestant Orphans Home. With the introduction of per diem rates, funding to the Catholic orphanage rose to $1,593, a 2.4 per cent increase over the amount allotted to the Protestant Orphans Home. In terms of poorhouses, the Catholic House of Providence received an increase of more than 300 per cent in provincial funding after the implementation of the Charity Aid Act.[13] In effect, the act weakened the advantageous

Table 2.1
Provincial grants to Toronto charities, 1874–1875

	Protestant House of Industry	Catholic House of Providence	Protestant orphanage	Catholic orphanage
1874				
Total grant	$2,900	$1,000	$640	$640
No. of inmates	205	273	137	396
1875				
Total grant	$2,900	$3,298*	$657**	$1,593**
No. of inmates	176	351	159	384

SOURCE: Archives of Ontario, *Report of the Inspector of Asylums, Prisons and public Charities*, 1874, 1875.
* Calculated at the rate of 5 cents per day for each inmate, plus a supplementary grant of 2 cents per day's stay (not to exceed one-fourth of money received from sources other than government).
** Calculated at a fixed rate of 1½ cents per day for each inmate, plus a supplementary grant of ½ cent.

position of Protestant charities by ensuring that Toronto's Catholic charities received provincial funding commensurate with the disproportionately higher number of the city's Catholic poor.

The passing of the Charity Aid Act evoked considerable opposition from Conservative Orangemen, who attacked the "privileges" accorded to Catholic organizations. Langmuir, however, was able to defend his proposal in the name of rational fiscal management and good government. The Liberal Party, led by Oliver Mowat, which had come to power in 1871 in part because of its ability to attract Catholic voters, was no doubt a contributing factor. Under a Conservative government, such a proposal would not likely have succeeded. Regardless of the backdrop, as Valverde asserts, the act was "a significant intervention in church-state relations in Ontario because it removed the Protestant lobbying advantage by taking grants to charities out of the realm of politics and into the realm of administration."[14] The collection of statistics through audits and accounting practices meant that technical criteria replaced political connections as the basis for allocating funding.

It should, however, be noted that the Charity Aid Act applied only to indoor relief – that to individuals housed within institutions. Government funding for outdoor relief continued to privilege Protestant organizations. Outdoor relief was a significant aspect of the benevolent work undertaken by houses of refuge. Many working-class families earned barely enough to subsist and therefore relied on social assistance from voluntary associations to make ends meet. In 1875 the Protestant House of Industry's outdoor relief work had kept 2,340 individuals from falling further into destitution. This Protestant effort was generously subsidized by the provincial legislature; comparable work by the Catholic House of Providence, however, was not. The province saw no inconsistency in its refusal to subsidize the House of Providence's work with 1,093 Catholic poor. The lack of contributions forced the House of Providence to refer many Catholics to the publicly supported House of Industry.[15] Hence the advantageous position of Protestant charities continued to characterize Ontario's funding to benevolent organizations.

EFFICIENT BENEVOLENCE AND BUREAUCRATIC CHARITIES, 1900–1930

By the early 1900s, Toronto's charity sector was increasingly influenced by and modelled after business management precepts. Business philanthropists and local politicians lobbied to introduce a corporate-style benevolent infrastructure that would maximize charity dollars and eliminate the ingrained inefficiency which was said to plague social welfare delivery. This new logic of scientific management that pervaded benevolent work was in part a response to the fiscal crisis that engulfed Toronto's municipal politics in the early 1900s. The rapid expansion of the city into a metropolis was accompanied by sizable levels of public debt. In the area of social welfare alone, the city's expenditures rose by 400 per cent between 1905 and 1915.[16] Coupled with this increase were the successive waves of recessions in 1907–08, 1913–15, and 1920–23, which exacerbated the problem of financial shortfalls. During such periods of economic uncertainty, government spending became highly scrutinized, particularly in the area of social expenditures, where civic officials were determined to ensure greater accountability.[17]

It was within this context that the doctrine of efficient management took hold among reform-minded politicians and businessmen. A new urban progressive movement had developed with a mandate to introduce "business and efficiency" into every aspect of municipal government.[18] The market logics of efficiency, bureaucracy, and centralization formed the centrepiece of this new ethos. In Toronto the effort was led by the political economist Morley Wickett; elsewhere it was influenced by such prominent individuals as J.S. Woodsworth in Winnipeg and Herbert B. Ames in Montreal. While the movement was an outgrowth of the Urban Reform Movement of the 1880s and 1890s, which called for government regulation of the economic sector, the emphasis on restructuring institutions along market principles distinguished it from earlier crusades.[19]

The ideological foundations of the movement were rooted in the writings of Frederick W. Taylor, notably his book entitled *The Principles of Scientific Management* (1913). It argued for the centralization of administration, the specialization of tasks, and the introduction of cost accounting procedures to provide managers with the information they needed in their role as administrators.[20] Initially deployed on factory shop floors, Taylorism reshaped labour processes throughout Canada. Taylor's ideas soon came to pervade many types of organizational structures. He himself argued that "the same principles can be applied with equal force to all social activities: to the management of our homes; the management of our farms; the management of the business of our tradesmen, large and small; of our churches, our philanthropic institutions, our universities, and our governmental departments."[21] The appeal of scientific management lay in its promise to eliminate waste, needless repetition, and mismanagement. It also promised maximum profits at minimum cost.[22] We should note that the influence of business reform on philanthropic institutions was not unprecedented. Valverde discusses how commercial practices in the Victorian era resulted in philanthropic institutions functioning like "joint-stock charities, with boards of directors and procedures modeled on those of the emerging capitalist enterprise."[23] Moreover, the underlying philosophy of philanthropy itself was premised on investment/return imperatives, in which money "invested" in the poor would generate a return in the form of "moral capital." Taylorism, however, by exposing the daily operations of organizations and individuals through new reporting methods, promised to redesign and optimize benevolent work through efficient management.

In the charity sector, as James Pitsula notes, scientific management "coincided with the extraction of maximum value for every charity dollar spent."[24] Charities were depicted as imbued with a deep-rooted inefficiency that resulted in wasted resources and funds. Business philanthropists and politicians were eager to re-engineer and recreate the charity sector in accordance with Tayloristic business ideals, which would ensure the elimination of duplicated tasks and the mismanagement of philanthropic dollars. Such attempts would bring under greater scrutiny not only the individual organization but those in receipt of aid as well. Peter Miller and Ted O'Leary argue, in their work on accounting practices, that scientific management was as much about "optimizing the efficiency of each individual action" as it was about redesigning organizational behaviour. They note that "the efficiency of the individual was considered to be something that could be acted upon and improved."[25] Thus scientific management practices were seen as a way of protecting voluntary agencies from unscrupulous individuals who exploited social services with fraudulent claims.

Catholic charities became particularly suspect under this new business ethos. Concerted attempts were made to cut funding to Catholic charities that were deemed to be duplicating Protestant services, and hence wasting scarce fiscal resources that could be redirected to Protestant charities. Such perceptions were further fuelled by the advent of social work, which sought to replace the lay knowledges of volunteer work with academically trained experts. Despite the fact that Catholic aid workers were increasingly being trained in new social work principles (as discussed in the next chapter), Catholic charities were continually chastised for their reliance on religious or lay volunteers. As such, Catholic benevolent organizations often found themselves the target of government cutbacks.

The Beginnings of Centralized Bureaucracies: The Social Service Commission

The formation of the Social Service Commission (SSC) in 1912 was one of the first attempts by Toronto's municipal government to introduce a management model to the charity sector. The SSC superseded the Associated Charities, formed in 1881, but unlike its predecessor, the SSC was officially appointed by the city. The five businessmen appointed to the commission sought to combine benevolent commitment with corporate ethics. An elaborate system of accounting and financial management was imposed, which required aid organizations to maintain extensive bookkeeping and statistical records. Annual grants were replaced by per diem rates allocated on the basis of the perceived need, the extent of care provided, and compliance with SSC requirements. (Many of these measures, such as per diem rates, had been introduced at the provincial level in the 1870s, but were not used in a direct way to impact on the internal policy decisions of individual agencies.) Voluntary agencies that had previously applied directly to the municipal government for grants now had to appeal to the SSC for public funding. Non-compliance with the commission's accounting mechanisms meant that charities risked either reductions in or the loss of their funding.

Essentially, the SSC extended government regulation over the charity sector. It did so by making visible the minute operations of the individual agencies through the application of scientific management practices.[26] The commission, armed with information and annual reports on each institution, began introducing new cost-accounting measures. These extended far beyond mere funding decisions; they impacted on the internal policy practices of voluntary associations. For example, in the name of fiscal responsibility, the SSC deemed the placement of children in foster homes a more financially viable option than institutional care in orphanages. Per diem grants were withdrawn from orphanages if the commission felt that alternative arrangements could be made for a particular child. This practice was particularly worrisome for Catholic agencies, which cared for 60 per cent of orphaned children in the city. To maintain their level of funding, they had to prove that alternative care was not available. Through such measures, the work of Catholic orphanages declined precipitously. In other areas, the work by the Sisters of St Joseph with the incurably sick was targeted as a waste of resources and an unnecessary duplication of services provided by non-denominational agencies. As such, it too was subject to budgetary cuts.

Such repeated interference in the work of individual agencies soon led to the downfall of the SSC. It was criticized for a lack of social work representatives on its board. Many felt that businessmen were ill-equipped to assess the importance of different varieties of voluntary work. Clashes with aid workers eventually led to the scaling down of the SSC's responsibilities. In 1918 its duties were limited to the supervision of relief provided by the House of Industry, and two years later it was replaced by the Social Welfare Division of the Department of Public Health.[27] Despite its short career, the SSC was important for initiating the move towards bureaucratic management and the centralization of relief work at the municipal level. Moreover, it forced charitable institutions to respond to the growing demand for the maximization of charity dollars and the efficient administration of service delivery.

Centralizing Charity Management

Determined to pre-empt the municipality's attempt to impose a new governing body, charity leaders organized their own bureaucratic structures, which, while partially financed through public coffers, were relatively independent of government intervention. If social aid workers were to have a say in shaping and directing social welfare policy, they needed to develop an administrative mechanism that could interact with government departments. Within Catholic circles, the Catholic Charities organization (renamed the Catholic Welfare Bureau in 1922) was formed in 1913 to coordinate the work of previously independent Catholic benevolent institutions.[28] The Neighbourhood Workers Association, formed in 1914, was the Protestant counterpart.[29] These umbrella organizations were designed to coordinate and centralize the work of previously independent voluntary institutions and to oversee admissions to individual charities. Local charities were to limit their mandate to service delivery; eligibility and funding structures would be determined by central bureaucracies. Both the Catholic Charities and the Neighbourhood Workers Association were promoted as ways of assuring professional standards by pooling resources, which would thereby ensure a reduction in duplicated tasks and abuses of almsgiving. Charity consolidation was touted as a means of minimizing costs while maximizing the quality of service. It also served to reduce the autonomy of individual associations, such that they could no longer embark on independent initiatives. Charities run by lay organizations or religious orders, many of which were administered and staffed by women, now had to submit to regulations and forms of accountability determined by central agencies typically headed by men.

The formation of the Catholic Charities brought individual voluntary organizations under greater diocesan control. Although some church leaders feared that the emphasis on efficient management would undermine the spirit of Catholic voluntarism, the archdiocese was eager to introduce a central agency that would operate under its command. The proliferation of relatively autonomous voluntary institutions had made it difficult for the archdiocese to exercise its authority over all associations. The consolidation of Catholic charities resolved this problem. Moreover, since the 1880s Catholics had been becoming more entrenched in the city's social fabric, and by the early 1900s collaboration with non-Catholic voluntary organizations was deemed essential. Cooperation with mainstream organizations and municipal departments was critical if the church was to ensure that it had a voice in social welfare debates.[30] In order to accomplish this, it required the power to direct the internal operations of individual charities. Although the Catholic Church had distanced itself from philanthropy, it was not opposed to new administrative techniques that would enhance charity delivery. Indeed, the Archdiocese of Toronto welcomed innovations that would extend its central authority. The Church may have been opposed to philanthropic methods of governing the poor, but it did not object to modern methods and techniques for governing charities.

Parallel developments in the United States also influenced the incorporation of modern management practices in Toronto's archdioceses. After World War 1, archdioceses throughout the United States, in cities such as Boston, Chicago, Detroit, New York, and Pittsburgh, formed central organizations to bring independent charities under the direct control of the archbishop.[31] According to Dorothy Brown and Elizabeth McKeown, in the United States, consolidation and modernization were "the dominant concerns of charities leaders between 1900 and 1930."[32] This consolidation also extended to the centralization of fundraising campaigns, which ensured archdiocesan control over church finances. Centralization was a means of ensuring fiscal, professional, and administrative accountability. This accountability was essential if the church was to maintain public funding and influence welfare legislation. In Toronto, as in the United States, modernization anchored Catholic charities in social welfare.

The Politics of Fundraising

The secular Federation for Community Services, formed in Toronto in 1919, was yet another umbrella organization designed to coordinate the funding of voluntary associations. It was the brainchild of the Bureau of Municipal Research, founded in 1913. A private organization of prominent businessmen interested in civic reform, the bureau was committed to restructuring civic affairs according to sound management practices based on science, expertise, and rational decision-making. In a 1917 pamphlet on philanthropic work in the city, *Toronto Gives*, the Bureau advanced its strategy for amalgamating the fundraising efforts of Toronto's charities into a single operation to be known as the Federation for Community Services (the predecessor of today's United Way). Unlike the Social Service Commission, the Federation for Community Services would be run by a board composed of charity workers and local philanthropically minded businessmen. This proposal for joint fundraising appealed to both the Neighbourhood Workers Association and the Catholic Charities, as they would retain at least some direction over funding decisions. The alliance nonetheless ensured that market principles would still permeate the voluntary sector.[33] The federation continued to impose new techniques of budget discipline, cost accounting, and audit procedures. Under the federation, each member organization was required to forgo all independent initiatives to raise money on its own. The amount of funding given to charities would no longer be determined by benefactors who gave money to their favourite charities; rather, the federation would base its funding decision on an in depth assessment of anticipated need determined according to economic necessity. Through such governing practices, individual charities increasingly lost their autonomy to determine the direction of their organizations. The future of charities now depended on the federation's agenda.

In 1919 the Catholic Charities joined the federation. The archdiocese was understandably reluctant to place its institutions under the direction of a secular agency, since Catholic agencies had been successful in financing their own ventures in the past. In 1915 the House of Providence had secured $33,582 in donations, which far exceeded the $3,621 raised by the House of Industry in that same year.[34] The Roman Catholic Orphanage Asylum and the Good Shepherd Refuge also collected private donations that far surpassed the amount received by their Protestant counterparts. Nonetheless, given the disproportionate number of Catholic poor, Catholic charities continued to be underfunded in relation to many Protestant services. Therefore, the archbishop acquiesced to the Catholic Charities joining the federation after it was assured that Catholic agencies would receive their fair share of charity funds. And indeed, the Catholic Charities did benefit from participation in the federation. In the first fourteen months of operation, the Catholic umbrella organization received a total of $104,828, about a quarter of the federation's revenues.[35] This alliance, however, soon came under attack.

Plummeting funding drives, notable during the 1920–23 recession, severed relations between religious and secular agencies. Tensions increased when several members of the federation took offence at the proportion of funds allocated to the Catholic Charities. These members saw no reason why Catholic services should not be amalgamated under non-sectarian agencies. They justified their arguments by pointing out that the duplication of services for purely religious reasons ran counter to the federation's underlying goals of efficient management, and that, in times of fiscal restraint, such additional costs were unjustifiable. Secular agencies claimed they were suffering financially because a substantial amount of money was "lost" to Catholic charities. Moreover, they supported their views by denouncing the common use of volunteers by Catholic agencies, which, they argued, reflected an outdated practice that failed to conform to the professional standard of social work.[36]

In May 1924 the federation's executive wrote to Toronto's Archbishop Neil McNeil requesting the amalgamation of Catholic charities. The organizations to be merged included the Catholic Big Brothers, the Catholic Big Sisters, the St Vincent de Paul Society, and the St Elizabeth Visiting Nurses. The archdiocese flatly rejected the proposal. In retaliation, the federation "unceremoniously expelled" Catholic institutions in September 1927. It justified its actions by announcing that declining revenues were directly attributed to the refusal of many donors to subsidize Catholic benevolence.[37] Left to its own devices, the archdiocese incorporated its own Federation of Catholic Charities in November 1927. All agencies belonging to the Catholic Welfare Bureau (formerly the Catholic Charities) were brought under the supervised control of the Federation of Catholic Charities. It assumed responsibility for coordinating the work of individual agencies and for fundraising campaigns, while the Catholic Welfare Bureau was reduced to a casework agency.

This centralization of financial administration at times drove a wedge between the federation and the Catholic orders involved in benevolent work. The federation was adamant that no institution be allowed to raise revenues on its own, which meant that the amount allocated to individual charities by the federation was their only source of funding. Some agencies did contravene these measures. In April 1930, for example, the Carmelite Sisters – whether knowingly or not – violated the federation's policies by organizing a fundraising concert. Angered by this deviation, the federation appealed to the archbishop to quash such blatant defiance. According to the federation, benefactors who had already donated to a particular charity would be less likely to participate in annual diocesan collections. It argued that the financial viability of the federation, and ultimately all Catholic charities, was jeopardized. In the end, the Sisters were forced to cancel their concert.[38] This example illustrates how the centralization of funding authority curtailed the ability of religious orders to make independent decisions about their own affairs.

Attempts to impose efficient management by amalgamating Toronto's charities continued throughout the twentieth century. In 1943 all charitable federations operating within the city were united under the auspices of the United Welfare Fund. In addition to the Catholic and secular federations, the Federation of Jewish Philanthropies joined this fundraising initiative. In 1944 the fund was renamed the Community Chest of Greater Toronto, and it became the United Community Fund in 1957. This union continued until 1976, when the Catholic charities broke away over the abortion issue and formed the ShareLife funding organization.

By elaborating new ways of documenting the internal operations of charities through the use of inspectors, accounting methods, and centralized bureaucratic organizations, the charity sector became an ever-increasing object of regulation. Key market-based techniques brought charities under administrative control by making their internal dynamics more visible, thereby making it possible to subject them to bureaucratic regulations. These new business-inspired practices extended the ability of power structures, whether they were government bodies or church bureaucracies, to intervene and direct the internal operations of individual charities. In essence, these methods made possible new ways of governing charities. The end result was that servicing the poor and needy became a secondary concern to the primary objective of the maximization and efficient management of charity dollars. Services could be expanded, curtailed, or eliminated, not on the basis of need, but in accordance with the business ethos of scientific management. Each institution would be evaluated, not primarily in terms of the extent of its services to Toronto's poor, but rather, according to its efficiency and its ability to manage costs, reduce duplication, and ensure that recipients were not taking advantage of services. If voluntary efforts were seen as duplicating existing services, as was often believed of Catholic charities, they risked losing their funding.

This bureaucratic control, however, was not simply an extension of government power over private relief. As the Federation for Community Services demonstrates, it was often initiated by charity workers themselves. Charity workers, including those in the Catholic Church, participated in creating structures that would submit their organizations to new methods of governance. As the Foucaultian use of "governance" suggests, "it is not only governments that govern but all sorts of levels or forms of social relations that are involved in governance."[39] In sum, the restructuring of the charity sector by scientific management techniques can be understood only as the outcome of multiple competing forces that combined to negotiate a process of change.

3 From Catholic Charity to Catholic Welfare: The Impact of Social Work

In 1930 Toronto's Archbishop Neil McNeil circulated a statement to all parishes as part of the annual campaign for the Federation of Catholic Charities:

During several years we have been learning how to translate our faith into better service of the poor and the suffering ... We have learned that the distribution of money among them ... is far more effective and does more good when done through trained workers ... We have learned that the work of distribution among needy families requires equal efficiency acquired either by a course of training in a school of social service or by experience under competent direction. ... Without the trained workers the distribution would be hap-hazard, wasteful, and tending to pauperize. With the trained workers the assisted family is often led to become again self-supporting, and means of help in addition to resources of our [Catholic Welfare] Bureau are often found. These and other advantages more than justify the salaries paid to trained workers.[1]

Under Archbishop McNeil, social service to Toronto's poor would be entrusted to professional agents working within Catholic institutions. By the 1920s the Catholic Archdiocese of Toronto had begun to train and hire its own social workers, while restructuring its charity infrastructure to reflect the directives of the social work profession. The principles of social work were integrated into most aspects of charity delivery.

The extent to which social work pervaded Toronto's Catholic charities is not reflected in most historical accounts of the evolution of social work. The emergence and widespread acceptance of social work during the interwar period is most often interpreted as a secular scientific development replacing the "traditional" practices of religious charities. In her work on social service in Toronto, Gale Wills describes how "professional social work became, above all, a secularization of moral reform and a reaction against the evangelical purpose imposed by organized religion."[2] Allan Irving argues that out of the "decline of religiously based social reform emerged the secular profession of social work."[3] And Sara Burke, in her study of the University of Toronto's Department of Social Service (later the School of Social Work), traces the chasm that widened between the ideals of Christian benevolence and social work education.[4] Social work was undoubtedly influenced by the social gospel, but as Ramsay Cook documents, the scientific impulse that infused the reform movement provided the "vehicle" for its secularization.[5] By the 1920s the social work profession is said to have supplanted theocentric solutions with social scientific explanations of society's social problems.[6] Canadian historians have argued that social workers conceived of and promoted their profession as a modern, rational science that sought to detach itself from the amateur practices of religious volunteers.[7]

This chapter, in examining the social reform and social work practices of the Catholic Archdiocese of Toronto, challenges this conventional wisdom. It begins with a critical reflection on the underlying tenets of the secularization thesis. While the Protestant social gospel may have waned during the interwar period, Catholic social action continued well into the post-1918 era. The chapter then discusses the emergence of Catholic social action, a parallel movement to the social gospel, and its growth during the 1930s. In the following section I examine how social work techniques were integrated into Catholic charities. By the 1930s the logic of social work had penetrated many aspects of Catholic charity. The development of professional social work may have diminished the importance of voluntary efforts, but it did not replace the work of Catholic benevolence. Instead, the Catholic Church became an active promoter of professional expertise. Finally, the chapter explores the logic and techniques of social work, in particular how they operated within the Catholic Church. Social work is discussed not simply as a method for alleviating poverty but as a new paradigm for governing social problems and, specifically, dependent families. The works of Nikolas Rose, Peter Miller, David Howe, and Nigel Parton are used to highlight the logic of welfarism. Their emphasis on how social work legitimated intrusions into family life through claims that it promoted the "well-being" and best interests of society is particularly salient.[8]

WAS SOCIAL WORK A SECULAR PRACTICE?

The rise of professional social work has, in part, been traced to late-nineteenth-century attempts to introduce bureaucracy, efficiency, and scientific management into the practice of social service.[9] Allan Irving describes its origins as a threefold phenomenon: a scientific and empiricist impulse; a new concern with the measurement of poverty; and the social reform impulse of the social gospel.[10] Darwinian challenges to theocratic authority, beginning in the 1860s, laid the groundwork for turn-of-the-century social scientific challenges to religious truths. In Canada, moral and religious opinion was supplanted by the social scientific investigation of prominent academics and social reformers, including J.S. Woodsworth, the first leader of the CCF, Montreal businessman Herbert Ames, child welfare activist Charlotte Whitton, and Harry Cassidy, director of the University of Toronto's School of Social Work.[11] The application of social science methods to the study of social problems, fostered in part by the social gospel movement, helped to facilitate the subsequent development of social work. Social workers would address the causes of poverty, not through moral proselytizing, but through the quest for objective facts informed by the social sciences.

Though a social scientific perspective imbued the voluntary sector, it did not result in the displacement of religious influences. The secularization thesis, as taken up by historians such as Ramsay Cook, Richard Allen, and David Marshall, was undeniably a significant trend during the interwar period, but its comprehensiveness is overstated.[12] By the 1920s, Protestant church attendance had fallen off, and a mounting number of religious charities were adopting secular governing structures. Nevertheless, the thesis presents an exaggerated picture of a "golden age" of religious dominance juxtaposed against a later rational and enlightened secular era. By relying on a "top-down" analysis – that is, a narrow focus on leading theologians, academics, and religious and cultural elites – the thesis downplays the continuing influence of religion, particularly in the area of social services.[13] The "view from the pew"[14] as Mark McGowan puts it, has until recently received far less scholarly attention.[15] While religious authority may have been diminished in anglophone Canadian social thought, the Protestant churches continued to play a prominent role in social reform, social service, and social scientific research. In their study of Protestant social welfare, Nancy Christie and Michael Gauvreau challenge the thesis that the social importance of religious institutions declined after 1920. Rather, they suggest that Protestant churches should be viewed "not as the garrisons of antimodernism but as the chief harbingers of cultural change before 1940."[16] As Christie and Gauvreau point out, the Protestant churches "enjoyed their greatest cultural influence during the first four decades of the twentieth century," since they were at the forefront of social investigation, the rise of the social sciences, and the expansion of the welfare state.[17] Cook, while contesting much of Christie and Gauvreau's claims concerning the post–World War 1 Protestant revival, acknowledges their important contribution in documenting how "church people were in the vanguard of reform," notably in matters "relating to the needs of the family and child welfare."[18]

A number of sociologists – Peter Berger, David Martin, David Lyon, and Bryan Wilson, among others – have begun to "rethink" the secularization thesis, which they argue has oversimplified the complexity of church-state relations.[19] These scholars are critical of the way in which the term has been used to connote a unified, consistent linear progression from religious dominance to a secular modernity that traverses continents and diverse religions and practices in much the same way. British sociologist David Martin has gone so far as to call for secularization to be "erased from the sociological dictionary."[20] While this is a radical proposal, his intent is to challenge the grand narratives that blind researchers to the multiple ways in which various churches across diverse regions of the country were differently transformed and "restructured" in response to secularization. A recent collection edited by David Lyon and Marguerite Van Die, *Rethinking Church, State, and Modernity*, draws attention to how secularizing processes "produced not 'no religion' but rather, deregulated, reshaped, relocated, and restructured religion."[21] As Lyon states, "The dangerous thing about secularization is not so much that it is false, as that it has taken root as a taken-for-granted, unproblematic assumption of much academic and media analysis, which makes it one of the most misused and abused concepts in history and sociology today."[22] In the area of social welfare, the secularization thesis has prevented an examination of the continually shifting mixed social economy. The presumption of a linear progression to modernity has obscured the ways in which institutions such as the Catholic Church embraced and furthered the modern impulse in unique ways. The following discussion attempts to document the Catholic Church's active involvement in and promotion of social reform and professional social work.

CATHOLIC SOCIAL ACTION

An examination of the demographic makeup of Toronto's Catholics reveals a rapidly growing congregation during the early decades of the 1900s. Between 1900 and 1940, immigration boosted the Catholic population in Toronto by over 100,000, and Catholic services – churches, rectories, new religious orders, separate schools, and charities – expanded accordingly. Twenty-five new churches were constructed within the city boundaries, and another eighteen were erected in surrounding areas.[23] The archdiocese invited nineteen new religious orders to Toronto to assist in providing services to its expanding congregation.[24] Moreover, Catholic social action, Catholicism's counterpart to the social gospel, gained popularity during the 1930s, brandishing its own social reform ideas.

Catholic social action, a movement that in Toronto began at the turn of the century, represented a relatively new way of thinking about social and political experience. Problems facing society came to be understood as "social problems" necessitating the intervention of both private and public institutions. In many ways, Catholic social action paralleled the Protestant social gospel in its demand for political, social, and economic reforms. Catholic social action had emerged in Italy in 1863 as an attempt to counter anticlericalism and anti-Catholicism. In Toronto some have traced its roots to the rise of charity structures in the 1850s,[25] while others suggest that it was largely a response to the 1891 papal encyclical, *Rerum novarum*.[26] As previously noted, the encyclical, while principally an attack on socialism and the vicissitudes of laissez-faire capitalism, called for greater state intervention to protect the rights of workers. In 1931 the Vatican renewed its commitment to social action in a second encyclical, *Quadragesimo anno*, translated as "The Social Order." In response to the failures of capitalism, which by 1929 had resulted in widespread poverty and unemployment, and concentrated power in the hands of a wealthy few, Pope Pius XI called upon Catholics to demand basic human rights and social justice.[27] He advocated the development of vocational organizations and cooperative approaches as a way of countering the "most modern and menacing of the problems" facing society, namely, communism and excess capitalism.[28] Religious virtue was no longer to be limited to theology or a once-a-week display of devotion; piety was to be expressed through social activism. Catholic social thought sought to impress upon clergy and laity alike the importance of social and political responsibility.

These teachings were the impetus for the creation of a North American Catholic social action movement determined to promote social justice, civic participation, and social change. One of the central goals of the movement was to persuade state officials to intervene, where necessary, in economic and private spheres to ensure workers' rights. It also encouraged government responsibility in areas of public health, social welfare, and labour legislation. Charity continued to be of paramount importance, but in and of itself it could not secure workers, rights; protective legislation was essential. According to Brian F. Hogan, "the emphatic support for the right to a living wage and for workers' associations, and the balanced appreciation of the duties incumbent on ownership of private property, provided the direction for the development of Catholic social thinking until the Second Vatican Council" in 1961.[29] It also further opened the door for cooperation with Protestant and other social groups promoting the rights of the poor and marginalized. In the United States, the Social Action Department of the National Catholic Welfare Council worked to advance Catholic interests in Washington. According to David O'Brien, the NCWC "gave strong backing to most New Deal reforms, from the National Industrial Recovery Act of 1933, through the National Labor Relations Act and the Social Security Act of 1935 to the Fair Wages and Hours Law of 1938."[30] In many ways, this movement exemplified the growing concern with "the social," a modern mechanism for governing private life.[31]

In Toronto a range of strategies were advanced under the general rubric of Catholic social action. Indeed, many attempts to address issues of poverty were identified as extensions of this approach. Some examples include cooperative initiatives, support for trade unions, and lobbying for legislative changes in social welfare.[32] The Catholic press was a principal vehicle for disseminating social action ideas. Henry Somerville, editor of the *Catholic Register*, wrote numerous articles on social issues during the 1930s. Many of these appeared in a weekly column, "Life and Labour," a forum developed by Somerville to educate readers on the economic crisis and the need for greater private and public commitment in the area of social welfare.[33] The objective was to demonstrate how Catholic teachings on social justice could be applied to current labour problems.³⁴ In this vein, his columns called for greater job protection and the enactment of comprehensive labour and social welfare laws. Somerville advocated social insurance for the unemployed, and when the federal government introduced an unemployment insurance program in 1938, he criticized it for not going far enough to include protections for workers against mass layoffs.³⁵ Low-cost housing and family allowances were championed as necessary to ensure the stability of the Christian home. Affordable housing was promoted as a defence against the ills of the market, and family benefits were supported as a means of ensuring the well-being of children and stimulating the birth rate, which had fallen off precipitously during the Depression.³⁶ Hogan describes Somerville's editorials as part of an overall campaign to strengthen and stabilize marriage and family relations. For Somerville, "a harmonious familial foundation was perceived simultaneously as the basis for the worker's life-satisfaction, and as one of the goals and results of his labour."³⁷

The social activism of the Basilian priests teaching at St Michael's College in the University of Toronto is particularly noteworthy. A broad spectrum of activities was advanced by the Basilians, including courses, study groups, and public lecture series, all designed to explore the application and significance of the papal encyclicals for social and political action. Much of the impetus for these endeavours derived from the work of Moses Coady, of St Francis Xavier University.³⁸ Coady encouraged the Reverend T.O. Boyle, of St Michael's College, to establish a program to educate priests, students, and the laity on the need for social action work.³⁹ The study group emerged as the most effective strategy for promoting social awareness on campus. In 1935 the St Michael's Social Ethics Club was created, and a year later the Study Club, the Social Justice Club, and, most, prominently, the St Michael's Social Guild were formed. The guild's Friday night meetings were regularly attended by over one hundred people, among them professors, students, the clergy, and members of the general public. As Hogan notes, "it was at the club level that the most intense study and discussion developed, and the most concrete expression of social action as well."⁴⁰ The emphasis was on analyzing Christian social responsibility and the need for active participation in defending democratic rights, as well as the role of the state in the social sphere. "One of the favourite devices employed by the Guild was to introduce a piece of 'legislation' concerning some social question before a parliamentary-type forum and to debate the issue to a close."[41] Among the topics of discussion were a range of social welfare issues affecting Toronto's poor, including poor relief, labour laws, family allowances, and unemployment insurance. Creating a social consciousness was one means by which the church sought to extend its teachings and to pressure government for progressive legislation.

The success of the social action movement is evident in the range of cooperative ventures that emerged throughout Ontario. Hogan documents the birth and operation of dozens of such efforts and hundreds of credit unions from 1930 to 1950.[42] Catholic settlement houses for the poor, such as Catherine de Hueck's Friendship House in Toronto (see chapter 5), were other examples of social action in benefit of the poor.

The "back-to-the-land movement" was another example of social action, which also bore Coady's influence. Farm resettlement projects were advanced by members of the church as a solution to Ontario's relief program. The federal government was itself fond of back-to-the-land resettlement projects as a way of dealing with urban unemployment, congestion, and moral decay.[43] For the church, the countryside was glorified as a healthy retreat where destitute families could be nurtured by the serenity of nature and be removed from the perils of the urban slums. For the government, it was a way of reducing relief rolls and maintaining a constant "reserve army." Two settlements were initiated by the Catholic Church: the Mount St Francis Colony, founded by Father Francis McGoey in 1934 in King Ridge, twenty-five miles north of Toronto; and the nearby Marylake Farm School, established in 1936 by Father Michael R. Oliver, director of St Michael's Social Guild. By March 1936, 117 people, including 48 children, had moved to the Mount St Francis Colony. According to McGoey, his project had saved city ratepayers some $25,000 in two years. These projects, he argued, were ideal solutions to the unemployment problem. Not only did they restore individual dignity and self-sufficiency, but as he often pointed out, they cut the city's expenditures on poor relief. As he proclaimed, "we must forget about taking care of people on relief temporarily. They must be provided for permanently. Segregating them in separate settlements outside the town on which they were on relief will not only save the town great expense but will restore to recipients their self-respect."[44] McGoey proposed the relocation of an additional 500 relief families if the municipal government agreed to provide two years' funding, after which, he argued, the families would be able to maintain themselves. Although the colonies initially showed some promise, they were disbanded in 1940 when the war stimulated urban employment.[45]

CATHOLIC SOCIAL WORK

Along with Catholic social action, Toronto's Catholic archdiocese by the 1930s was championing modern scientific methods of social service. Catholic charities had begun to adopt the imperatives of modern social work, and increasingly, professionally trained social workers took over the work of volunteers. The move towards social scientific methods of charity was in part animated by a pragmatic desire to ensure Catholic prominence in the charity sector. If the Catholic Church failed to keep abreast of modern methods for administering benevolence, it risked losing part of its flock to the Protestant churches. The Toronto church was also greatly influenced by developments in American Catholic charities, which had earlier adopted modern methods to deliver social services. By the 1910s, social work practices were a common feature in progressive archdioceses throughout the United States.

By the post-1918 era, tensions between the social sciences and Catholic theology, which may have existed in the late nineteenth century, had largely been resolved. Theoretical developments in the natural sciences, in particular Darwin's theory of evolution, posed a challenge to religious authority. However, developments in medicine and the social sciences – sociology, psychology, criminology, and social work – generally presented a less direct challenge to religious dogma. (Today, theories of evolution and "the big bang" are no longer refuted by the Vatican.) Even Freudian theories were not completely rejected by the church. As Rudolph Villeneuve argued, "Catholic social work does not reject completely the Freudian psychology, especially in regard to its contributions to the understanding of the dynamics of human behaviour, it nevertheless rejects the basic Freudian concept which conceives of man as little more than a bundle of emotions and man's actions as the overflow of deep unconscious surging."[46] Moreover, in Quebec the Roman Catholic Church figured prominently in the development of academic social science programs during the 1930s. The Catholic School of Social, Economic, and Political Sciences, established at Laval in 1938, espoused social scientific methodologies and theory alongside a commitment to church doctrine.[47]

Thus the central tenets of social work were viewed as compatible with Catholicism.[48] Catholic social work fused scientific knowledge with theology, enabling charity to be "Christ-like as well as scientific."[49] The Catholic Church had been opposed to Protestant philanthropy, and social work continued to extol the importance of advice over material aid and the instilling of "proper" habits among the poor, but it dispensed with the philanthropic practice of classifying the poor according to the deserving and the undeserving. Instead, the underlying premise of social work was to identify the root causes of social dislocation, in order to restore problem families to a normal state. The social worker "probed beneath the symptoms of impoverishment" and, rather than making moral judgments, asked "why the family had fallen into that condition. Having made the diagnosis, the social worker was confident that he could prescribe the cure."[50] Once a diagnosis of the problem was achieved through objective expert inspection, a prescribed course of treatment could be applied to rehabilitate those in need.[51]

Training

The rise of Catholic social work in English-speaking Canada was influenced greatly by developments in the United States. The National Conference of Catholic Charities (NCCC), founded in Washington in 1910, shaped many of the ideas about Catholic welfare in both the United States and Canada. The NCCC had its genesis in the secular National Conference of Social Work. Catholics who attended the latter, secular conference often held informal discussion groups to review the specific spiritual and social needs of their communities. Out of these grew the NCCC, an organization committed to reforming the standards and practice of Catholic charities. Initially, the NCCC was run primarily by voluntary lay initiative, but after World War I it increasingly recruited social workers. Its main goals were to modernize Catholic charities, to root out antiquated practices through investigation and social surveys, and to promote the adoption of new methods of social work. The NCCC was influential in initiating social work instruction at Catholic universities such as Loyola and Fordham in 1913 and 1917 respectively. In 1921, along with the National Catholic Welfare Conference, it sponsored the first Catholic Service School in Washington.[52] By 1941, seven Catholic social work programs were operating in American universities.[53]

Most of the directors of Toronto's Catholic Charities had trained in American schools of social work. Of the five priests who headed the Catholic Charities (renamed Catholic Welfare Bureau in 1922) between

1913 and 1960, four had been educated at American schools of social service. Only the first superintendent, Father Bench, had not received such training. Brother Barnabas, who ran the Catholic Charities in 1921–22, had over thirty years of experience in New York's welfare sector. He had served on several state commissions and had been active in the founding of the NCCC. Father Joseph Haley, director of the Catholic Welfare Bureau from 1922 to 1931, had been educated at St Francis Xavier University and had attended the New York School of Social Science in 1922. As well, both the Reverend F. Hugh Gallager and the Reverend John G. Fullerton, directors in 1932–46 and 1946–60 respectively, had studied at the Catholic Social Service School in Washington.[54]

Most social workers employed by the Archdiocese of Toronto received their training at the University of Toronto's Department of Social Service, which opened its doors in 1914.[55] By 1921 the Catholic Charities had hired its first two professional social workers, both of whom held degrees from the Department of Social Service. The number of trained professionals steadily rose; and by 1940 the Catholic Welfare Bureau employed twelve social workers. By 1927 "none but [university] graduate social workers" were to be hired by the Welfare Bureau, and "the absence of graduate workers was the only reason that any consideration was given to the employment of untrained workers."[56] The Catholic Children's Aid Society hired its first professionals in 1932, and that year it began its role as a work-training site where students from Toronto's Department of Social Service could pursue their field training. By the 1950s some twenty social workers were on the society's board.[57]

Much of the research on social work describes the gendered nature of the field, wherein overworked women performed most of the casework duties, while men held administrative positions. According to James Struthers, women, "it was assumed, were willing to work primarily for love, not money."[58] A typical social worker salary at the Catholic Welfare Bureau in the 1930s was roughly $1,400 per annum.[59] Within Catholic charities, control over the funding structure resided with the Federation of Catholic Charities, an organization dominated by men, but of the fourteen voluntary agencies administered under the Catholic Welfare Bureau, six were headed by women, mostly women belonging to religious orders.[60] Indeed, in Toronto, as in Quebec, religious orders often played a leading role in welfare work. In her pioneering work *Taking the Veil*, Marta Danylewycz attests to this trend in Quebec, where "religious life opened the door for some women to a variety of educational and social opportunities." While other women were barred from positions of leadership in social service, nuns were not.[61] Those religious orders of women involved in social service were also determined to supplement practical experience with educational training. In 1935 the first two nuns graduated from Toronto's Department of Social Service.[62] Despite the significant role played by Catholic sisters, their work tended to be concentrated in orphanages and maternity homes, areas where women were thought to have a "natural" affinity. The administration of central agencies such as the Catholic Welfare Bureau continued to reside with the clergy.

Catholic voluntary organizations also showed a commitment to social science. The Toronto Knights of Columbus, an association of Catholic men who sponsored the Catholic Big Brothers, the Catholic Boy Life Council Camp for underprivileged children, and the Columbus Boys' Club, offered its members training in "boyology." The boyology courses were designed to instruct volunteers about contemporary research in boy guidance, including recreation, education, and applied religion. The idea had germinated at Notre Dame University, where the Knights had been successful in organizing a master's program in "Boy Guidance." A graduate of the Notre Dame school was hired in 1929 to run the Knights' programs in Toronto. In the summer of 1929 the Toronto chapter began offering boyology courses, consisting of thirty hours of training over ten consecutive days. Catholic professionals and businessmen were expected to give up their summer vacation to study the social difficulties facing boys in society. The average attendance in the first year was approximately 250. While boyology courses were widely popular, no courses were offered in "girlology." The Catholic Big Sisters ran occasional workshops on the problems facing girls, but these were in no way formal courses steeped in social scientific methods.[63]

Catholic social work in Toronto was soon recognized beyond sectarian circles. In the 1920s Father Haley, superintendent of the Catholic Charities, was appointed director of the Child Welfare Council of Canada. He also held positions in the Canadian Association of Social Workers and the non-denominational Big Brother Movement.[64] In 1920 the provincial attorney general solicited Haley to help draft a bill on "the child of the unmarried mother."[65] In 1928 he was invited to speak at the First Canadian Conference on Social Work, where he discussed modern techniques of interviewing clients and the causes of and solutions to unemployment. In 1940 the Reverend F.H. Gallagher, of the Federation of Catholic Charities, was asked to work with Charlotte Whitton, of the Canadian Welfare Council, to organize the "Community Planning and Interpretation" panels at the Seventh Canadian Conference on Social Work.[66] Archbishop James McGuigan was among the speakers at the First Ontario Conference on Social Welfare in June of 1947.[67] Toronto's Catholic leaders were frequently invited to discuss their innovations at the NCCC.[68] And Montreal and American Catholic organizations such as the Sisters of St Joseph in Waterton, New York, sent representatives to study Catholic developments in Toronto.[69] By all accounts, Catholic social work was deemed an accepted practice by both religious and secular organizations, and was not dismissed as an anachronistic practice.

Restructuring Catholic Charities

During the 1920s the Archdiocese of Toronto began to focus attention on raising its standards of social service. Responding to the rise of social work, the business ethos of efficiency, and the growing number of poor in need of relief, Catholic charities underwent a significant restructuring process. Earlier, individual agencies had been coordinated under the Catholic Charities, the central umbrella organization formed in 1913. Its primary responsibilities were largely confined to the coordination of member agencies. By the 1920s, however, it had increasingly moved into the areas of direct relief and family casework. The rise in poverty during the early 1920s, coupled with the overall increase in the Catholic population as a result of immigration, meant that more families were in need of assistance. At the same time, American uses of scientific methods in social services put additional pressure on the church to incorporate family casework into its activities. Social work experts in the United States had already managed to commit many American Catholic charities to scientific methods of provisions, and these models made their way to Toronto via the NCCC. Moreover, in Toronto, university-trained social workers from the Department of Social Service were promoting their knowledge and expertise in the charity sector. As it became apparent that existing structures were inadequate to respond to these social challenges, Archbishop McNeil sought to redefine the role of Catholic charities.

In 1922 he commissioned the "Social Welfare Survey of the Archdiocese of Toronto" to study the operations of benevolent work, in a bid to prescribe structural readjustments that would raise professional standards. The survey method was a technique that had gained popularity during the early 1900s. It relied on the gathering of objective information by social work experts; such information was to be used to inform and improve changes in the design of charitable organizations.[70] Dr John Lapp, from the National Catholic Welfare Council of Washington, was brought in to conduct the research. His team included two American social researchers and Mary Irene Foy, a Toronto public health nurse who would later become executive director of the Catholic Welfare Bureau. The survey method included in-depth interviews with the directors of all Catholic welfare agencies and with seventy parish priests. As well, questionnaires were administered to the local St Vincent de Paul Societies.[71]

The report's findings denounced the Catholic Charities for its meagre scientific basis. The office was said to be "badly managed" and lacking in statistical reports on welfare recipients. Detailed information on recipients was not maintained. For example, there were no data on the frequency with which particular families were assisted. The report found that "every record in the office shows a lack of thorough investigation. This means not only that there had been insufficient data received, but also that most of the facts have not been verified. They show a lack of effort to obtain [information] from the usual available sources, as pastors, doctors, visiting nurses, hospitals and clinics." While Catholic charities emphasized efficient management, they lacked modern techniques of casework and a systematic plan for restoring families to self-sufficiency. According to the report, once a family was assisted, there was no follow-up system in place, and "no real constructive re-habilitation work was done." The lack of a systematic plan for long-term maintenance meant that many families became dependent on agency services. The survey recommended the immediate restructuring of the Catholic Charities and ordered that "at the head of each division should be a trained worker."[72]

The archdiocese immediately responded by inaugurating the Catholic Welfare Bureau in September 1922 to replace the Catholic Charities. The bureau combined efficient management with scientific principles of social work. Its mandate was "to direct and coordinate the institutions and societies engaged in works of charity, to act as intermediary between them and the Governments which assist them, to maintain friendly and helpful relations with non-Catholic institutions and societies doing similar work and to supply trained social workers who can assist in the duties thus outlined, and in dealing with needs not met by existing institutions and societies."[73] Structurally, the bureau was divided into two main departments: the Family Welfare Division and the Child Caring Division. The former continued the coordination and referral tasks carried out by the Catholic Charities; in addition, it was charged with the task of conducting all family casework assessments. Counselling through casework would become the division's main responsibility, and later, during the Depression, this department emerged as one of the main relief agencies in the city. The Child Caring Division, in cooperation with the St Vincent de Paul Children's Aid Society, was to provide temporary care for children in need, supervise children in boarding homes, oversee admissions to child-care institutions, and assist unmarried mothers and their babies.[74]

WELFARISM

The term "welfare," part of the names of both the Social Welfare Survey and the Catholic Welfare Bureau, suggests a new rationale for managing charities and their recipients. Welfarism is not simply a synonym for the interventionist state; it introduces new processes for governing the social sphere and, in particular, social problems. A brief outline of how welfarism has been defined by those adopting a Foucaultian approach to the study of "the social" is appropriate. Nikolas Rose and Peter Miller describe welfarism as a particular form of governance that emerged in conjunction with the rise of the social sciences.[75] Allan Hunt and Gary Wickham suggest that the term "welfare" is probably a better translation of what Foucault had in mind when referring to security, a situation in which the social professions came to induce self-regulation.[76] The rise of social experts – those in psychiatry, psychology, criminology, sociology, and social work – introduced new methods for the conceptualization, classification, and regulation of social problems. This knowledge enabled the production of new ways of programming and transforming the social field. Improving national health and enhancing national growth were tied to the well-being of society and the minimization of social risk through social security programs and social scientific expertise.

The establishment of modern social work was one element of the welfarist project. Welfarism provided the rationale and social work the techniques for regulating the private lives of individuals. According to Nigel Parton, social work, and welfarism more generally, promoted the idea that "measured and significant improvements could be made in the lives of individuals and families through judicious professional interventions."[77] Social workers claimed to be improving the well-being of individuals through expert, scientific knowledge. Thus social work was conceived of as working towards the welfare – or social solidarity, in the Durkheimian sense – of society and ultimately of the nation-state. This focus on welfarism eschews the dichotomous evolutionary framework in which the growth of state welfare is seen as displacing the work of religious charities. It facilitates an analysis of the multiple groups involved in the governance of social problems. In this manner, the contributions of Catholic social work can be seen as an integral feature of the welfarist project.

The principal target of welfare practices was "the family." The techniques of assessment were central to both the Family Welfare Division and the Child Caring Division of the Catholic Welfare Bureau. Preserving the sanctity of the family was the principal mission of the Catholic Church, but it was also of paramount importance within welfare rationality. The family was identified as both the source of and the solution to social problems. Legislation increasingly came to focus on provisions for the well-being of the family. The family was the central socializing unit where children were taught the responsibilities of citizenship, behaviour was shaped, and morals were learned. It was the institution through which society transmitted its values, its culture, and its spiritual heritage.[78] A 1929 statement by the Catholic Welfare Bureau noted:

The family ... is the great storehouse in which ... the inheritance of spirit and character from our ancestors are [sic] guarded and preserved for our descendants ... The formative years, years rich with experience that endure a lifetime, are spent within the family group, and even if [one] is temporarily outside the family circle, there are home influences that bind and cling ... Therefore, those who furnish behaviour problems, both the adult offender and juvenile delinquent, cannot be classed under the category of mere personality problems, but must be realized both for diagnosis and treatment, each, as an integral part of the family unit. For it is within the family's past history and present situation that we must seek according to case work methods for symptoms, causes and part of the standing symptom indicating that all is not well within the family group. It is essential that we grasp and interpret the social, mental and physical facts beyond the symptom, if we may hope to affect a cure.[79]

Poverty was interpreted as symptomatic of family breakdown.[80] Illegitimacy, dependency, truancy, delinquency, alcoholism, and other social dysfunctions were understood as having their genesis within the family unit. Concerns over the family were not new, but with welfarism, the degree and mode of intervention in the family was intensified.[81]

Paradoxically, if the family was the cause of social maladjustment, it was also the source of solutions. The task of the social worker was to reconstitute, reform, and normalize the dysfunctional family. He or she was to discover the internal and external pressures that interfered with the functioning of a normal family unit. For if left unchecked, "the insidious problem of maladjustment [could] snowball from generation to generation as each child learns from his parents and passes on to his future children a learned distortion of himself, the people around him, and society in general."[82] In a *Catholic Register* article, sociologist Paul Hanley Furfey, of the Catholic University of America, used American eugenics studies to argue that anti-social behaviour and delinquency were necessarily transmitted to future generations:

A number of degenerate families had shown a history of vice, crime, and social inadequacy generation after generation ... Martin Kallikak had an illegitimate son by a feeble-minded girl during the Revolutionary War. Four hundred and eighty descendants of this union were studied and their history was a history of vice and crime ... It was felt that there was a hereditary type of socially inadequate individual for whom society at large could do nothing ... The last twenty years have seen an almost complete about face in regard to this problem. Social scientists no longer feel utterly incapable of dealing with the Kallikaks ... Their long histories of vice and inadequacy can be explained almost as well by environment as by heredity ... Studies of social problems began to realize that.[83]

Explanations for the dysfunctional individual had shifted from biology to sociology, and the root cause of such problems was family socialization. Social work promised to delve into the minute details of family life to uncover the customs, habits, and actions that triggered anti-social behaviour.

Social Casework

The most popular method for probing the family was differential casework. The application of casework in English-speaking Canada was informed by American developments, in particular the pioneering work of Mary E. Richmond. Two of her books, *Social Diagnosis* (1917) and *What Is Social Case Work?* (1922), presented methods and techniques that would dominate the practice of social work by the late 1920s.[84] One observer referred to *Social Diagnosis* as "a [quasi]-legal textbook on the collection, classification and admissibility of evidence."[85] Richmond's approach was to apply methods used in medicine and social science to the study of the individual. According to the Catholic Welfare Bureau, casework was a modern method for "treating the trouble, not as a sudden misfortune or accident, but as a doctor would treat a disease, by a careful building up of information and then a diagnosis of the case, and lastly a steady and sure treatment."[86] Training in casework involved intensive instruction in the collection of evidence from the client, the family, neighbours, and outside agencies, and included education on interviewing methods. The preparation of records was an integral component of professional education, as were techniques of assessment and methods of treatment. Each individual problem differed, and the ideal social worker would be attentive to the particularities of each case. In a presentation to the 1928 Canadian Conference on Social Work, Father Haley revealed the complexity involved in "the art of interviewing":

the interview necessarily involves considerable questions as it is through it that statistical information must be secured ... the manner of the social worker has much to do with the success or failure of an interview, a soft voice, little courtesies, such as asking the client to be seated, enquiries regarding the health or the particular interests of the family, help to relieve tension and to put the client at ease ... The physical setting for the interview requires careful consideration ... It is evident that in a home visit there will be found many openings, many opportunities to break down the wall of reserve between client and interviewer which are absent in an office – the children, the pictures and photographs, perhaps pets or a garden, suggest natural topics of conversation and it is not necessary to ask as many direct questions. In fact, it would be impossible to do good casework without an occasional glimpse of the home. But the office also has advantages ... The man of the family can as a rule be interviewed with greater ease in the office.[87]

Detailed reports, including chronological accounts and observations, were compiled for critical examination. Case records provided the necessary material for formulating objective decisions about the proper course of treatment. Moreover, as Richmond noted, "a record so made becomes not only an indispensable guide to future action on behalf of the person recorded; it can be unexcelled material for training other case workers." Such records also served "as a basis for industrial studies made by case work agencies themselves."[88] They might also prove useful in juvenile court cases, as well as in family court, hospitals, and schools.

Essentially, casework provided a legitimate method for monitoring, regulating, and reforming private life. The accumulation of social evidence would form the basis for actions attempting to transform human behaviour. As Howe suggests, social work was "thoroughly immersed in one of modernity's key projects – to bring discipline and order, progress and improvement to the human condition."[89]

Richmond's social diagnosis and her focus on the environment as the root problem of poverty appealed to those Catholics seeking to legitimate their own separate professional schools of social work. By the late 1910s her method came to form the basis of instruction in Catholic social work schools, but it was modified to conform to Catholic dogma and was underwritten by Thomistic philosophical teachings. The outcome was a specifically Catholic social casework approach that combined social diagnosis with an emphasis on the sanctity of the family, marriage, and reproduction. Brown and McKeown discuss how, in American Catholic schools, the concern over the promotion of birth control, sterilization, abortion, and divorce "drove Catholic leaders to especially strenuous efforts to address [these] in the training of their own social workers. Along with extensive instruction in the church's view of the inviolability of marriage, the 'Catholic philosophy of social work' stressed the social workers' obligation to oppose the use of artificial birth control by clients."[90] This distinctive approach was used by Catholic charities to defend their work and to ensure that religious background remained an important consideration in relief work.

By the late 1920s Richmond's approach began to be eclipsed by a new therapeutic diagnostic practice informed by developments in psychiatry. This latter approach instructed social workers to be equally committed to the welfare needs of the poor, but focused attention more on individual psychology than on social environment. Increasing state involvement in relief work resulted in mounting pressure on voluntary agencies to adopt new psychological advances in social work. To ensure their ongoing presence in welfare work, Catholic charities increasingly accepted these new techniques, but continued to underwrite them with their religious teachings.

The Impact of Social Work on Institutional Practices

Social work's focus on reconstituting "normal" families fundamentally altered the practice of child care within Catholic charities. In the past, child care had often meant taking children at risk away from their parents and placing them under institutional care. With the advent of social work, institutionalization was seen as furthering anti-social behaviour, since "normal" child development could only occur in natural family settings. Only in extreme cases should the child be removed. Social workers were first to make every attempt to restore normal family life. The goal of child care was to improve the life of children through judicious and expert interventions that would rehabilitate the child and the family as a whole, rather than merely rescuing children from family neglect or abandonment. It was this new child-care ethos, which viewed the placement of children in such family environments as foster homes or boarding homes as preferable to institutions, that resulted in the "death of orphanages." As one Catholic Welfare Bureau article indicated, "A few years ago all homeless and dependent children were placed in institutions ... It is a recognized fact that children reared in institutions are in abnormal relations to family life and society ... there is a new development in child-caring which will save the child from all of these institutional handicaps – that of placing these children in suitable foster homes."[91] Extensive campaigns were launched to locate adoptive families and suitable boarding homes. The Catholic Church participated in and endorsed province-wide adoption campaigns initiated by the Ministry of Public Welfare.[92]

Even in cases of illegitimacy, every effort was made to keep mother and child together, whereas in the past many pastors and agency workers had encouraged their separation. Historically some parishes had set up homes where single pregnant women were kept hidden from their families until the birth of their child. After a nursing period that could last up to eight months, women were returned to their communities, and their children were placed in orphanages to await adoption. Such practices became unpopular with the advancement of social work, which advocated that "children should never be kept from a home when that can be re-established."[93] Unwed mothers were to be encouraged to retain their children, but they were also to submit to social work strategies aimed at rehabilitating their "immorality." Social work would promote "the rehabilitation of the mother in society, the protection of her reputation, the prevention of further wrong doing, and the assurances of the welfare of the child. There must be sympathetic help for the mother and at the same time the rights of the child ... must not be ignored."[94] An explicit goal of the Child Caring Division of the Catholic Welfare Bureau was to provide social casework "to help the girl make a plan for herself and her expected child, and to work through any emotional difficulties she may have."[95]

The focus on restoring the family unit was not new; the Catholic Church had historically endeavoured to preserve the sanctity of the family. Social work, however, introduced new strategies for governing and "politicizing" the private sphere of the family. Casework methods focused on the specificities of each problem family, rather than pontificating about "the family." While priests may have preached the same Sunday sermon on the family, and voluntary workers may have treated all families alike, Catholic social work endeavoured to discover what was unique about the problems confronting each family. It adopted specialized knowledge and curative techniques in diagnosing and treating problems on a case-by-case basis. An exclusive focus on Catholic theology would point to a creed out of touch with modern notions of family and child psychology. Yet a study of technologies used in day-to-day practices reveals the extent to which modern scientific knowledge and clinical approaches were integrated into Catholic charities. The activities of the Catholic Church during the interwar period, specifically the work of Catholic social action and Catholic social work, are not indicative of a religious retreat in the face of secular social welfare reforms. Rather, Catholic social action and Catholic social work became integral to the formation of the modern welfarist project.

4 Social Casework during the Depression

The economic collapse of the 1930s was a catalyst for the expansion of state welfare programs. As the number of families on state relief soared, governments struggled to devise an administrative structure that could respond to the plight of the burgeoning poor. The new public relief programs, far from displacing the work of charities, intensified cooperative ventures, or "partnerships," between voluntary institutions and municipal departments. In Toronto, for instance, the Catholic Welfare Bureau, along with other organizations such as the Neighbourhood Workers Association, became the central agencies through which the city funnelled its relief to the poor. As Ontario's director of unemployment research, Harry Cassidy, attested, the "stimulation and coordination of private effort" was one of the central strategies adopted by Toronto's City Council.[1] Such collaborative endeavours, however, have received little attention in scholarly debates. Considerable attention has been paid to municipal, provincial, and federal reactions to the Depression,[2] but as John Douglas Belshaw observes, relatively "little is known about the extent and character of economic relief provided by the various churches."[3] Even less is known about the interrelations between the state and the voluntary sector in devising a welfare structure. It is this gap that is the focus of this chapter.

More specifically, the analysis focuses on the connection between Toronto's municipal relief programs and the Catholic Welfare Bureau from 1928 to 1935. Particular attention is paid to the implementation of three policy initiatives devised by the municipal government to manage poor relief: the introduction of casework assessment in 1929; the implementation of a two-tiered relief system in 1930; and the regulations imposed by the Department of Public Welfare between 1931 and 1935. For each initiative, private agencies such as the Catholic Welfare Bureau provided essential social casework assessments that formed the basis of the city's relief programs. By 1928 every applicant for poor relief had to submit to a mandatory social casework assessment.

Casework provided municipalities with a unique mechanism for "governing at a distance."[4] Governments could not intervene directly in the rehabilitation and moral reform of the dependent poor. Doing so would not only be too costly, but it would also breach conventional liberal rights in which the state limited its intervention in the private life of citizens. Hence governments licensed a growing cadre of social workers to intervene, police, and regulate relief applicants. Since family casework was conducted, not by government bureaucrats, but by trained social workers employed by voluntary agencies, it appeared devoid of partisan politics and state control.

Casework was an essential prerequisite for the development of a multi-tiered welfare system. Rather than relying on one common eligibility criterion for relief, casework enabled distinctions to be made between different categories of poverty. For example, those in need of health care or psychiatric services could be differentiated from those whose problem derived mainly from lack of work. Hence the poor could be classified into bureaucratically administered categories and then separated and regulated by distinct programs. The work of Linda Gordon and Nancy Fraser on the welfare state is insightful here. They describe how contemporary social services are constructed along a two-tiered system: the first tier consists of contributory insurance programs, such as unemployment insurance, disability pensions, and workers' compensation, for which participation in the labour market entitles an individual to benefits when in need. By contrast, the second tier, funded primarily through general tax revenues, consists of means-tested, non-contributory, stigmatized social programs such as welfare benefits. These provisions are associated with a range of discretionary supervision, testing, and regulation, and are administered as a form of charity rather than as a right of citizenship. The latter category is most often criticized for causing welfare dependency. Within this two-tiered model, the former group is always privileged, encompassing those "social citizens" entitled to pensions and other non-social-assistance benefits. Second-tier recipients are characterized as less deserving, are not considered "rights bearers," and consequently are subject to greater surveillance.[5] While Fraser and Gordon examine these practices as part of the contemporary welfare state, my work demonstrates how these processes emerged in the 1930s and were born, in part, of a mixed public-private welfare program that relied on social casework.

While the focus here is mainly on the cooperation between Toronto's municipal government and the Catholic Welfare Bureau, the analysis has wider relevance. This interrelationship typifies the dealings between city officials and other voluntary organizations in Toronto; similar exchanges also took place in other urban centres.[6] This account is not intended as a comprehensive or definitive history of poor relief in Toronto, but as an examination of how various forms of assistance involved both public and private administration. One obvious omission is the lack of reference to many federal and provincial relief strategies. Municipal policy was indeed shaped by directives from Ottawa and Queen's Park. The impact of these directives on charities, however, was largely filtered through local governments.

THE CONSTRUCTION OF THE CATHOLIC POOR

Catholics in Toronto were one of the groups hardest hit by the Depression; they constituted 14 per cent of the general population, but made up 25 per cent of the relief rolls.[7] Employment opportunities for Catholics were hampered by Orange dominance in Toronto and general xenophobia during the Depression years. Discriminatory practices, such as requiring applicants to state their religion on employment forms – adopted by companies such as Eaton's, Bell Telephone, Loblaws Groceries, and Consumers' Gas – restricted job opportunities for Catholics. Transient seasonal labourers, many of whom were Catholic immigrants, were unable to find year-round work during the 1930s. Transient men were especially reliant on private benevolence, since eligibility for poor relief in Toronto required that one be a British subject and a resident of the city for a minimum of one year. In addition, a significant number of Catholics were recent immigrants who did not meet the five-year requirement for naturalization and hence were not eligible for relief work.[8] Many of those fortunate enough to be employed were concentrated in low-end, semi-skilled jobs where meagre wages often did not cover the cost of basic necessities. Moreover, on average, Catholic families had more children than Protestant ones and thus required greater amounts of relief. And private funds for Catholics paled in comparison to those provided to welfare agencies by more wealthy Protestant societies such as the Masons, Rotarians, Kiwanis, and other lodges. Their members also worked to secure employment for fellow lodge devotees, a practice that discriminated against many Catholics.[9]

CASEWORK AS PUBLIC POLICY, 1928

Prior to the Depression, Toronto's House of Industry was the only private agency delivering publicly funded outdoor relief in the form of food and fuel. All those eligible, Protestants and Catholics alike, were referred there for public relief. Ineligible Catholics were sent to the local St Vincent de Paul Society or the House of Providence. Public funding to the House of Industry was, however, minimal, and hence the poor relied on such private agencies as the Catholic Welfare Bureau or the Neighbourhood Workers Association, among others, to provide for basic necessities such as clothing, help with rent, light, and gas bills, legal services, and other essentials, including employment counselling.[10] The city's fear of subsidizing idleness was used to justify such meagre support. The city did operate the Social Welfare Division of the Department of Public Health, which cared for the chronically ill poor and investigated House of Industry beneficiaries. It also ran a small municipal relief office that referred clients to various private agencies, but it otherwise was not involved in direct relief.[11] For the most part, municipal and provincial governments were reluctant to take on direct responsibility for social assistance, preferring instead to finance existing private agencies.

When economic downturns forced an unprecedented number of families onto public relief, however, the city began to be directly involved in the coordination of relief.[12] First-time applicants to the House of Industry rose from 1,802 in 1921 to 4,354 by 1928.[13] For the city, the rise in numbers translated into increased expenditures. Concern over this growing trend prompted the Social Welfare Division to conduct a study in 1928 into the causes of poverty. The sample group of seventy-six first-time applicants revealed that poverty was not simply the result of unemployment. It was a product of a much more complex set of social, cultural, and psychological issues. The city's investigation thus concluded that much more than mere economic relief was required: in the majority of instances, "there was evidence of the need for personal service and guidance, and frequently of medical and other treatment."[14]

The results of the study coincided with the claims put forth by social workers seeking to promote casework principles. In the early 1920s, social work had yet to emerge as a widespread accepted profession. It lacked the legitimacy accorded to the more established discipline of psychology. But as governments were searching for solutions to the relief problem and were being called upon to take a more active role in social welfare, social workers found a unique opportunity to promote their professional expertise. They moved swiftly to convince politicians of the need for a larger plan to rehabilitate families, a policy that integrated casework with outdoor relief. In her study of social work in Toronto, Gale Wills reveals how agencies during the 1920s, including the Neighbourhood Workers Association, the Catholic Welfare Bureau, and the Social Welfare Division, seized any "golden opportunity to 'sell' casework principles to the Board of Control and to the Taxpayer."[15] Their lobbying efforts did not go unnoticed, for in April 1929 the municipality officially adopted casework as its formal solution to the rising cost of relief. Henceforth, social workers were backed by a legislative mandate that officially directed them to intervene, monitor, and regulate the private lives of the poor. As governments determined policy and eligibility criteria, private agencies were made responsible for the rehabilitation of dependent families.

Whereas prior to 1929, first-time applicants had been able to apply directly to the House of Industry for outdoor relief, under the new municipal regulations, every applicant first had to undergo a casework assessment. These assessments were to be conducted by one of the city's eight private welfare agencies, which included the Catholic Welfare Bureau. Once completed, the assessment was submitted to the city's Social Welfare Division, which determined if applicants were eligible for public relief from the House of Industry. As applications were being assessed by the Social Welfare Division, private charities were "expected to tide the family over for a period of several months, and in the meantime do all they [could] to re-establish the families without the assistance of public relief."[16] The new casework policy thus helped the city reduce its relief budget by forcing private organizations to share the financial costs. Voluntary agencies received little financial compensation; the Catholic Welfare Bureau was allotted a one-time grant of $3,000 for its additional work and expenses.[17] According to the city, this amount was sufficient to ensure an effective and pragmatic relief system that would curtail indiscriminate charity to those on relief.

Apart from its fiscal benefits, the casework program appealed to city bureaucrats because it enabled the collection of data on various types and conditions of poverty. In the past, relatively few data were available on the causes of poverty. There were estimates of the number of poor, but not of the reasons leading to their condition. For example, there were no statistics on the number of cases resulting from illness, desertion of a spouse, or unemployment. Casework enabled the computation of such information. In effect, it provided a singular opportunity for the state to govern at a distance, as private agencies regulated, reformed, and compiled information on the destitute for public scrutiny. At the same time as casework functioned to ensure that individuals received guidance and counselling, it also allowed governments to gather systematic information on the subjects of social policy, thereby enhancing the scope of administrative power.

Paradoxically, the municipal government adopted casework at the same time as it was being questioned in academic circles. In her analysis of the University of Toronto's Department of Social Service, Sara Burke examines the skepticism surrounding the practice of casework. The department's director, E.J. Urwick, viewed casework's emphasis on specialized skills as putting at risk "any vision of the wider social facts."[18] He saw a danger in "the increasing tendency among social workers to overemphasize the value of psychological insight in casework."[19] In contrast to the differential casework model promoted by Mary Richmond, casework, by the 1930s, was increasingly influenced by Freudian diagnostic perspectives. This shift was in part a strategy promoted by social workers, who sought to imbue their profession with scientific authority.[20] Urwick feared that the emphasis on administrative technique would lead to the development of a bureaucratic "machinery" promoting efficiency and economy over the assessment of structural social conditions. These concerns were not unfounded. The social casework policy adopted by the municipality indeed served to consolidate an image of poverty as a moral-psychological problem, rather than as a consequence of economic hardship.

THE FORMATION OF A TWO-TIERED RELIEF STRUCTURE, 1929–1931

The stock market crash of 1929 was the catalyst for a renewed partnership between the city government and voluntary agencies. Widespread unemployment, coupled with changes in public opinion, which increasingly attributed poverty to economic, rather than social or psychological, problems, impressed upon the government the need for a more interventionist role. Moreover, as benevolent organizations found themselves unable to deal administratively or financially with the soaring number of citizens on relief, they began to demand greater government involvement. In 1930 Toronto's voluntary agencies, frustrated with government inertia, refused to assist any new applicants. For Catholics, the outcome was the transfer of over 1,500 families from the Catholic Welfare Bureau to the Social Welfare Division.[21] Such strategies, which were spearheaded by the Catholic Welfare Bureau and the Neighbourhood Workers Association, marked the beginning of a concerted effort by private charities to convince governments of the need to address unemployment as an economic, rather than a moral, problem. Charity, they claimed, was designed to alleviate moral and social problems; it could not rectify the failure of capitalism. Nor was its purpose to manage economic or national crises.

Forced to take on responsibility for a growing number of the homeless and destitute, city officials began re-examining their relief structure. A commission, the Civic Unemployment Relief Committee, was struck in October of 1930 to investigate and restructure relief in the city. The committee's conservative approach is evident in its three administrators: Howard S. Rupert, a senior official of the Civic Works Department; G. Arthur Lascellas, of the Central Treasury Department; and Frank D. Tolchard, general manager of the Board of Trade.[22] It took the committee less than a month to conclude its study, and by December 1930 its recommendations were integrated into new policy directions. The final recommendations reflected municipal priorities to minimize social spending while maximizing control over the unemployed.

The new relief program specifically targeted single unemployed men and women. Previously, all poor were governed by a uniform relief policy; one either met the eligibility criteria or not. With the implementation of new regulations, all recipients were classified and separated into one of two groups – families and single individuals. These groups were consequently administered by different welfare processes. Gordon and Fraser's analysis of the two-tiered welfare state can be applied here to describe how the first tier, consisting of poor relief families, continued to be regulated by private agencies and were identified as the deserving clients. Single unemployed men and women, however, were construed as a potentially unruly mass of layabouts soaking up scarce resources.

Under the new regulations, relief for the single unemployed became a complex exercise infused at all levels with surveillance. To apply for poor relief, these applicants first had to register with the newly established municipal Central Bureau for Unemployment Relief. Following a thorough investigation, the bureau separated the eligible residents from the undeserving. Those who met the stringent criteria for assistance obtained an eligibility card entitling them to seven days' worth of food and lodging from a private charity, after which they would be reassessed by the bureau and then issued a new card. Relief assistance continued to be provided through privately run charities (see appendix 5). But henceforth, private shelters were expected to service only those in possession of a card; the others were to be evicted. Private agencies were also responsible for monitoring the single unemployed. They were to record on the eligibility cards the number of meals consumed and nights spent at a shelter. This information could then be used by government officials to monitor the whereabouts of relief recipients. Alan Bass's study reveals that one night's missed accommodation was sufficient to incur intensive questioning to determine if the recipient had access to independent sources of funding.[23] The fear of interrogation – or, worse yet, the possibility of being cut off relief – was seen as a way of preventing individuals from participating in protests, petitions, militant union action, or communist activities.

Toronto City Council sought to legitimize its policies by construing the single unemployed as a largely indolent class, which if left unchecked would continue to exploit the limited resources of private agencies. As Cassidy argued, "before the Civic Unemployment Relief committee brought order into the care of single men in Toronto, it was very common for men to move about from one soup kitchen or mission to another, getting two or three lunches or dinners in different places until they were satisfied."[24] What municipal officials never mentioned in public was the way in which this new policy would dampen civil unrest and the growing popularity of communism among the unemployed. In their early work on the American social service sector, Frances Fox Piven and Richard Cloward argued that one of the primary objectives of welfare programs was the suppression of political dissent, particularly during periods of mass unemployment.[25] The eligibility card in essence operated in Toronto as a new technology of government that ensured a method of bringing single transients under the vigilance of state officials. Interestingly, this rigid supervision was maintained through a joint private-public system. Private agencies continued to monitor and regulate the daily activities of the unemployed on behalf of the state, but now the state was also directly involved in scrutinizing the behaviour of these individuals.

Of the 683 unemployed who registered with the Central Bureau on its first day of operation, 200 were Roman Catholic, double their proportionate representation in the city.[26] The bureau's investigation of these men revealed that many of them were not drawing on Catholic charitable organizations but on Protestant ones. Howard Rupert, of the Civic Unemployment Relief Committee, wrote to Archbishop McNeil in December 1930, imploring the church to bring these men under its care. The Church complied with the request, and in January 1931 it opened a new homeless shelter, the St Vincent de Paul Hostel, to accommodate 100 young men. The lodging was reserved for "innocent" young boys on Toronto streets.[27] Social welfare services had a long tradition of separating impressionable young boys from the "rather poor character" of older men. From this perspective, poverty was construed as contagious, necessitating barriers to prevent youths from being drawn further into a life of indolence or criminal activity. A concerted effort was made to remove youths from regular hostels and place them in lodging where they could be taught the virtues of order, discipline, and hard work.[28]

If relief to single men provided only bare subsistence, services for unmarried women were practically non-existent. Women in Toronto were generally left to the care of groups such as the Young Women's Christian Association. With few resources, the YWCA sought to place women in domestic service rather than provide relief.[29] Bass notes that hostels for women were generally non-existent during the 1930s. The Sisters of Service, however, did operate the Catholic Women's League Hostel. The hostel was initially designed to assist immigrant women, but was later converted to accommodate the growing number of nurses, clerks, and domestics thrown out of work. The Sisters promoted the home as a place where single women could enjoy "healthy and safe recreation." Intensive instruction was offered in a range of areas, including English, arithmetic, writing, and gender-specific courses such as sewing and household science. And of course, religious devotion was incorporated into the daily activities. The Sisters also sought to provide work opportunities for their "girls"; in 1933 over five hundred women were placed in employment. If a woman refused a job, she could be cut off relief.[30] As the number of women seeking assistance grew, the existing accommodations proved insufficient. Inadequate bedding meant that some slept on the basement floor, and many others were turned away. Attempts were made to find places for women in "approved" rooming houses that had been "carefully inspected" by the sisters in charge. The Sisters applied to the city for a grant to expand the hostel, but were denied permission on the grounds that such funding would set a precedent and encourage other women's groups to seek government aid.[31]

The low priority placed on relief for single women underscores the gendered construction of welfare provisions. The Central Bureau was largely preoccupied with regulating single men, who could threaten the status quo; it was far less interested in the plight of single women. In 1933, for instance, Catholic single women were no longer required to register with the Central Bureau. Their control was relinquished to the Catholic Welfare Bureau. Although their status presented a moral dilemma, unlike single men, they were not seen as a political risk, and hence private casework was deemed more appropriate than government control.

While single men fell increasingly under the control and surveillance of city officials, families on relief continued to be regulated by private institutions. Family casework was thought to be the most effective means of restoring households to self-sufficiency. It was identified not only as the most efficient means of curtailing fraudulent applications but also as the least expensive way of dealing with the situation, since it relied more on philanthropic funds than on tax dollars.[32] The municipality channelled a mere $160,000 to Toronto's charities for the explicit use of family casework. Some $20,000 of the full amount was reserved for the Federation of Catholic Charities.[33] Authority over how the money was to be spent, however, rested with the board of Control.[34] Voluntary agencies had to agree to terms identified by the board and were subject to various forms of inspection to ensure they complied with established conditions.

REDEFINING "SOCIAL PROBLEM" FAMILIES

The establishment of the City of Toronto's Department of Public Welfare in June of 1931 marked the beginning of a new, intensified relationship between private agencies and the municipal government. The department, whose formation had been proposed in the 1930 report of the Civic Unemployment Relief Committee, was promoted as a means of centralizing social services by amalgamating and coordinating the administration of all the city's welfare relief functions.[35] It would be given the power to "govern the soliciting of alms, food, clothing, money and contributions of any kind for charitable or benevolent purposes in Ontario."[36] In effect, it would be invested with the power to regulate "the officers, staffs, servants, employees and agents and the powers and duties" of all institutions, private or public, involved in charitable work. This would essentially amount to complete control over the administration of charities.

Social workers, determined to preserve control over their work, launched a campaign to limit the department's mandate. Charlotte Whitton, executive secretary of the Canadian Council on Child and Family Welfare, was at the forefront of this opposition. On 25 March 1931 she wrote to Archbishop McNeil to solicit his support for a united front against the City Council's agenda. As she stated, the proposed legislation would give a "tight measure of control over the internal management of institutions which the Department at present has no staff to enforce."[37] The efforts were of no avail. The provincial government approved the formation of the municipal Department of Public Welfare. And as expected, the department succeeded in permanently restructuring the charity sector in Toronto.

Albert W. Laver, a former chief tax collector, was appointed the first public welfare commissioner. Within a year, he had devised new funding criteria which brought private resources under greater government regulation. Annual lump-sum grants to charitable institutions were terminated, and from 1932 on, subsidies were provided on a per capita/per diem basis. Applications were to be submitted to the department, which would investigate "each case to determine eligibility on the grounds of legal residence and indigency, as well as the social justification of the City's assumption of payment for either full or partial maintenance as required."[38] This new fiscal method, as one Catholic Welfare Bureau official complained, was "becoming monthly more difficult and intricate ... To secure a refund for any item of relief a visit must be made to the home and a long and complicated type-written report must be submitted. No matter how much arrears are owing, only $15.00 rent, $3.50 gas and $2.00 light can be paid: a consecutive month's rent or a consecutive gas or light bill cannot be paid."[39] This procedure, as Laver himself noted, "enabled the Department to maintain a thorough working knowledge of the functions of these various organizations to the end that duplication is avoided, and uniformity of practice maintained."[40] It also meant that decisions as to the extent and type of relief given to a particular family were no longer determined by private agencies.

The new funding arrangements limited the ability of benevolent institutions to respond to the growing relief crisis. By August 1931 some 2,432 families totalling 11,130 individuals relied on the Catholic Welfare Bureau for relief, an increase of 77 per cent from the year before. In 1932 roughly 1,000 more families were added to the relief rolls[41] (see appendix 6). The city's per diem rates were insufficient to meet the needs of the thousands of applicants lined up at the Catholic Welfare Bureau's doors. Moreover, the archdiocese had its own financial troubles, which prevented it from covering part of the bureau's debt. By February 1933, sixteen parishes within the Archdiocese of Toronto had defaulted on their interest payments.[42] Unable to deal with the growing caseload, the Catholic Welfare Bureau appealed to the Department of Public Welfare to assume a greater share of the expense. The bureau requested that the department take full charge of those families where chronic disability, neglect of children, or imprisonment of the breadwinner was a problem. In June of 1932 the Neighbourhood Workers Association, the umbrella organization for secular and Protestant charities, had issued a similar plea. By June 1933 the department had agreed to a limited transfer of cases where household heads were fifty years or older or were veterans. Another 1,500 families were then handed over to the department, leaving some 2,500 families under the care of the Catholic Welfare Bureau.[43] This shift was the start of a process that firmly established unemployment relief under the authority of the Department of Public Welfare.

Two months earlier, in April 1933, Laver's office had begun its campaign to take control over direct relief. When the number of unemployed surpassed 27,000, Laver convinced City Council to transfer responsibility for outdoor relief from the House of Industry to his department. A new voucher system replaced the traditional bags of food and fuel distributed by the House of Industry, and home investigations of families on relief were intensified. According to historian James Struthers, "about the only aspect of Toronto's relief operation that remained unchanged" under Laver's administration "was the level of food, fuel and shelter allowances," as these were set by provincial standards.[44]

In 1934 Laver extended his reform agenda by targeting poor families. As tens of thousands of families faced misery and despair, public opinion in Canada began shifting. The traditional stigmatization of relief recipients was slowly being displaced by a new discourse emphasizing social rights. Governments across the country were being called upon to enhance their role in social welfare. In Ontario this new mood was exemplified by the election in 1934 of Mitchell Hepburn, whose platform called for "a new deal for the unemployed."[45] In Toronto, relief to the "unemployed" was intensified, but only for those fortunate enough to be categorized as the "true" victims of economic hardship.

Under Laver's 1934 policy, families on relief were separated into two tiers: "unemployed" cases and "social problem" cases, with each category being administered through different welfare practices. The "unemployed cases," those families whose dire circumstances could be directly attributed to lack of work, were cast as a public priority and entitled to immediate state benefits. Their administration was transferred from private agencies to the Department of Public Welfare. Poverty among "social problem" cases, on the other hand, was identified, not as the result of an economic downturn, but as emanating from a defective family structure. Those belonging to this category were defined as "a) social cases where unemployment is not a factor, such as desertion, illness, etc.; b) social cases where relief is not a problem but where an acute family condition exists requiring guidance, and c) cases where unemployment is a factor but where family demoralization and other serious family problems render necessary skilled and sympathetic casework service."[46] These families were subjected to constant supervision and regulation. In order to obtain assistance, they first had to apply through a private organization, which conducted an initial assessment to be forwarded to the Department of Public Welfare. To maintain their eligibility, they were forced continually to prove their worthiness by opening their homes to monthly inspection. Under this program, approximately 1,000 "unemployed" Catholic families were handed over to the Department of Public Welfare, leaving some 1,400 "social problem" families under the administration of the bureau.[47] The reduced load of the bureau meant that caseworkers had "more time for home visiting."[48] But, as Marion Bell's research on the bureau suggests, social workers did not always follow up on the required monthly supervision.[49] They were, however, required to establish that every effort was made to return families to self-sufficiency.

A casework assessment form used by the Catholic Welfare Bureau reveals the detailed information collected for the classification of families (see appendix 7). Catholic caseworkers used a checklist to differentiate between twenty-nine possible causes of dependency. These included health, legal difficulties, marital disputes, parent-child conflicts, illegitimacy, common-law unions, alcohol abuse, and mental deficiency. These

Table 4.1
Social problems outlined in the Catholic Welfare Bureau 1935 annual report for family agency

Type of problem	Percent
Father deserted	18
Parent serving prison term	5
Domestic trouble	8
Drunkenness, immorality, neglect of children	12
Mother dead, in mental hospital, or in sanitarium	8
Widows ineligible for mother's allowance	7
Families not eligible for public relief*	42

SOURCE: "Catholic Charities: Annual Report for Family Agency," *Catholic Register*, 24 October 1935.
* This category typically consisted of cases where the head of the household had employment, but was receiving an insufficient wage to support a large family.

perceived social problems were rarely considered to be the result of economic circumstances. The Catholic Welfare Bureau's 1935 annual report outlined the distribution of some of these conditions (see table 4.1). Topping the list are desertion, drunkenness, immorality, and neglect of children. One should also note the apparently gendered construction of these classification schemes. Although there are no actual statistics on the gender breakdowns between the two tiers for Toronto, in 1943, 59 per cent of Ontario's relief population were women.[50] One can presume that the social problem cases consisted of a higher percentage of women since they were less likely than men to hold regular employment during the 1930s. They were also more likely to head single-parent families as a result of illegitimate births, family dislocation, or desertion by men. Men often left their families behind when they went in search of employment. Thus women continued to be defined by their incapacity and dependency as appropriate recipients of charity.

The application of these categories was significant in that it enabled the reconfiguration of poverty into concrete bureaucratic designations – for example, the "unemployed," the "alcoholic," or the "single mother." Once such categories were established, governments could devise specific practices to govern the various relief constituencies. The process allowed for a new technique of governing that could address specific types of social problems. For instance, during the 1930s, various attempts were made to promote the use of birth control among dependent families, and sterilization was advocated for those of "low grade" intelligence on relief. Albert Laver, the public welfare commissioner, himself supported such strategies. In 1936 he argued that the "lack of sterilization law is yearly increasing the relief burden in Toronto – this was partly because women of low mentality, giving birth to illegitimate children, usually come to the city to lose themselves – 63% of the whole social case load is caused by illegitimacy and immorality of all types ... I think the laws should be so drafted that any person asking state aid could be compelled to be sterilized if a fully qualified board were of the opinion that he should be."[51] The Catholic Church strongly opposed such measures. For Catholics, all interference with "natural" reproduction, including birth control, sterilization, and abortion, was completely immoral. The vociferous condemnation of all forms of birth control by the Catholic Church, according to Angus McLaren, "was clearly important in attenuating the success of the eugenicists in Canada."[52]

With the Depression, a multi-tiered system of poor relief emerged in Toronto that reflected a new discourse on poverty. Prior to the 1930s, public officials had attempted to disassociate poverty from economic conditions. It was understood to be a question of immorality, a social problem requiring disciplinary and moral reform.[53] Such assumptions could no longer be maintained during the Depression. It was at this juncture that economic questions come to infuse the discourse of poverty, but only for some of the poor. Certain sectors of the poor were deemed economic victims, a group of unemployed who need not be reformed since they already possessed the proper work ethic.[54] The category of unemployment did exist well before the turmoil of the 1930s; Struthers locates the emergence of unemployment in Canada "as a major political issue in the late nineteenth and early twentieth centuries as progressively more people made the transition from self-employment in agriculture to wage employment in industry."[55]

But although unemployment was identified as a distinct condition, it did not figure in welfare policies until the 1930s. Even though distinctions between the "chronic poor" and the "unemployed" were identified prior to the 1934 policy, as Cassidy posits in his 1932 report, "both groups, from the standpoint of existing public policy, belong to the poor, and both receive the same treatment ... without any distinction being made between them. Both are equal in the sight of our relief system."[56] Two years later, however, these groups were regulated by different welfare practices. William Walters's study of unemployment in Britain illustrates how mass unemployment during the 1930s "designate[d] an arrangement whereby, for the first time in industrial history, a large majority of the victims of industrial depression [were] registered, relieved and counted, i.e., governed, as 'unemployed' persons – as opposed to vagrants, paupers, deserving cases, etc."[57] As Walters argues, the distinction does not reflect nineteenth-century concerns over the deserving and undeserving; rather, "it is a distinction which is made at the level of statistical analysis." Distinctions were made not between individuals but between types of poverty.[58] These distinctions did not simply reflect differences of categories, but were related to concrete ways of governing the poor. Once the unemployed were redefined as an economic problem, they became a public priority, a group that could claim a right to public assistance. This construction of the unemployed as being entitled to state benefits culminated in Canada's unemployment insurance legislation in 1940.

At the same time, those considered "social problem" cases became stigmatized as a class whose loose morals, lack of control, and unsanitary habits were the root cause of their dependency. Dependency was differentiated from poverty, and it continued to be construed as a social and moral problem. Thus the state could justify a distant supervisory role that left these cases primarily under the control of private social workers. This does not mean that those receiving direct government relief were entirely devoid of moral regulation. Margaret Little's analysis of Ontario mother's allowance attests to the state's involvement in the moral scrutiny of the poor.[59] Moreover, the public regulation of single men was infused with efforts to govern their behaviour. However, the logic that underlay the methods of investigation used for each group was quite distinct. While the unemployed were governed as an economic problem, regulation of the social problem cases was aimed at reforming a moral, physical, or psychological condition. Public assistance to the former category was aimed at *preventing* poverty, as it was designed to support families until work became available. Relief to the social problem cases was administered as charity (not as a right), and recipients continued to be subjected to a range of practices aimed at *treating* the causes of indigence.

5 Private Policing and Surveillance of Catholics, 1920–1960

"The Holy See is terribly afraid of Communism, the centre of which, in Canada, is Toronto," wrote Toronto's Roman Catholic archbishop James McGuigan in 1937 upon returning from the Vatican.[1] "It is unfortunately making progress here and I would not be at all surprised if, within a few years, we have a real persecution similar to that in Spain." While exaggerated, such beliefs framed the perceptions of many English-speaking Catholics in the city.[2] Threatened by what appeared as a profusion of socialist organizing,[3] the Archdiocese of Toronto had by the 1930s developed an extensive infrastructure to seek out, regulate, and prevent the spread of communism.[4] As the Toronto Red Squad, a branch of the police department, was using coercive tactics to thwart communist-related activities, the Catholic Church was deploying a variety of means to avert this apparent danger, including the surveillance and infiltration of socialist groups and a pervasive moral and educational campaign aimed at newly arriving immigrants. While it conducted its own investigations, the church's endeavours were supported by state officials. It obtained intelligence information from the Red Squad as well as secret Royal Canadian Mounted Police (RCMP) reports. These actions went far beyond the realm of religious proselytizing or philanthropic endeavours. The strategies employed by the church amounted to an active policing and surveillance of individuals that operated independently from law-enforcement agencies but were intertwined with state political initiatives.

This chapter highlights the historical role of the Catholic Church in the private policing of citizens and the maintenance of national security. The analysis introduces a broader definition of policing and surveillance, one that examines how these operations functioned within a mixed social economy involving public and private institutions. While Mariana Valverde and others use the mixed social economy to analyze philanthropic social services, this approach is adopted here to illuminate the multiple, contradictory, and interlocking techniques and technologies used to uphold national security. Such an approach highlights how private lives are policed by a variety of moral, social, and legal bodies.

The activities by non-state organizations are, for the most part, overlooked in studies on political surveillance. Most analyses of political or national security emphasize the state as the apex in the maintenance of social order.[5] For example, in historical works by Gregory S. Kealey and Reg Whitaker, among others, surveillance tactics adopted by extra-state institutions, when examined, are typically discussed as incidental to public order. These works reflect the common understanding of policing as consisting solely of the state-sanctioned actions of the criminal justice system. An examination of the activities of the Archdiocese of Toronto, however, reveals a church that was actively involved in the private policing and surveillance of individuals. The anti-communist activities of the Catholic Church point to a need for re-evaluating and extending commonplace notions of the processes and techniques involved in safeguarding national security.

The term "private policing" is typically used in the criminology literature to distinguish non-state organizations involved in preserving social order from the criminal justice system. It commonly refers to an earlier practice when much of the responsibility for public order rested with individual citizens.[6] This is contrasted with the development of the modern police force in early nineteenth-century London in response to a changing industrial society. More recently, the term "private police" has been applied to community-based programs such as Neighbourhood Watch or private security personnel hired by corporations.[7] These definitions, however, rarely consider non-state policing and surveillance as a continuous historical phenomenon that has often been intertwined with and operated alongside the criminal justice system. The term "private policing" tends to be almost exclusively used to describe a corporate agenda concerned with securing private property; the role of private philanthropic policing and surveillance is rarely considered.[8]

This oversight might in part be attributed to how private philanthropic institutions enforce discipline, which, most often, does not conform to traditional forms of surveillance and punishment. Public authorities secure social control through the threat and deployment of coercive force, and private corporate police attempt to prevent crime through the knowledge that one is being monitored, as in the use of video cameras. Philanthropic control, although it may at times resort to punishment, is more concerned with minimizing social risk by regulating and reforming behaviour.[9] It is this concern with moral regulation that distinguishes philanthropic policing from private corporate policing. In evaluating the role of corporate security systems, Shearing, Stenning, and Addario posit that corporate policing is concerned less with moral reform than with reducing risk.[10] Philanthropic institutions, by contrast, are concerned specifically with instilling the "right kind of character." These institutions, as demonstrated in Valverde's work, promise to deliver a subjectivity that will solve social problems by reforming the way we govern ourselves.[11] In fact, Valverde proposes that non-state organizations are often more successful than the state in reforming citizens. This outcome reflects the public-private relationship, in which institutions operating within the private realm, including philanthropic and corporate institutions, are much less confined by the legal boundaries and limits of privacy. For their part, governments often participate in moral-reform efforts by providing the legal framework for voluntary action and by supporting private campaigns through funding and information.[12] It is precisely this interaction between private and public institutions that is central.[13] This conceptualization disrupts the image of two clearly defined, bounded, and separate spheres. It opens up the possibility of exploring how the public sector is linked to private forms of social reform, and as well, how private policing and surveillance participate in securing public order. In the exploration of these interconnections, the idea of the state as the sole guarantor of social order is deconstructed, thereby bringing to light the role of the private charity sector in preserving public order and national security.

ENGLISH-SPEAKING CATHOLICS AND THE IMMIGRANT "PROBLEM"

Most analyses of the Canadian Catholic response to communism have dealt exclusively with the church in Quebec. Few works, if any, reference the activities of Catholics in Toronto. Yet the Catholic Church in Toronto, under the direction of Archbishop Neil McNeil from 1912 to 1934 and Archbishop James McGuigan until 1971, developed a number of strategies and techniques to prevent communist infiltration among newly arriving immigrants and to ensure a loyal English-Canadian Catholic community.[14] Seditious acts that threatened to destroy the Canadian social fabric also challenged the now entrenched patriotism of English-speaking Catholics. Thus Catholic anti-communism reflected both a religious ideological opposition and the interests of a privileged class attached to its private property and liberal institutions.

By the mid-1920s the hierarchy of the Roman Catholic archdiocese consisted primarily of Scottish and Irish immigrants. This hierarchy was especially worried that communism would take hold among the thousands of immigrants arriving from central and eastern Europe. The majority of these recent arrivals, many of whom were practising or nominal Catholics, had emigrated from Hungary, Italy, Malta, Poland, Lithuania, and Ukraine. The Catholic population in the Archdiocese of Toronto increased from 85,000 in 1920 to over 164,000 by 1935. In 1941, Catholics in Toronto represented 16 per cent of the city's population.[15] These immigrants' working-class backgrounds and their lack of fluency in English meant that many were concentrated in low-paid, unskilled jobs.[16] Deeply rooted prejudices against foreigners and lingering hostility towards Catholics further hampered their employment prospects. In addition, the church viewed their religious devotion, which did not conform to Irish standard practice, as promoting idolatry. Their foreign values and customs were taken as evidence of their predisposition to superstitious beliefs and radical ideologies. With little relief and few jobs available, Catholic leaders feared that these immigrants were potentially ripe for communist organizing. After all, the Communist Party of Canada had been quite successful in recruiting immigrants.[17]

Founded in May 1921 in Ontario with twenty-two members, the Communist Party of Canada (CP) operated underground until 1924. Although the executive was largely British-born, by 1929, 95 per cent of the rank and file was composed of immigrants, primarily from the Finnish, Ukrainian, and Jewish ethnic groups.[18] Despite some gains, by 1929 the party had yet to draw a significant following; its membership totalled 2,876, and in the Ontario provincial election that year, the CP polled a mere 1,440 votes.[19] During the Depression, its membership did increase, particularly among the poorest elements of society. While the party did poorly in the 1935 federal election, by 1936 two communists had been elected to the Toronto Board of Control and one to the Board of Education. In the 1939 Toronto municipal election, Tim Buck, the party leader, registered 45,112 votes.[20] Most of those voting for the CP, however, were not full-fledged communists, but supported communist attacks against low wages and insufficient government relief. At a time when few groups championed the cause of the destitute and the unemployed, many turned to the CP for hope. Nevertheless, the party never gained sufficient support to significantly challenge the status quo. Its national membership barely exceeded 16,000, a level achieved only by 1939. Moreover, as Ivan Avakumovic notes, most of the east European membership "was often unwilling or unable to participate in those Communist activities ... the CPC considered essential."[21] They tended to limit their participation to communist events within their respective ethnic communities.

POLICING RADICALS: THE RED SQUAD, THE RCMP, AND THE ARCHDIOCESE

For the Archdiocese of Toronto, however, the party's denunciation of religion as the "opiate of the masses" and its promotion of atheism and (supposedly) free love threatened to undermine the sanctity of the family and eradicate religious freedoms. Catholic leaders were determined to prevent this "evil menace" from taking hold within ethnic communities. The church's first task in fighting communism was to gain intelligence about the party's clandestine operations, propaganda techniques, and various strategies. Obtaining such information was not a difficult task, as the church relied on its pre-established relationship with the local police. Although the Toronto police force counted many Orangemen on its staff, it collaborated with the Catholic Church on a number of occasions. For example, the two organizations worked together on initiatives to reduce crime in the city, and often the inspector of police, bypassing official channels, would place delinquent youths under the supervision of Catholic youth leaders to prevent them from appearing before the courts.[22] Moreover, at an ideological level, the anti-communism shared by the two organizations was coloured by fascist overtones; the Vatican at this time supported Mussolini's government, and some Catholics in Canada viewed fascism in a favourable light.[23]

Furthermore, the church defended both federal and municipal police attempts to subvert communism.[24] The Toronto Red Squad, a branch of the municipal police department under Chief Constable Brigadier-

General Denis C. Draper, was notorious for its brutal treatment of dissidents. The squad, commonly known as "Draper's Dragoons" for its heavy-handed repression of communists, would beat and jail members for distributing propaganda; it prohibited meetings in "foreign" languages, prevented the party from campaigning during elections, and used tear gas – for the first time in Canada – to break up meetings. And in August of 1931 the Red Squad arrested nine of the party leaders under section 98 of the Criminal Code, a broad statute suggesting that strong criticism of the government could merit incarceration.[25] While labour groups, even those estranged from the Communist Party, demanded a public investigation of the harsh actions deployed by the Red Squad, members within the Catholic Church counteracted public indignation by applauding the police actions. In a *Globe* article, Catholic clergy and members of other religious and financial groups sanctioned the squad's attempt as an effort to uphold justice and democracy.[26]

The church endorsement of the Red Squad and RCMP operations enabled it to elicit secret information on communist organizing within the city. Confidential RCMP surveillance records compiled in 1923 appear among archdiocesan files. The records chronicled the range of communist activities throughout Canada and particularly focused on the vulnerability of immigrant groups, specifically Ukrainians and Finns. Page after page revealed the extensive means by which the party attracted youths into the communist ranks.[27] "The principal subjects taught are the Ukrainian language, ... revolutionary songs, and such smatterings of history, economics and science as will implant in the children atheistic, revolutionary and communistic opinions and prejudices. Every effort is made to induce the children to regard Russia (including the Soviet Ukraine) as a model country; to hate religion, patriotism, and the government ... and to desire and expect a revolution by violent methods."[28] This report recounted how at least ninety Ukrainian children were attending communist after-hours schools in Toronto.

When, in 1932, Archbishop McNeil requested information on communist activities in Toronto, Chief Constable Draper readily forwarded extensive intelligence reports compiled by Inspector Douglas Marshall of the Red Squad. One report documented the range of communist movements in Canada. Other files provided detailed accounts of propaganda techniques and emphasized the party's success among immigrants. Ethnic societies suspected as subsidiary organizations of the party were disclosed (many of which later appeared in the *Catholic Register* as associations for Catholics to avoid). Still other reports exposed how many youth organizations were in fact communist fronts designed to indoctrinate the future generation. The inspector was particularly outraged at the concerted effort to entice youth into the Young Communist League, and as he stated, "With the training that is being given the children of tender years, to oppose Law and Order, defiance of Police Order, and no check being made on these teachings, the result can only be one thing, revolution. These children will, say in ten years time, be militant and absolutely revolutionary, and unless steps are taken ... we are going to have a huge population of foreign extraction who will be prepared to go to any length to attain their own ends."[29] Although Inspector Marshall conceded that he did not know the exact number of communists in Toronto, his estimate, based on the circulation of the party paper, *The Worker*, was in the range of 40,000, an obvious exaggeration.

In effect, these reports painted the Communist Party as an organized movement of sedition determined to subvert democratic freedoms and manipulate people into becoming pawns of Soviet power. Communists, according to police sources, were playing on the misfortune and destitution of immigrants. While the party achieved only mediocre success in municipal and provincial politics, the reports depicted it as an imminent danger that would ultimately culminate in generalized civil unrest.

These reports, coupled with the information gathered through the archdiocese's own surveillance, were taken as confirmation that a communist conspiracy was at hand. According to Archbishop McNeil, 28,000 Catholics in his archdiocese had joined the Communist Party, and he was determined to find out the causes of this dissident behaviour.[30] In the 1930s the archbishop commissioned a systematic survey of each parish in his diocese. Initially, the archdiocese relied on its own informants, lay Catholics who attended ethnic functions and reported on any inkling of communist meddling. But Archbishop McNeil opted for a more systematic method: he hired his own spy, Catherine de Hueck, to police ethnic organizations within local parishes.[31] De Hueck, a Catholic who had fled the Russian Civil War, was an optimal choice. Her Russian heritage and ability to speak several Slavic languages allowed her easy entry into communist organizations.[32] In October of 1931, living among the immigrant poor, de Hueck began infiltrating communist organizations and compiling a survey of their activities. Each week she would update the archbishop on the operations of the Communist Party. Part of her assignment included a visit to New York, the communist headquarters in North

America, to obtain newspapers and periodicals destined for Canada and to elicit information on communist activities in Toronto.

In 1932 she presented Archbishop McNeil with an extensive survey of her investigation, a ninety-five-page document on communist activity in Toronto.[33] The report included a comprehensive analysis of membership profiles, party structure and activities, propaganda techniques, and various schemes to attract immigrants. Communist promotional campaigns in Toronto were successful, she suggested, because they employed systematic planning; the city was divided into sectors, each with its own organizer, who was responsible for canvassing the area and for attracting workers and the unemployed to communist events. De Hueck recounted how educational and recreational activities, the ethnic press, and foreign-language speeches were designed to appeal to the sentiments of immigrant communities. She claimed that the Communist Party in Toronto published forty-eight papers in eighteen different languages. All forms of relief, including professional assistance from lawyers, doctors, and dentists, were provided to the poor as a means of luring them to the party. She described attempts by party leaders to infiltrate non-communist organizations. What de Hueck found most jarring was their work among school-aged children. Debating societies, social newspapers, summer camps, after-hours schools, and underground activities were organized by professors and teachers to inculcate radical ideologies among these youth. Moreover, "Atheistic Sunday Schools," as de Hueck referred to them, were held in private homes under the guise of national language schools. Their location was moved each week in order to avoid police detection. A further tactic, she noted, was the organization of societies such as the league of Youth against War and Fascism, which lacked an outward communist association, but was in fact used to draw new members to the party.[34]

In addition to the report, parish-by-parish surveys were conducted. These surveys included extensive maps of parish communities, on which black dots marked the locations thought to be the sites of communist activity. On one map entitled "Communist Activities in St. Patrick's Parish," a downtown Toronto parish, thirty-three black dots pegged the location of residences, rooming houses, bakeries, restaurants, pubs, theatres, non-Catholic churches, bookstores, and a "suspicious looking store," all thought to be places of communist activity. A good number of these establishments were owned by Finns or Ukrainians.[35] Mapping was a means of documenting the "character" of the street, and such forms of social mapping to plot urban poverty had been undertaken by social reformers such as Charles Booth in Britain and Jane Adams in the United States. This technique enabled the church to identify and regulate problem alleys, slums, and residential and business locations seen to be in "need" of infiltration, reform, and conversion. The surveillance reports confirmed the archbishop's suspicions that communists were preying on innocent, ignorant immigrants, who, although not inherently rebellious, were being swayed by cunning and unscrupulous communist propaganda.[36]

The archdiocese's surveillance and use of spies to police and map ethnic communities illustrates the historical importance of private policing by philanthropic institutions. It also demonstrates that policing was not limited to the criminal justice system, and that religious organization did more than preach. To characterize the church's operations as an extended branch of the state would be misleading; the Catholic Church had its own vested interests in eliminating "atheistic communism" and was much more influenced by anti-communist directives emanating from the Vatican.[37] Moreover, there is no evidence to suggest that the church circulated its reports to the local police. Yet both institutions benefited from an exchange of services; the church backed police retaliation and in return was kept abreast of the CP's activities. This relationship points to how securing citizens, a project undertaken by both the state and voluntary organizations, operated at multiple and intersecting levels. The means adopted to govern individuals, however, were quite distinct.

CREATING A BULWARK AGAINST COMMUNISM: THE DEPRESSION YEARS

While the Toronto police department relied on repressive coercion to punish dissidents, the Catholic Church secured its congregation by seeking to reform beliefs and instill a sense of moral fibre. The excessive deployment of force exercised by the Red Squad may have been successful in forcing many communists underground, but it was limited in its ability to effect a conversion of mind and always risked hardening attitudes. Legally entrenched democratic rights prohibit the explicit involvement of public authorities in the moral reform of individuals. The church, however, specifically sought to morally regulate private behaviour. As Archbishop McNeil stated in a 1933 brochure, *The Red Menace*, "by intensive action we must educate the people to a conversion of mind. It cannot be done by force or by law. It must be done by the power of the word, written and spoken. Then, and then only, can we hope for a return to Christian ideals and to Christian institutions, where charity and justice reign."[38]

During the 1930s the archbishop successfully launched an anti-communist campaign to ensure a bulwark against communism. In his view, the education of immigrants was paramount. Sunday sermons warned members to steer clear of subversive organizations, and afternoon radio broadcasts spoke of the ills of communism.[39] Catholic demonstrations reminded audiences that religious gatherings were outlawed in the USSR,[40] and study clubs were formed to educate the unemployed on the ideological dangers lurking in their midst. Services were provided in foreign languages, and new ethnic churches were built to retain the loyalty of immigrant families. To protect the impressionable minds of youths, a concerted effort was made to enrol immigrant children in separate schools. The Legion of Decency, a branch of the Catholic Welfare Bureau, was devised to root out indecent and objectionable community events. The legion protested against stage shows promoting "red propaganda" and denounced communist fundraising events. It monitored labour organizations suspected of being organized by left-wing radicals, such as the Ontario Federation of the Unemployed and the Federation of Democratic Associations. Blacklists were compiled of films, books, and magazines promoting socialist ideals.[41]

The Ontario Catholic press regularly printed articles on the persecution of religion in the USSR, as well as on clandestine activities within the country. At the same time as the Communist Party newspaper, *The Worker*, promoted Bolshevik ideologies, the *Catholic Worker* was circulated at factories and communist rallies throughout Toronto. Food wrapped in the *Social Forum*, another Catholic paper, was often left behind for workers in factories.[42] The editor of the *Catholic Register*, Henry Somerville, was unrelenting in his editorials on the communist exploitation of immigrant poverty. To distribute newspapers and leaflets, the church recruited university students from St Michael's College.[43]

Speaking engagements supporting Christian freedom were encouraged among the laity. Catherine de Hueck was often invited to speak publicly on the "Red Menace." As a former spy, she was considered an expert on the issue. At one address in 1933, de Hueck, accompanied by lay Catholic Mrs Harris McPhedran, addressed over five hundred women from different religious denominations. Their lecture, entitled "What Can Women Do to Help in the Present Crisis?," encouraged women to enter the homes of "these homesick lonely foreigners"; for only with "a little sympathy and understanding by voluntary workers" could communism be "successfully combatted." This sympathy, however, did not extend to a condemnation of the destitute conditions to which many of these immigrants were subjected during the Depression. Instead, de Hueck and her supporters denounced direct relief for promoting idleness, humiliation, and vagrancy. Rather, they suggested, "how much wiser [it is] to have each person work for what he or she receives if they only sweep the streets." As McPhedran noted: "What are we doing to conserve the fruit and vegetables which go to waste each year in Ontario? ... We could use the unemployed to pick, preserve and store them at little cost to the Government."[44] The dignity and pride of men, she and de Hueck argued, could only be maintained if they were transformed into contributing members of society. To provide concrete evidence of what "women can do to help," de Hueck, McPhedran, and Catholic reformer Helen McCrea opened a Russian restaurant, the Tachainick. They boasted that through their efforts, thirty-three people had been removed from the relief rolls in only three weeks. Their success was extended to other business ventures, such as a tailor shop, a bicycle repair store, and a handicraft workshop, all opened in Slavic residential areas. Initiatives such as these, they claimed, reduced men's dependence on society: they "restore[d] their self respect and incidentally rescued several of them from communism."[45] Work, not the dole, would prevent contact with the numerous halls spreading left-wing propaganda. The great appeal of these lectures is evidenced by the range of associations seeking de Hueck as a speaker, including the Toronto Board of Trade and the Toronto Rotary Club, where she was the first woman to address that organization.[46]

The extent of the church's anti-communist hysteria is evident in the controversy that emerged over the Canadian Commonwealth Federation (CCF) in the 1930s. Until the 1940s, any group espousing left-wing ideas was suspected of communist ties. The confusion over the CCF, founded in 1932, emanated from the Canadian Catholic Church's interpretation of the two papal encyclicals *Rerum novarum* (1891) and *Quadragesimo anno* (1931), which spelled out the Vatican's position on political movements.[47] While, in England, Catholic bishops did not consider the Labour Party as falling under the Vatican's repudiation of socialism, the Canadian Catholic Church was confounded over whether, as a socialist party, the CCF was condemned under the papal encyclicals. Adding to this dilemma were exaggerated accusations that the CCF was in effect overrun by communists. A report to Archbishop McNeil in the 1930s alleged that "the communists have driven a wedge in the socialist party known in Canada as the CCF ... [they] have bored deeply into the directing organism of the CCF Party in Canada."[48] While fabrications, such reports did place the CCF under the suspicious gaze of the church. In 1934 a pastoral letter issued by Archbishop Gauthier of Montreal denounced the CCF as a radical organization opposed to Christian doctrine. Church leaders throughout the rest of Canada were more cautious, merely warning Catholics of the party's potential socialist underpinnings but not formally denouncing the CCF.[49] Nonetheless, even though Archbishop Gauthier's declaration applied only to his diocese, Catholics across Canada believed that the CCF had been condemned by the church.[50]

In Toronto the editor of the *Catholic Register*, Henry Somerville, took issue with the Quebec declaration, arguing that the CCF platform in no way offended Christian values. He, along with Murry Ballantyne of the Catholic *Beacon* in Montreal, lobbied church officials to persuade them that the CCF was not a communist front but, rather, was akin to the British Labour Party. Indeed, as Ballantyne argued, the CCF "was perhaps even capable of being made our strongest defense against communism."[51] Somerville convinced McGuigan that to forbid Catholics "from supporting the CCF would alienate the working class and identify the Church in their view as the supporter of an unreformed and oppressive capitalism."[52] The debate culminated in a plenary meeting of the Canadian bishops on 13 October 1943. By then the CCF had modified its platform, giving assurances to the business community, and had become involved in an open conflict with the Communist Party over control of unions.[53] The bishops' conference concluded that, in a way similar to "the older parties," the CCF platform was "indifferent" and not opposed to Christian principles. The official report released by the bishops, however, simply declared that Catholics were "free to support any political party upholding the basic Christian traditions of Canada," and it did not specifically name the CCF.[54] According to Walter Young, the decree was so "ambiguous as to amount to almost a reiteration of the original condemnation."[55] Hence many Catholics continued to assume that the CCF was censured by the church. Eventually, Catholic editorials in both the *Catholic Register* and the *Beacon* clarified the church's position.[56]

In light of its strong reaction to left-wing movements, the church's response to fascism is of particular interest. Throughout the 1930s the church maintained a reserved response towards fascism. At one point in 1938 it issued an apology for having suggested that fascism was a menace equivalent to communism. Even after public opinion in Canada turned against Mussolini following his invasion of Ethiopia, and despite the clash between the pope and the Italian government over domestic policy in 1936 and the adoption of Nazi-like racial laws in 1938,[57] the Archdiocese of Toronto refrained from taking a strong position against fascism. While the archbishops opposed anti-Semitic activities and participated in mass protests against the persecution of Jews in Germany, they failed to seriously question fascist ideology.[58] When the archdiocese initially proposed a demonstration in Toronto against both communism and fascism in 1938, for example, pressure from the German and Italian Catholic congregations convinced Archbishop McGuigan to revoke his stand on fascism.[59] In the end, the parade was limited to a protest against communism. In an attempt to prevent any strife with the ethnic parishes, McGuigan forwarded an apology to German and Italian Catholic legionnairies stating that "there certainly never was any intention to condemn any particular form of Fascism now existing or to hurt the sensibilities of any of our Catholic people ... sorry that any misunderstanding has arisen and I'm very eager to dispel it."[60] The apology was also sent to an Italian priest, the Reverend Pellicelita, who was latter interned by the RCMP during World War II; McGuigan eventually obtained his release.[61] While socialist groups were being condemned, the archdiocese was, at least indirectly, defending Catholics sympathetic to fascist ideologies.

CATHOLIC RELIEF AND ANTI-COMMUNISM

The most invasive means by which the archdiocese enforced its moral regulation was not through intervention in party politics but through the Catholic Welfare Bureau, which had been established in 1922 to administer welfare activities for Catholics. Initially, private agencies such as the bureau worked to supplement public relief from the House of Industry and aided those ineligible for the dole, such as transient men. But in 1931, with the establishment of new regulations under the Department of Public Welfare, every welfare recipient had to first apply through a private agency.[62] This new arrangement, designed to root out fraud, had the effect of augmenting the intervention of voluntary agencies in the private lives of individuals. Those in need of relief were now forced to divulge their private selves to philanthropic workers who maintained detailed files on each case. Hence Catholics who relied on benevolent agencies became increasingly vulnerable to the moral reform efforts of the church. Given its increased ability to monitor families, the Catholic Welfare Bureau was also able to ensure that children were enrolled in Sunday school and that families were participating in what the church deemed "appropriate and acceptable" leisure activities.[63] The state was not directly involved in moral regulation, yet it clearly provided the legal infrastructure for Catholic benevolent agencies to interfere in private lives.

The superintendent of the Catholic Welfare Bureau, Father Michael Jo McGrath, was notably active in rooting out communist activities among the unemployed. He supplied Archbishop McNeil with any evidence about communist activity obtained from bureau case records. In a 1938 report to McNeil, he confirmed suspicions that the Unemployment Workers' Association, an organization advocating work and welfare initiatives for the unemployed, was, in fact, operating under the auspices of the Communist Party. The association, McGrath said, was "plan[ing] to forcibly seize Grace Hospital and to [hold] a sit-down strike in one of the large department stores ... and force the city to provide them with food, clothing and bedding equipment as specified by the association."[64] The church, he emphasized, should act promptly to circumvent such an "outrageous" plot.

According to McGrath, the best means of averting such communist activity was to find single men employment, preferably on farms far from the city. He undertook an extensive work-finding project in which lists were erected in parishes across the city to register businesses, households, or farms with opportunities for the unemployed. The majority of these employment positions offered little in the way of monetary compensation. For instance, the most common type of employment in the city was construction work, at which men could expect to earn a total of 63 cents a day ($3 to $4 per week). Farm work typically consisted of room and board and a meagre allowance of $5.00 per month. In 1934 approximately 1,071 men were found jobs in the city, and over 100 men were placed on farms each year. Unemployed Catholics were forced to accept these positions or risk being thrown off relief.

The Communist Party of Canada actively targeted those receiving aid from Catholic charities. It accused the church of ignoring the unemployed and of further demoralizing and pauperizing those on relief by providing insufficient aid. Members of the party tried to entice those lined up at Catholic soup kitchens with promises of better relief and services at communist halls. Police reports verified that such tactics were quite successful in luring men away from the Catholic House of Providence.[65] Father McGrath, outraged at the number of men receiving aid from non-Catholic houses of refuge, wrote to the city in 1939 complaining that "now there [was] no means of offering them work or [to check] whether they [were] involved in any part of the present crime wave."[66]

In addition to the Catholic Welfare Bureau, a settlement house was established to provide aid to those who failed to meet the stringent criteria for government relief. In September 1934 St Francis Catholic Friendship House opened at 122 Portland Street, in a working-class area of Toronto inhabited mostly by Czechoslovakians, Poles, Russians, Ukrainians, and Jews.[67] Although the settlement house was first proposed as a means to counteract Protestant efforts at luring new Canadians, the catalyst for its opening was the growing fear of communist "conversions." The house, founded during the Depression, was strategically positioned across from the Protestant Church of All Nations and a communist hall. This location enabled Catholics to counteract the appeal of communists among the unemployed. During elections, settlement workers posted "VOTE FOR CHRISTIANITY" signs across from the "VOTE COMMUNIST" slogans.[68] To run the house, the archdiocese hired Catherine de Hueck.

The Friendship House offered a range of services: soup kitchens, clothing distribution, English-language classes, and a shelter for single men. In the first month it provided 1,200 meals, and by February 1935 this number had increased to 2,300 per month.[69] Suitable activities to prevent adults from engaging in vice or, worse yet, communist subversion took the form of drama and dance classes, cooking lessons, religious study groups, and book talks. To attract children, after-school recreation was available. These activities functioned to inculcate a sense of inner-self improvement and responsibility, and moral education was a component incorporated into every event. For example, dinner in the soup kitchens was always followed by a discussion of social issues and Catholic teachings. These strategies, de Hueck claimed, saved hundreds of transient workers and poor immigrant families from communism.[70]

In a paradoxical turn of events, de Hueck's accomplishments soon came under attack. Opposed to the Friendship House, several priests called for an inquiry into its canonical status. Many objected to the house's financial status; funds were obtained largely through soliciting donations. Moreover, the clergy disapproved of de Hueck's personal life; she was a single mother as a result of her estrangement from her husband. Added to this, she was, ironically, accused of being a communist herself. Her constant discussions of communism were mistaken by some as evidence of communist sympathies. Furthering these unfounded allegations was the accusation that one of the staff at a similar house in Ottawa had been deported as a communist.[71] On 15 August 1936 a commission of five priests was established to look into the matter. The members concurred, not surprisingly, that the settlement house would be best administered by local priests. Following de Hueck's dismissal, Archbishop McGuigan requested that she continue investigating communist activity, which she did until 1938, when she left for the United States to set up additional settlement houses there.[72] She returned to Ontario in 1947 and founded Madonna House in Combermere, a training site for lay apostolates to the poor.

COLD WAR POLITICS WITHIN THE CATHOLIC CHURCH

As the federal government pursued collective security through international military alliances and nuclear deterrence, national security on the home front was also being safeguarded by extra-state institutions.[73] During the Cold War the Catholic Church was involved in its own practices of containment. It continued to police suspect communities and maintained a pervasive moral and educational campaign designed to curtail internal dangers and preserve freedom and security. These activities, however, have been largely ignored in accounts of the Cold War era, which tend to be framed by a state-centred approach. For example, Whitaker and Marcuse's extensive work on the Cold War includes a detailed discussion of extra-state and non-corporate institutions, but their analysis maintains a state-centred bias.[74] Those extra-state institutions that participated in a Canadian version of "McCarthyism" – right-wing groups, the media, avid anti-communists such as Watson Kirkconnell and Pauline McGibbon, and the Toronto Alert Service, to name a few – are characterized as having played a rather minor role in the formation of a Cold War outlook. As Whitaker and Marcuse suggest, "it is hard to know how much, if any, influence such services actually had, since the numbers and importance of their subscribers is unknown. Certainly, they had little influence relative to comparable groups in the United States at this time."[75] The Catholic Church may not have been as influential as the state or business in shaping a political and popular agenda, but it nonetheless was an important force that helped consolidate a post-war outlook. Catholic anti-communism and reform efforts permeated the private lives of thousands of Catholics and others living in Toronto. That the church had a significant impact on the communist movement is evident in the party's attempt to defend itself against the archbishop's accusations. In 1949 the Communist paper *The Tribune* reproached McGuigan for his "fascist plot" to destroy democratic freedom and militant trade unionism.[76]

The Cold War was not simply an international, state, or corporate concern: rather, it operated as a mixed social economy in which government interests merged with the goals of private voluntary institutions. The activities of the Catholic Church demonstrate how extra-state institutions were involved in engendering moral behaviour and political values that worked to consolidate the Cold War agenda. It is the interlinking between public practices and private initiatives that explains, in part, the success of post-war strategies in ensuring a Canadian public that supported an arms race and a doctrine of collective security.

During this era, federal and provincial interests used Catholic anti-communism to their own benefit. The Catholic vote in Quebec was essential to the federal strategy of collective security and to an increased international role in NATO. Politicians, including Prime Minister Louis St Laurent and Secretary of State for External Affairs Lester Pearson, not to mention Union Nationale premier Maurice Duplessis, sought to capture the Quebec electorate by dramatizing the Soviet peril to Catholic audiences. St Laurent, for instance, in a 1949 speech at the Richelieu Club in Quebec city, singled out a bishop in the audience and suggested that Soviet domination could result in the bishop's imprisonment, as had occurred to so many men of the cloth under communist rule.[77] Such Liberal practices, Whitaker and Marcuse note, were successful in convincing Catholics that Canadian troops in Europe and later in Asia "were standing on guard for God, church, and family against the armies of darkness."[78] This federal anti-communist rhetoric, although directed to French-speaking Catholics, gave more legitimacy to the Catholic crusade throughout the country.

Moreover, in Ontario the conservative government of George Drew was likewise seeking an ally in the archbishop of Toronto for his war against the "commies."⁷⁹ In a June 1945 letter to Archbishop McGuigan, Premier Drew outlined his concern over the growing momentum of Soviet power within the province: "the fact is that the communists have more votes than ever before. They have an active, vigorous, well financed organization. I believe their propaganda will continue to be as active as ever." As he fuelled the archbishop's fears, Drew encouraged an intensified Catholic moral campaign. For, as the premier claimed, "there is a very real need for an educational campaign showing what their purpose really is."⁸⁰

Attempts to sway the Catholic vote do not suggest that the church was a malleable instrument shaped by government interests. Anti-communism was well entrenched in the Archdiocese of Toronto before the Cold War. Rather, state initiatives and Catholic goals can be seen as merging over a common agenda to secure the nation against revolutionary movements. Federal and provincial governments may have had a greater advantage in creating a Cold War national outlook, but a pervasive pro–Cold War public opinion would not have been achieved without the consent and, more importantly, the participation of extra-state institutions. In this regard, the Catholic Church in Toronto was indeed a compelling force, actively involved in containing the spread of communism.

Just as the Gouzenko affair had disclosed how trusted public servants had engaged in espionage, so too was the church concerned with disloyalty amidst its own congregation. Rumours that the church itself had been infiltrated by "commies" intensified the surveillance of ethnic communities. By the late 1940s, suspicions were mounting over communist aims to penetrate all aspects of immigrant life, including ethnic parishes and local priests. Within Toronto, allegations regarding the Slovenian community led to a commission in 1949 on the "Religious Condition among New Canadians of Slovenian Descent."⁸¹ The investigation concluded that many Slovenian families living in Toronto were estranged from the church, and that this was indeed the outcome of communist propaganda. The names of individuals living in Canada under assumed identities who, before emigrating, had been associated with the CP were also divulged to the archbishop. One of these was the president of the Slovenian branch of the Holy Name Society in Toronto. Ironically, the society was a Catholic devotional confraternity known for its anti-communist activities.⁸² Moreover, complaints from parishioners revealed that at least two priests were affiliated with the Communist Slovenian People's Party. One was denounced by churchgoers for advocating communist ideals and "basing his treatment [of Slovenians] on their political affiliations." He was also accused of hosting meetings of the Slovenian People's Party in church halls.[83]

In the late 1940s, when concern was mounting over the presence of extreme leftist groups on university campuses, McGuigan promoted the formation of Catholic committees to "quietly size up the extent of communist activities" in universities.[84] Catholic students warned the archdiocese that university associations were being overrun by the Reds, and reports informed McGuigan that some recent immigrants had obtained teaching posts at Canadian universities for "the explicit agenda of spreading communism in Canada."[85] In response, the Canadian Federation of Newman Clubs (CFNC), formed in 1942 to foster unity among Catholic students, resolved in 1947 to combat communism on university campuses.[86] McGuigan encouraged the development of surveillance committees and financed the activities of the University of Toronto Newman Club.[87] The CFNC was successful in convincing other student bodies to protest the penetration of communist ideals into the National Federation of Canadian University Students, the main secular student body.[88]

In addition to policing by Catholics, McGuigan was closely associated with the Toronto Alert Service, a secular organization "dedicated to the task of gathering information" and alerting citizens to subversive operations in Canada and Soviet domination abroad.[89] Marjorie Lamb, the director of the service, in stipulating its objectives, claimed that "it is not the function of the RCMP to distribute information concerning Communists or communist activity. In the area of communist infiltration of ideas and psychological warfare ... their job is not to act, but watch and know. To see that the communists do not obtain their objectives in these areas is the job of every loyal Canadian."[90] The service was in part subsidized by the Catholic Women's League.[91] Moreover, McGuigan supported Lamb by circulating the service's publications, encouraging Catholics to attend her anti-communist study clubs, and inviting her to address Catholic gatherings. The Civic Election Alert, a branch of the Alert Service, would inform the archbishop about candidates sympathetic to communism. Not only did McGuigan distribute these names to all the churches in the various wards, but he also requested that pastors encourage their congregations to vote against Labour Progressive (Communist) candidates.[92]

At the same time as the federal state was ensuring deterrence through an arms race, the church was participating in containment through its moral and educational campaign. The archdiocese's strategies, including weekly sermons and social study clubs on "atheistic communism," continued to denounce communist threats.[93] The *Catholic Register* exacerbated concern over Soviet domination with such headlines as "Over Nine Thousand Priests and Nuns Killed or Arrested by Reds."[94] Speakers' series were organized by the church; at one conference, Watson Kirkconnell, an extreme anti-communist university professor, was invited to speak.[95] Kirkconnell had written the government pamphlet on communism in Canada, a distorted analysis of a country about to be overrun by Soviet power.[96] As new evidence of communist penetration surfaced, the church immediately attempted to quash its success.

To counteract the communist penetration of unions, the archdiocese formed labour schools in the 1950s. Involvement in the workers' movement was a priority for the church, as the Vatican encyclicals *Rerum novarum* and, more so, *Quadragesimo anno* encouraged labour associations as a means of protecting workers against unscrupulous capitalists. The development of communism was blamed on the excesses of capitalism, and as McGuigan noted in 1961, "Communism has had its appeal for one reason: because it presents itself as a solution to the economic problem."[97] Although the Vatican promoted participation in trade unions, it opposed any revolutionary activities; unions were to seek more cooperative approaches, rather than attempt to dominate business relations.

A National Catholic Union emerged in Quebec, but the expediency of a similar movement for the rest of Canada was a contested issue.[98] Since the early 1900s, the Quebec church had opposed affiliation with the American Federation of Labour or any international labour organization, insisting instead that Catholics participate in confessional unions. Such proposals placed Catholics outside Quebec in a precarious situation. In response, Archbishop McNeil argued that a National Catholic Union was not feasible. His alternative was the formation of labour schools to promote Catholic leadership in the workers' movement. Father Charles E. McGuire, who was placed in charge of the schools, drew on his contacts in the union movement and obtained prominent leaders to address his students. The schools were popular; they boasted over seven hundred participants and became known for their "leading role in unmasking communism."[99] Several union members, including those affiliated with the International Chemical Workers and the United Packing House Workers of America, sought out McGuire's schools to assist in liberating their unions from communist control.[100] The schools worked, in part, to counter the formation of a strong labour activism, and they reinforced a Cold War outlook.

The goals pursued by the Catholic Church during the Cold War were not dissimilar to those of the state. Internal security in the public sphere was ensured, as Whitaker and Marcuse note, through the "erection of controls to screen out 'security risks' among civil servants and immigrants; the elaboration of internal surveillance techniques to keep watch over dissident political activities; the dissemination of propaganda warning citizens of the dangers of Communism and celebrating the benefits of the Free World."[101] The Catholic Church was pursuing a similar agenda through its spies, informants, and surveillance of immigrants, its university committees to assess subversive activities, and its moral and educational campaign to create a Canadian Catholic bulwark that would defend not just religious freedom but the nation as a whole.

The activities pursued by the Roman Catholic Archdiocese of Toronto are evidence of how national security and a political Cold War ideology was ensured through the interplay of a multiplicity of forces extending beyond state or corporate powers. Extra-state organizations have historically participated in the policing of citizens; they have not simply been confined to religious devotions or to social welfare.[102] These extra-state forms of surveillance point to the pervasive nature of policing and the extent to which it permeates private life. Policing is not merely a coercive force; it operates at multiple levels. In this sense, private policing is emblematic of Foucault's work on discipline.[103]

Such private means of monitoring and regulating behaviour, however, cannot be subordinated and subsumed under state power or dominant interests. Securing citizens is ensured through the intersection of public and private institutions, and voluntary organizations are capable of making their own claims on the state. For instance, during the 1930s the Toronto Red Squad relied on endorsements from social groups to justify its heavy-handed approach to the Communist Party. And the government's anti-communist policy would not have been as successful, were it not for groups within civil society that shared this concern.

6 The Role of Catholic Private Agencies in Community Corrections, 1890–1940

By the 1890s the subjectivity of the delinquent child had shifted. No longer were young offenders thought to be hardened criminals to be punished for violating the law; they were now seen as misguided youths in need of understanding and rehabilitation. Social reform groups, such as the Child Savers Movement, and Protestant and Catholic children's aid societies condemned the incarceration of children in reformatories or adult prisons. Their efforts ushered in new crime control strategies that involved industrial and training schools as well as parole and probationary programs. These innovations were designed to remake young offenders, turning them into productive, law-abiding citizens. Privately run benevolent organizations were thought to be best suited for this remoralization process. As such, Catholic voluntary services were able to become key players in this new law-enforcement initiative. The Catholic Archdiocese of Toronto, for instance, operated two industrial schools by the 1900s, and soon after, Catholic agencies were administering parole and probationary programs for Catholic delinquents.

This chapter focuses on the interrelation between the Ontario government and the Catholic Church with respect to the juvenile justice system. It begins with a brief treatment of the church's initial foray into the field of corrections, namely, penitentiary chaplaincy. This is followed by an analysis of the church's involvement in the industrial school movement. The Archdiocese of Toronto built two institutions to house Catholic young offenders: St John's Industrial School for boys

(1895) and St Mary's Industrial School for girls (1900). These schools marked the beginning of the church's direct role in the juvenile justice system. Importantly, the analysis centres on techniques of discipline, practices of normalization, and the importance of casework in the governance of delinquents. Finally, I explore the parole and probationary services offered by the Catholic Big Brothers and Big Sisters, among others. The Catholic Church's work in the area of juvenile corrections served to blur the line between the voluntary and law-enforcement sectors. Public authorities were able to govern at a distance because private agencies compiled information and reformed young offenders on behalf of the state.

THE BEGINNINGS OF CATHOLIC PRISON WORK

The 1834 Penitentiary Act, which appointed a Protestant chaplain to the Kingston Penitentiary, exemplifies the importance placed on religion by the criminal justice system. The Protestant clergy were deemed an integral component of the rehabilitation process, since religious conversion was viewed as essential in the moral reform of convicts. Catholic priests, however, were initially barred from prison work. The Penitentiary Act included no provisions for Catholic clergymen, and prison wardens took it upon themselves to deny them access to penal institutions. Catholic priests, who feared that Protestant chaplains were converting Catholic inmates, lobbied the government to allow them to pursue their work in prisons. The unification of Upper and Lower Canada in 1841 increased the number of French-speaking Catholics sentenced to the Kingston Penitentiary and intensified public pressure to acknowledge Catholic prison work. In 1843 Father Angus MacDonnell was granted permission to begin his mission to Catholic inmates, and in 1846 the revised prison statute ensured the future recognition and financial compensation of Catholic clergymen. Later, in 1892, the Catholic Church of the Good Thief was built on prison grounds. Women detained in the Mercer Reformatory and those in the Don Jail also received regular visits by local priests, and in 1885 the Catholic Ladies Visiting Society began its moral reform work with female convicts, providing them with blankets, reading material, friendly advice, and other forms of aid.[1]

Catholic chaplains' first-hand knowledge of conditions within penal institutions placed many of them at the forefront of the prison reform movement. The devastating conditions faced by imprisoned young offenders were especially deplored by the clergy, who advocated the separation of children from adult criminals. In 1855 Father MacDonnell argued for the construction of juvenile reform institutions that would be "remedial, industrial and penitential. The end to be aimed at ought to be, a reform [of the delinquent], by discipline approaching as near as possible, that followed in a Christian and well-regulated family."[2] His statement echoed the sentiments of a growing reform movement that called for an end to repressive corporal methods and the formation of new institutions which would ensure the rehabilitation of juvenile delinquents through disciplinary education.

The construction of St John's Industrial School for boys and St Mary's Industrial School for girls reflects the Toronto Roman Catholic archdiocese's commitment to the prison reform movement. These institutions were built to house the growing number of Catholic juveniles sentenced by the courts. Both schools were administered by religious orders, with the Christian Brothers operating St John's, which opened with sixty beds, and the Sisters of the Good Shepherd running St Mary's.[3] The Sisters of the Good Shepherd had been involved in prison work since 1875, when they founded the Good Shepherd Female Refuge for Fallen Women, an asylum for adult female prisoners and prostitutes. In the early 1900s the asylum also housed a number of young female delinquents sentenced by the courts, particularly when overcrowding became a problem at St Mary's.[4]

THE CHANGING DISCOURSE OF JUVENILE DELINQUENCY

Before we review the internal practices of the schools, a discussion of the wider significance of the industrial school movement and the development of juvenile delinquency legislation is warranted. In Foucault's study of penal history, *Discipline and Punish*, he argues that modern prison systems differed from earlier penal practices in that disciplinary power came to replace corporal forms of punishment.[5] Although repressive forms of punishment were not done away with, modern penalization became more preoccupied with correcting and normalizing behaviour than with dispensing punishment.[6] The formation of industrial schools in Canada echoes this shift. Industrial schools were advanced as disciplinary educational institutions that, for the most part, did away with the corporal methods prevalent in reformatories.

Reformatories themselves, when first constructed in the 1850s, were deemed progressive institutions because they removed children from the harsh living conditions of prisons and from association with adult criminals.[7] Nevertheless, by the 1870s they were depicted as antiquated institutions whose austere practices and excessive corporal procedures fostered anti-social behaviour.[8] According to historian Paul Bennett, reformatories were depicted as nothing more than holding cells from which children more often "graduated to the Central Prison and the Kingston Penitentiary than to gainful employment and 'upright citizenship.'"[9]

By contrast, industrial schools promised to reform their wards through the implementation of a rigid system of moral discipline and training that would ensure the production of useful, contributing members of society. Industrial school advocates did not perceive young offenders as inherently evil felons deserving punishment, but as misdirected, irresponsible children who had been marred by family dislocation and improper socialization. The aim of industrial schools was to reform the character of the deficient child, rather than to penalize him or her for crimes committed. Modern penal practices, as David Garland argues, shift attention "away from the offence itself towards questions of character, of family background, and of the individual's history and environment."[10] The industrial schools aimed to mould subjectivity to a point where children would come to internalize normative middle-class values, behaviours, and work habits. Discipline, as Foucault claims, is an "art of correct training"; it "makes individuals"; it produces obedient, law-abiding, industrious, and hard-working citizens, and this was the objective of industrial schools.[11]

These new disciplinary institutions were increasingly seen as constructive not only for those youths who broke the law but for any child displaying a potential for criminal behaviour and, in particular, for the neglected and wayward children of working-class parents. If those children, foreshadowing the onset of deficient behaviour, were left unchecked, the middle class feared that future transgression of the law could be expected. Industrial schools offered a convenient solution to this problem.[12] The removal of children from city slums and their detention in industrial schools was promoted as a benevolent scheme that would save them from a brutish life of crime and vice. Industrial schools would provide children with the discipline and proper socialization that were lacking in their own families. They offered children a stable "home life environment where they could be given proper care, educated, taught a trade, and prepared to earn an honest living."¹³ It was this benevolent rhetoric that came to legitimize the incarceration of hundreds of poor children.

With the enactment of the 1874 Industrial Schools Act, the courts were empowered to incarcerate juveniles not only on the basis of criminal transgressions but also on the perceived criminal potential of the child. The act allowed for any children under the age of fourteen to be brought before the courts who were "found begging or receiving alms, found wandering in the streets and had no settled place of abode, who were found deserted or whose parents were in jail, whose parents or guardians claimed they were unable to control the child or who, owing to the vice of the parents, was growing up without salutary parental control."¹⁴ Later, other behaviours such as truancy and sexual immorality were added to the list. In effect, the act legislated the courts to make assessments based not exclusively on criminality but also on "normality" – that is, on the extent to which children fit within societal norms. The courts thereby wielded a tremendous power over the regulation of working-class and dependent families, whose children could be labelled neglected and thus incarcerated.¹⁵ Increasingly, neglected, abandoned, and working-class children were governed as potential criminals.

Interestingly, these schools were administered as educational institutions, not as penal institutions. The 1874 Industrial Schools Act made both public and separate boards responsible for the construction of industrial schools. School boards, however, were reluctant to take on the administration of industrial schools. Consequently, the provincial government revised the act in 1884, enabling voluntary organizations to undertake the task. Private agencies were already in the business of reforming defective and dependent families in need of benevolence, and juvenile delinquents were increasingly conceived of as neglected and misdirected cases, the traditional subjects of charities. The business of voluntary agencies was never limited to financial and material assistance or to furthering religious devotion; they were always involved in reforming and rehabilitating the moral character of individuals. Hence the revised Industrial Schools Act of 1884 marked the beginning of a historical partnership between voluntary agencies and the criminal justice system.

The birth of industrial schools has most often been associated with the rise of an urban industrial economy. The growth of industrial capitalism and the crowding of urban centres with newly arrived immigrants is said to have stimulated public alarm over juvenile crime, thus fuelling legislation to control young offenders.[16] This account, however, is disputed by studies that examine industrialization processes in Ontario, such as the works by Michael Katz, Gordon Darroch, and Michael Ornstein.[17] Their analysis reveals that cities in Ontario of the 1870s had hardly begun to be urban or industrial. Darroch's work and that of Bruce Curtis and Chad Gaffield can be used to advance a different understanding of the rise of industrial schools.[18] In a recent article, Darroch argues that widespread support for public schools, like the popularity of privacy, domesticity, and child nurture, reflected, not the imposition of middle-class interests, but a general cultural transformation. This transformation was located in "the social needs and commitments of farm, small town, rural labouring, and probably, from urban working-class life in the context of expanding proletarianization."[19] In the case of industrial schools, this argument can be applied to interpret their emergence, not as the extension of middle-class social control, but as the outcome of "a continuously negotiated attempt of privileged sectors of that class to express, direct and turn to advantage a wider, uneven movement, the origins and dynamics of which they might wish to have, but could *not* script."[20]

DISCIPLINING CATHOLIC DEVIANTS

As industrial schools fell under an educational, rather than criminal, jurisdiction, the Catholic Church maintained a constitutional right to operate its own separate schools. The British North America Act guaranteed Catholic school boards the right to erect and receive funding for separate facilities, a provision that was not enjoyed by other religious groups. Thus, when tensions erupted over religious instruction in the Protestant-run industrial school, the Catholic Archdiocese of Toronto opted to build its own school. Ontario's first two industrial schools, the Victoria Industrial School for boys and the Alexandra Industrial School for girls, built in 1887 and 1891 respectively, were administered by the Protestant churches. The Catholic archdiocese objected to the Victoria school's practice of subjecting all children to Protestant religious education. For the Catholic chancery, this was tantamount to a breach of religious civil rights, and as such, it threatened to revive the Catholic school controversy of the 1850s (see chapter 1). Consequently, St John's Industrial School was opened by the Christian Brothers in 1895, and soon after, in 1900, the Sisters of the Good Shepherd took on the administration of St Mary's Industrial School.[21]

Table 6.1
Number of juveniles in Catholic industrial schools, 1930–1935

Year	St Mary's	St John's
1930	69	149
1931	80	167
1935	68	202

SOURCE: Archives of Ontario, Ministry of Correctional Service, RG 20, J 2, vol. 22, "Report of the Committee Appointed to Investigate the Present Juvenile Reformatory School System of Ontario," 1935, 37.

The St John's Industrial School, which opened with 60 beds, by the height of the Depression in 1935 had expanded to accommodate 202 charges. In the 1930s St Mary's cared for approximately 70 to 80 girls. In the four-year period between 1929 to 1933, some 35 per cent of the industrial school population in Ontario were Catholic (569 out of a total of 1,623), a significantly high number, given their 22 per cent share of the province's population. Half the children came from non-English-speaking families, the largest groups being Italians and Poles, which represented 21 and 12 per cent respectively. Working-class children comprised the overwhelming majority of cases, in part because of biases in arrest patterns but also, presumably, because poor families had few other avenues for disciplining misbehaving children. Moreover, during the Depression many families had barely enough on which to subsist, and placing children in industrial schools alleviated some of their hardship.[22]

A comparison of these two Catholic schools reveals that boys were two to three times more likely to be institutionalized than girls (see table 6.1).[23] In general, most children were committed for stealing or incorrigibility. The latter category encompassed anyone who had not actually committed a crime, but was thought to be at "moral risk." The following statistics on the general industrial school population from 1929 to 1933 provide some indication of the frequency of offences. Statistics exclusive to Catholic institutions unfortunately do not exist; therefore the percentages reflect the total industrial school population. Boys were more likely to be incarcerated for stealing (49 per cent), breaking and entering (18 per cent), truancy (14 per cent), and incorrigibility

(12 per cent). Girls, on the other hand, were most often detained for moral misconduct, including incorrigibility (28 per cent), uncontrollability (22 per cent) and immorality (22 per cent). The frequency with which girls were institutionalized for minor offences reflects the general moral panic and the association of female misconduct with sexual promiscuity. Many were committed for being found in a "house of bad repute" or for failing to inform their parents of their whereabouts.[24]

The ages of the children in industrial schools ranged between eight and sixteen. Legislation prohibited younger children from being placed in industrial schools; they were typically sent to orphanages or foster homes. When children in orphanages or foster care were deemed too old for those institutions or when space was lacking, they were sometimes transferred to industrial schools. As mentioned earlier, industrial schools were not only reserved for the offending child but were seen as beneficial to any child deprived of adequate family care. In 1917, for example, 20 per cent of St Mary's residents (12 out of 61) had been transferred from the Sacred Heart Orphanage. As of 1900, children could be detained for a maximum of three years, but they remained under the supervision of the schools until the age of twenty-one. In a few cases, when release to parents or foster homes could not be arranged, they were detained for a longer period. In one case, for example, a child was institutionalized for nine years.[25]

Children in the industrial schools were offered a daily regime of academic, vocational, physical, and of course religious training. Adherence to a rigid schedule enabled social reformers to represent these schools more as private boarding schools than detention centres – schools in which every minute of the student's day was filled with productive re-education. Disciplined education was said to be essentially corrective and productive: it sought to repair the behavioural problems of children and was a "means of developing personality and encouraging self-expression."[26] Activities and courses were carefully chosen to maximize character-building and to instill industrious work habits that would turn inmates into useful, self-sufficient members of society. Each task was designed to mould juveniles into compliant, obedient citizens who would govern their behaviour according to normative social and moral rules. Hence coercive methods of control were to be used only as a last resort.[27]

At St John's the daily routine involved three hours of academic training and four hours of vocational work. A full academic curriculum was offered, as well as an "Opportunity Class" for the alleged "backward" boys (approximately 20 per cent of the school's population) who were thought to be in need of remedial education. Vocational instruction in a range of trades was designed to instill "habits of industry" and personal "satisfaction of accomplishment." Vocational training was offered in baking, tailoring, printing, shoemaking, barbering, and gardening – trades deemed appropriate for working-class children. Recreational activities were highly valued for their contribution to physical health, self-esteem, and team-work experience. More importantly, they were seen as a way of instilling acceptable leisure pastimes that could be pursued once the boys were discharged. School administrators believed that one of the greatest deterrents to juvenile delinquency was the provision of recreational pastimes. Hence the school sponsored a variety of outdoor programs, such as swimming, track and field, rugby, lacrosse, baseball, and hockey, which were supplemented with indoor activities, such as table games, hobby work, and music.[28] Religious and moral guidance was of paramount importance in the rehabilitation process. According to Brother Cyril, superintendent of the school, "by means of prayer, Mass, formal instruction, private interviews, selected readings, annual spiritual retreats and frequent opportunities for the reception of the Sacraments, we have endeavoured to build up desirable moral habits, to give the boys a real understanding of their obligations to God and to society and to convince them that their religion is a life to be lived."[29] Confession was also identified as a way of promoting self-reflection and redemption. The objective of religious education was not limited to spiritual or moral reformation; it was part of a larger goal to develop "democratic citizenship," not only by emphasizing patriotic duty but also by reforming those juveniles who had been tainted by communistic ideals.[30]

Industrial school training at St Mary's reinforced gendered stereotypes and traditional feminine skills. The girls were provided with some scholastic instruction, but the Sisters were ill-equipped to provide a full range of academic courses. Hence few of the girls gained entrance into high school. Likewise, the vocational program was limited to little other than household management. The girls were schooled in

personal cleanliness [as] the first study …They are instructed in the care of a household, and this comprises sleeping apartments, drawing room, living rooms, dining room, sewing rooms, kitchen and store rooms. The linen assigned to each of these must be made, marked, mended, sorted and kept in good order. They are taught dress-making, hand sewing, machine sewing, power machines and other, knitting, darning, embroidery, lace-making, mending, repairing and making over wearing apparel ... They are trained to a solid knowledge of the fundamentals with cleanliness and economy stressed.[31]

Particular attention was paid to educating the girls in modern household techniques, such as the proper "care of hardwood floors and good linoleum."[32] Such training prepared the girls for little else than a career in domestic service or motherhood. The future roles envisioned for these girls is also evident in the importance placed on grooming and hairdressing. The girls were encouraged "in everything which contributes towards personal attractiveness and daintiness."[33] Kelly Hannah-Moffat, in her study of female prisoners, describes how "emphasising a woman's appearance became a wider strategy to morally regulate her by creating 'a marriageable woman.'"[34] In essence, the Sisters were participating in state-formation by preparing these girls for their future roles as mothers of the nation.

THE NORMALIZING TECHNIQUES OF SOCIAL CASEWORK

By the 1920s the production and maintenance of case records emerged as a prevalent feature of industrial schools. Standardized forms were introduced to record information on the child's physical and emotional state, educational and moral progress, and family background. The alleged ability of social casework to probe beneath the symptoms of deviant behaviour to diagnose its underlying causes had licensed a range of experts – psychiatrists, psychologists, doctors, and social workers – to intervene in the administration of juvenile delinquents. These experts attempted to delve "behind the crime" to uproot the causes of delinquent behaviour, which could then be measured, diagnosed, treated, and normalized. The causes were often traced back to the home environment. Thus experts brought not only the offending child but whole families under professional scrutiny. The penal system came to rely on expert advice and casework governing techniques as a key component of its rehabilitative programs. Aspects of the child's past life and present behaviour were to be recorded in case records. This phenomenon, identified by Foucault, has also been referred to as the "tutelary complex" by Donzelot, the "psy" complex by Nikolas Rose, and part of socialized justice by Dorothy Chunn.[35] The integration of these forms of scientific investigation into almost every aspect of the penal process extended the powers of the judicial system.

The primary effect of this extensive assessment was to induce normalization. Children's behaviour was documented, measured, and compared against predetermined standards of "normal" behaviour. The nature of assessments presupposes normal versus abnormal categories that can be detected and distinguished. Those who failed to conform to prescribed norms could be identified and isolated, and their progress could be monitored over time. School administrators, empowered with the advice of experts, could then attempt to restore these individuals to a "normal" state. Positive techniques of intervention were employed to adjust the specific abnormalities of each child. Assessment techniques had existed prior to casework; medical doctors frequently remarked on the physical and mental state of children in industrial schools. But it was only by 1919 that this information was regularly recorded and collected on standardized forms to be maintained in case files.[36]

To see this process at work, we can examine how two standardized reports produced by the provincial government in the 1920s – the "Committal Report" and the "School Attendance Report" – operated as a technique of governance.[37] The Committal Report was completed by the Catholic Children's Aid Society prior to the sentencing of a young offender. It included details on the offence and background information to be used during the trial. The School Attendance Report, administered on a quarterly basis by the school supervisor, monitored the progress of the child within the institution. Once they were completed, copies of both records were submitted to the Department of the Provincial Secretary and, after 1930, to the Ontario Department of Public Welfare.

The reports included socio-biographical information on age, reason for committal, previous infractions, and scholastic standing, in addition to medical and psychological diagnoses.[38] A detailed family history profiling the child's upbringing was also contained in the Committal Report. As the root causes of juvenile delinquency were said to be located in the family, this section formed a significant part of the assessment. Information was compiled on parents' and siblings' occupations, general behaviour and appearance, church attendance, infractions of the law, the amounts of social assistance received, and the prevalence of such vices as alcoholism or gambling. Inspection of the home was mandatory, and evidence of uncleanliness, lack of furnishings or bedrooms for children, poor neighbourhoods, and other structural conditions were documented. The character of the mother was of particular importance, and much of the analysis was devoted to a detailed description of her activities. Working mothers were often reproached for leaving their children alone for the better part of the day.[39]

Medical and psychiatric exams were a requirement for each child. The general health of the child was noted, including the condition of the heart, tonsils, eyes, and teeth, the weight, skin conditions, and any habits such as nail-biting. Every attempt was made to correct any abnormality, for administrators believed that poor physical health was directly related to the propensity for delinquent behaviour. As the Industrial Schools Advisory Board noted in 1932: "the physical state of the child, such as diseased tonsils, decayed teeth and under-nourishment, has also contributed to delinquency and the medical reports have been of great assistance to us in recommending immediate treatment. We have found in a number of cases that the elimination of these defects has, in as short a period as six months, raised the mentality of certain inmates so as to admit of definitely higher standards of training."[40] In addition to physical health, evidence of sexual impropriety was closely monitored, particularly among girls, and any indication of venereal disease was accepted as proof of delinquency. Such close scrutiny was particularly evident in one report, which identified how "the hymen was partially ruptured, intromits admitting one finger."[41] Gonorrhea and syphilis tests were commonly performed on the girls, but were rarely reported in boys' case files. The concern with detecting venereal disease reflected prevailing fears that such illnesses could spread immorality as well as disease. Concerted efforts were made to transfer those infected out of the schools to local hospitals. As one government report stated in 1934, "the Girls' schools are not equipped to deal adequately with this problem; and we fear that by attempting to do so, the main purpose of the schools may be endangered, and that the health, morals and general training of the younger girls may suffer."[42] Medical examinations were not only used to identify actual health risks, but were laden with moral judgments.

Ontario was one of the first provinces to introduce psychiatric examinations of juvenile delinquents. IQ and other psychometric tests were regularly administered for the purpose of isolating "mental defectives" and the "feeble-minded." That 25 per cent of the industrial school population in Ontario in the 1930s was designated "mentally deficient" testifies to the indiscriminate use of such labels. This figure does not include the large number of children identified as "dull normal."[43] Apart from questioning the use of such methods to measure intelligence, Bennett also suggests that "little distinction was made between illiteracy and mental incapacity."[44] Illiterate or foreign-born children, for example, were frequently labelled "feeble-minded," and attempts were made to transfer them to the Orillia Hospital for the mentally defective. However, lack of funding meant that the majority remained in the industrial schools. St John's attempted to deal with this problem by instituting an "opportunity class." But apart from this initiative, little use was made of the tests within the schools. Psychiatrists and psychologists did not provide much in the way of treatment, and the schools lacked the resources to implement adequate remedial programs.[45] Where such assessments did have an impact was on decisions for release and after-care.

The production of case records enabled the state to monitor the activities of industrial school administrators and school inmates simultaneously. The forms, coupled with annual reports and routine inspections, meant that school administrators were under the constant gaze of government bureaucrats. Assessments could be made as to whether institutions adequately followed the priorities set out by the juvenile justice system, and these evaluations were then utilized to inform funding decisions. At the same time, these records were utilized by the industrial school to monitor the condition and progress of children, and were ultimately deployed to induce normative behaviour. The documents were used to identify problems, abnormalities, and deficiencies that, it was believed, could be reformed. The more that was known about the juveniles, the more controllable they became. Case records legalized and normalized the intrusions of experts and private social work agents into the lives of children and their families. These assessments, however, were never simply neutral judgments, but reflected class, gender, and racial biases. They were advanced as objective scientific procedures, but attempts at classification, categorization, and assessment are always shaped by official discourses and "competing truth claims."[46]

It was these reports, laden with "expert" knowledge and coloured by moral and social judgments, that became a key resource in the production of policy. The ability to make comparisons between and within institutions empowered governments to make predictions about juvenile populations and thus to legitimate policy decisions. Cloaked in the language of expert assessment, government decisions were rendered objective, neutral, and detached from partisan politics. For these reasons, the state was eager to sanction and open its doors to the governing practices afforded by experts and social work agents.

THE REGULATORY PROCESSES OF PAROLE

When children had completed their maximum three-year sentence, they were released on parole. In the early years they could be detained for an indeterminate sentence, but after 1900 they were to be released after a maximum of three years and could then be placed on parole until the age of twenty-one. Parole emerged as a post-institutional practice designed to assist children who were readjusting to community life while also monitoring their behaviour and activities. Parole supervision was to ensure both the proper conduct of juveniles and the detection of any breach of social norms and responsibilities. It extended the powers of the juvenile justice system into the community, as knowledge of the released child's habits, character, and daily activities continued to be made available.

The practice of parole again highlights the mixed social economy embodying private agencies and the state. With the introduction of the Act for the Prevention of Cruelty to, and Better Protection of Children, passed in 1893, responsibility for the welfare of children on release from industrial schools shifted from the state to the Children's Aid Societies. Previously, police officers had monitored those released from institutions, but this surveillance was deemed ineffective since there were no systematic plans for the continuing rehabilitation of children and their families. Administrators feared that children would be returned to environments that had caused their delinquency in the first place, with no services to help them readjust. Private agencies such as the St Vincent de Paul Children's Aid Society, among others, offered to continue rehabilitative programs in the community, thereby providing more effective means of regulation. Their reform programs were interpreted as benevolent social services and not as an extension of state repression. (After-care programs offered by Catholic organizations are further reviewed in the discussion of probation that follows.)

The provincial Industrial Schools Advisory Board was formed in 1931 to oversee the supervision of industrial schools and also the terms for releasing children into the community. Each eligible case for parole was forwarded to the board, which determined which children would be returned to their parents, placed in foster care, or employed. Its decisions were informed by comprehensive case records, which included a wealth of information on school performance, medical and psychiatric assessments, family history, personal letters from private individual agencies, appeals by family members, and any other pertinent information, including recommendations from industrial school administrators and the local Children's Aid Society.[47]

This system enabled the authorities to wield tremendous power over the future of young offenders and their families. For instance, before children could be returned to their parents, the board insisted on a detailed examination of their families and neighbourhood conditions. Members of the Children's Aid Societies were licensed to enter the homes of families and inspect every aspect of their lives. They questioned neighbours, local priests, and agency workers about the parents' character, habits, and values. Even parents who themselves had laid charges against their children came under the intrusive inspection of authorities. The decision to place their children in industrial schools opened the door to government and private agency regulation.[48] In effect, it displaced parental rights with those of bureaucratic administration. This was a serious concern during the Depression, when many working-class and destitute homes were deemed unsuitable for the upbringing of children.[49]

Once the child was released, a report on his or her progress conducted by the Children's Aid Society was to be submitted to the advisory board every three months. The "Placement Officer's Report," as it was known, included information on living conditions, general health, employment, and educational achievement. Leisure activities were closely monitored, and any sport, special interest, or church affiliations were recorded. Interviews were regularly conducted with family members, employers, educators, priests, social workers, and probation officers. Many aspects of the child's life were monitored, and any indication of potential delinquency could result in peremptory recommittal.

In effect, these reporting mechanisms ensured the continuous surveillance of children by the juvenile justice system.[50] Moreover, by licensing voluntary organizations to police and regulate children through parole, the state extended its scope, range, and penetration of legal control. These methods worked to intensify the state's ability to "govern at a distance."

GOVERNING DELINQUENTS IN THE COMMUNITY

Finally, we should consider the rise of probation as a new twentieth-century technology of governance. Probation emerged as a form of community-based correction that ensured supervision and rehabilitation without removing deviant children from their homes. The objective was not only to prevent lawbreaking but to ensure the moral reform of deviant youth through surveillance, social casework, and intervention in family life, as well as through the curative techniques of medicine, psychology, and social work. The reformist goal of the probation officer was the production of dutiful, hard-working citizens. In their efforts to turn delinquent youths into ethical citizens, these officers also sought to produce normative families. Thus probation, like parole, enabled the courts to extend their powers to police deviant children and their families beyond legal institutions into the private sphere through the active participation of voluntary organizations. Private agencies comprised the major support base for probation's emergence. At first, Children's Aid Societies and, later, organizations such as the Big Brothers and Big Sisters undertook the handling of probation.

The Child Savers Movement of the 1880s is often celebrated for pioneering the system of child probation in Canada. The movement, led by J.J. Kelso and other middle-class reformers, earned its name and reputation from its attempts to rescue children from familial cruelty and neglect and from incarceration in reformatories. In the latter case, it sought to heighten public awareness of the debilitating effects of institutionalization, which, it claimed, served only to reinforce anti-social behaviour. Instead, the movement's adherents advocated the adoption of community-based rehabilitative programs. If, as they argued, delinquency emanated from family dysfunction, then its solution too resided in the family. Children were not to be incarcerated for the misdemeanours of their parents. Even in situations of neglect, Child Savers refuted the use of detention centres and preferred placing children in foster care. It was through their efforts that probation came to be adopted by the justice system as an alternative to incarceration.[51]

The unrelenting pressure exerted on government officials by the Child Savers led to the 1893 Act for the Prevention of Cruelty to, and Better Protection of Children. This act, which was a landmark in the evolution of Ontario's child welfare policy, redefined the image and governance of juvenile delinquents; child welfare was essentially identified as a private, rather than a state, priority. Children's Aid Societies were granted guardianship over all children committed by the courts, whether they be in industrial schools, reformatories, or foster homes. The societies were also given the power to apprehend any neglected, mistreated, or criminal child under the age of fourteen. As well, the Act encouraged the formation of Children's Aid societies. The Toronto Children's Aid Society had already been formed in 1891, and within a year of the act, in 1894, the Roman Catholic St Vincent de Paul Children's Aid Society was created. Supervision over the societies was given to the newly created Office of the Superintendent of Neglected and Dependent Children, and J.J. Kelso was appointed its first superintendent.[52] The act was one of the first steps taken to integrate voluntary agencies into the juvenile justice system. According to criminologist D. Owen Carrigan, "agencies outside the correctional system could now intervene and bring a different philosophy and perspective to the treatment of young people in trouble with the law."[53] Henceforth, juvenile delinquency was not simply regulated as criminal activity, but was also designated as a problem of socialization that necessitated the intervention of philanthropic agencies.

The province, however, lacked constitutional authority under the British North America Act to legislate in substantive matters of criminal law, and thus the children's protection act was ultra vires. The Child Savers therefore appealed to the federal government, and in 1894 it passed the Youthful Offenders Act, guaranteeing private voluntary authority in child welfare. Under this act, Children's Aid societies became responsible for conducting investigations, for collecting information, and for the care of children appearing before the courts. The act reinforced the discourse made popular by the Child Savers Movement that delinquents were not criminals but, rather, children in need of supervision and tutelage.

In 1908 the federal government passed the Juvenile Delinquents Act. This act, along with various amendments, formed the basis of the juvenile justice system until the Young Offenders Act of 1984. It extended the jurisdiction of the provinces in criminal matters, made the formation of juvenile courts mandatory, reinforced the powers of Children's Aid Societies, and further opened the doors to community corrections. In most cases, Children's Aid workers became the courts' probation officers. Under the act, every juvenile court was to form a voluntary committee comprised of Children's Aid workers, either Catholic or Protestant, depending on the child's religion.[54] The committee would consult with probation officers and make recommendations regarding the disposition of cases before the courts. The act reinforced the state's commitment to have extra-state agencies assume responsibility for the rehabilitation of young offenders.[55]

Within this system, the police or Children's Aid Societies were given authority to determine whether a child would be brought before the courts or released. In 1921, of the 4,047 children apprehended, only 1,763 were brought before a judge. Once the case was in the courtroom, the judge would dispose of it on the basis of information collected by the probation officer and the advisory committee, which included a complete physical, mental, scholastic, and social family history of each child.[56] Historian Neil Sutherland provides a vivid portrait of the Toronto juvenile courtroom, which he describes as consisting of "an armchair behind a long table, at one end of which sat the agent of the Toronto Children's Aid Society, at the other the agent of the St. Vincent de Paul Children's Aid Society and, on either side of the commissioner, the chief probation officer, and the clerk."[57] In most cases, children were remanded into the custody of a probation officer, and only in extreme cases were they placed in an industrial school or other child-care institution for juvenile offenders.

The Catholic Church's foray into probationary work can be traced to 1895, when the archdiocese hired its first probation officer. Patrick Hynes, the first paid agent of the St Vincent de Paul Children's Aid Society, attended the Toronto juvenile court daily. In 1912, when the commissioner of the juvenile court requested the appointment of additional probation officers, the society hired two agents.[58] The Catholic Big Brothers Association was formed in 1918, and a year later the Catholic Big Sisters Association was established to oversee probationary work in Toronto.[59] These associations also supervised those on parole from industrial schools.

While, initially, the associations were administered by volunteers with little experience in child welfare, in time, professional social workers were hired. In 1920, two years after its formation, the Catholic Big Brothers had 50 active members, and the Big Sisters had 20 volunteers. To educate their members about the social problems facing delinquent children, the associations offered lectures and organized courses, such as the "Boyology" course, sponsored by the Toronto Knights of Columbus, which attracted 250 participants.[60]

The importance of the associations' work is evident in the number of children they serviced. In the first six months, 82 boys were placed on probation with the Catholic Big Brothers, while the Catholic Big Sisters received 65 girls within its first month of operation. In the mid-1930s, at the height of the Depression, the associations expanded their services to deal with preventative work that would address the needs of children before they appeared before the courts. In response to this activity, the numbers of children swelled, and in 1934 the Catholic Big Brothers reported assisting 654 children. At least 25 per cent of these had been referred to the association by the courts. The remainder were directed to the Catholic Big Brothers by a variety of social agencies, including the railway companies, which often picked up juveniles for minor misdemeanours. Some children also appeared voluntarily; they either were attracted to the recreational activities or truly believed they were in need of reform.

The goal of the associations was to reshape the moral character of the offending child. Since reformers identified a "lack of judicious home training" as the cause of "lawless behaviour," their task required intervening not only in the lives of delinquent children but also in the lives of their parents.[61] Unless the family as a whole was treated, rehabilitation efforts would be ineffective because once returned home, the children could regress to their prior immoral condition. J.J. Kelso himself voiced such sentiments when he claimed that "the modern conception of a probation officer is not that he should exercise constabulary powers, but that he should be the friend of the parent equally with the child ... It is not his duty to seize a child ... but by friendly tactics to bring about the cordial cooperation of the parents in securing the child's best welfare and its continuance in the home, which is its birthright."[62] Probation officers were thus to gain the confidence not only of the child but of the entire family, for "the home is the workshop in which the character and personality ... [are] moulded."[63]

The aim of the rehabilitation project was the regulation and reform of "habit." Probation officers sought to reform "bad habits." Valverde has discussed the category of "habit" as a key technology in the governance of behaviour.[64] Habit is an everyday behaviour that is not governed through expert-based or scientific knowledge, such as diagnostic categories produced by psychologists; rather, it is regulated through commonsensical, normative assumptions. Vice and habits, for example, are not discussed in terms of personality disorders but as reflections of a lack of self-control, as in smoking. According to the Catholic Big Brothers, habit "is such a common, everyday sort of term, with which everyone is more or less familiar, that it hardly seems necessary to discuss it at all. However, it is in this very fact – that habits are so commonplace and ordinary in the minds of the great mass of individuals – that the danger lies. All too frequently the fundamental importance of forming right habits in early life is minimized or overlooked altogether."[65] Reformers in the 1930s did not define their work as counselling, a term commonly used in the 1950s, but rather as the reforming of habits. Moral behaviour, as the Catholic Big Brothers noted, was "to a large extent, the result of habits of thinking formed in early life."

Probationary programs thus attempted to instruct parents on how to produce desirable habits in their children and on strategies for breaking deep-rooted "bad habits." The Catholic Big Brothers devoted a great deal of their energies to writing articles on the production of habit. They discussed a range of habits, including those of grooming, reading, and posture.[66] Parents were informed of the grave danger in "babying" children, for this fostered "habits of dependency."[67] When children displayed "slovenly habits," parents were advised not to scold or "nag" them. "Nagging will not improve him. He must be made to return to his room and wash or comb his hair, or adjust his clothing when he has neglected to do so. Praise, when he is properly groomed, is also quite effective."[68] Parents were told that if their "child has habits of sulking and pouting, break them at once. Do not argue, or punish, or scold, or try to divert his attention through bribery. Such tactics increase the condition of making him an object of special attention ... Ignore him completely and absolutely till he snaps out of it."[69] According to the Catholic Big Brothers, "any information which gives the interested parent a better idea of the mental life of the child, ... and suggestions for overcoming undesirable habits may be considered well worth while."[70]

Children, too, were governed in ways that would acquaint them with standard middle-class customs. They were encouraged in a range of recreational activities, including sports for boys, sewing for girls, and dual-sex pastimes such as reading and music. Those with academic interests were provided with scholarships and bursaries to pursue high school and technical or college education. Church attendance was an important convention that all children were encouraged to observe. Employment opportunities were also provided, and children were taught the value of saving their earnings for future endeavours. Big Brothers also worked to condition their "little" friends to proper grooming practices, such as the "use of a toothbrush, an article entirely foreign to many of [the] boys." As well, these organizations relied on other voluntary agencies to assist in their programs. Recreational clubs and summer camps sponsored by the Rosary Guild and the Knights of Columbus were made available to children. The camps, as the Catholic Big Sisters noted, "give the club supervisor the best chance to observe habits needing correction."[71] Habit training pledged to transform dependent, wayward, vagrant, and misbehaving juveniles into self-sufficient, productive, and contributing members of society.

The probationary activities were concerned with the practical problem of crime prevention and the moralization of the offender. Private agencies were well suited to this task because they could incorporate the curative techniques of the charity sector to morally, socially, and spiritually reform juvenile offenders and their families. In this effort, the Catholic Big Brothers and Big Sisters could summon the assistance of a vast network of services. For example, they relied on funding from the Catholic Welfare Bureau, on camps and clubs from the Rosary Guild and the Knights of Columbus, on court information from the Children's Aid Society, and on a number of volunteers who devoted their time to the cause. Over time, volunteerism was supplemented with the technical expertise afforded by social workers and psychiatrists.

The Catholic Church's involvement in the juvenile justice system highlights the interlocking sites between public law enforcement and private charity. It reveals how social practices made popular in the field of charity – social casework and moral reform – were brought to bear on penal strategies. The two spheres came to share logics of discipline and normalization. According to Garland, penal reform was increasingly "conceived of as a form of philanthropy, the prevention of crime being one specific aspect of a generalized campaign against vice, intemperance, pauperism and irreligion."[72] As punitive regimes gave way to disciplinary techniques, the door was opened to community involvement by private agencies such as the Catholic Church and non-legal experts in medicine, psychology, psychiatry, and social work. These extra-state actors were not co-opted by the state, but rather, they worked in alliance with governments to achieve common goals. Their involvement in juvenile corrections served to accredit their knowledge and legitimize their work, enabling them to expand their services and practices of intervention. It also granted them greater influence in legislative penal reform. They possessed, as did the state, the power of knowledge made available through case records.[73]

The rise of industrial schools, parole, and probation worked to decentre the role of the prison. Probation and, indeed, industrial schools were envisioned as alternatives to penal incarceration. Thus the schools were advanced as benevolent educational institutions and not as extensions of the prison system. It was this shift that opened the door to community corrections. Voluntary agencies directed their attentions to the welfare and rehabilitation of the deviant, not to punishing transgressions. The belief in the viability of community corrections extended the power of the state and the charity sector into the community, allowing for more effective policing, disciplining, and regulating of working-class youths and their families.[74]

Conclusion

The activities of the Catholic voluntary sector and the state have long been interwoven. From the inaugural Roman Catholic Orphan Asylum of the 1850s to Catherine de Hueck's settlement house of the 1930s, Catholic charities and public bodies have operated, not in isolation, but in close partnership. Local and provincial governments provided the legal framework, essential financial resources, and forms of bureaucratic supervision enabling the formation and proliferation of voluntary organizations. The ability of Catholic charities to expand rapidly to encompass a broad range of social services was made possible in part by government support. Public funding, however, was not unconditional; it was nearly always tied to monitoring techniques such as cost accounting, inspection, standardized forms, annual reports, and casework, all of which rendered charity practices and relief recipients visible and governable. They performed a similar function for the Archdiocese of Toronto, which throughout this period sought to enhance centralized control and accountability over the network of Catholic charities. They enabled both state and Catholic central agencies to "govern at a distance," as charity workers compiled information on, regulated, and reformed "deviant" families, a labour that in turn subjected the agency workers' own practices to forms of supervisory power.

Catholic-run agencies, while intermeshed with public institutions, were by no means simply co-opted by the state. Far from being a handmaiden of Queen's Park or Toronto City Council, the Catholic Church actively and successfully pursued its own interests. Catholic campaigns to moralize the poor, stem communism, and reform juvenile delinquents and their families promoted both church and state interests, and both parties viewed the arrangement as mutually beneficial. For example, information-sharing on communist activities enabled a much greater capacity for surveillance than would have been the case if either party had acted independently. While the church delivered social programs on behalf of the state, it in turn had its forays into people's private lives and homes legitimated by government legislation and regulations. Moreover, calls for state measures to alleviate social and economic hardships often emanated from voluntary agencies such as those belonging to the Catholic Church.

During the interwar period, municipal and provincial governments assumed greater responsibility for the provision of social services, a process that entrenched links with the voluntary sector. Historical studies of the Canadian welfare state generally hold that the rise of this modern, "secular" institution resulted in the near-eclipse of religious, voluntary organizations. But charities, as I have argued, were not casualties of state expansion. The 1920s expansion of community corrections programs and the Catholic Welfare Bureau's integration into municipal relief efforts during the Depression are but two of many examples of the private-public cooperation that characterized the workings of the criminal justice system and the delivery of social welfare. At the same time as governments were expanding their services and playing a more direct role in social services, so too were Catholic charities. The welfare state did not grow by shrinking the charity sector but, rather, by supporting and regulating it.

The Catholic Church's enduring and expanding presence in the charity sector reflected in good measure its adoption of and facility with modern social science methods. Historians of social work have argued that the understanding and treatment of social problems underwent an epistemological shift from a moral-religious paradigm to a social scientific one, beginning in the 1910s. This reconfiguration does not, however, preclude the possibility that religious organizations themselves could embrace social scientific methods to analyze and alleviate social problems. While the role of volunteers within Catholic charities diminished with the arrival of "expert" administrators, it does not follow that the voluntary sector as a whole was similarly marginalized. Catholic charity melded piety with social scientific practice. Social work's emphasis on technique and bureaucratic accountability conflicted neither with the tenets of Catholicism nor with the raison d'être of Catholic benevolence. Poor relief, parole and probation, and industrial schooling were all practices infused with social casework techniques. By the 1920s the church had tentatively embraced the social scientific ethos, hiring university-trained social workers and adopting policies and procedures modelled on expert curative methods.

The heady post-1945 expansion of the welfare state did not curb the importance of Catholic charities. For example, the number of children and family cases administered by Toronto Catholic Family Services (formerly the Catholic Welfare Bureau) rose from 12,776 in 1964 to 19,553 in 1968.[1] The introduction in 1966 of the Canada Assistance Plan, which saw Ottawa fund half of provincial social assistance and also saw a broadening of social welfare initiatives to include rehabilitation programs and community services, similarly did not limit the scale and scope of Catholic voluntary services or their levels of state funding. During the 1950s and 1960s the provincial government continued to pay all the operating costs of the Catholic Children's Aid Society, Catholic industrial schools, and the Sacred Heart Children's Village, which served disabled children. As well, municipal and provincial governments provided partial funding for a number of Catholic agencies, such as Rosalie Hall, a home for unwed mothers, Sancta Maria House, which offered rehabilitation services for sex workers and former female convicts, and Providence Villa (formerly the House of Providence), a home for the sick and the elderly.[2]

Strengthening the resilience of Toronto's Catholic charities was the rapid post-war influx of immigrants, many of whom were Catholic. Metropolitan Toronto's Catholic population vaulted from 483,000 in 1964 to just over 1 million in 1975.[3] In 1954 the archdiocese established the Catholic Immigration Bureau to provide planning, development, and support for community-based immigrant services. Under the bureau's direction, a number of "ethnic" centres were opened throughout the city, providing a range of social services and settlement assistance to the Italian, Portuguese, Korean, Filipino, and Chinese Catholic communities.[4] And in the 1970s the Catholic Church extended its outreach to encompass refugees. The public-private partnership model, whose origins date back to the nineteenth century, prevailed even as the welfare state broadened.

And so too did it prevail as the welfare state receded, beginning in the late 1970s. Buoyant economic growth during the 1950s and 1960s gave way to recession in the wake of the 1973 oil crisis. Economic "stagnation" – high levels of unemployment and inflation – along with mounting public debt, high interest rates, and public opposition to tax increases, coincided with the rise of neo-conservative economics, which denounced state spending and government regulation.[5] In this climate, state welfare projects were curtailed or rescinded entirely, beginning in earnest in the early 1980s. As government services were cut back, reducing the number of people qualifying for social assistance, private agencies stepped into the breach to offer an array of charitable programs. Such charities, like those of the Catholic Church, could fill the void left by state retrenchment because of their long-standing infrastructures of social service delivery. The cutbacks have provided the context for renewed voluntary-state partnerships since the Mulroney era. Since the late 1970s, Catholic charity services in Toronto have broadened and intensified. To combat substance addiction, the church set up Matt Talbot House, a residence for recovering alcoholics, and St Marguerite Centre, a drug and alcohol counselling centre, in 1981 and 1991 respectively. Members of the Catholic Madonna Apostolic were instrumental in devising the "food bank" concept and were close participants in the formation of the Daily Bread Food Bank in 1982. The Out of the Cold program, launched in 1987 by Sister Susan Moran, provided temporary shelter for the homeless in churches and synagogues. St Francis Table, a restaurant for the poor serving one-dollar meals, opened its doors in 1987. Municipal and provincial governments supported these voluntary efforts via subsidies, even as they curtailed their own spending on state social programs.

More recently, Ontario has witnessed the erosion of state funding for both public *and* voluntary sector social services. Soon after taking office in 1995, the Harris government slashed welfare rates by 22 per cent, and it later downloaded much of the costs of welfare programs onto municipalities. Ontario municipalities are now required to draw on property taxes to pay 50 per cent of the cost of family benefits, subsidized child care, nursing homes, and social housing. While embarking on its radical program of tax cuts and slashes to social spending, the government was espousing the voluntary sector's ability to care for the poor and the dispossessed, despite state funding cuts to their operations. For example, in 1996 Catholic charities in the Archdiocese of Toronto experienced a $2.8 million drop in their government funding, the bulk of the cuts coming from Queen's Park. Government officials claim that private donations to charities will increase in response to cuts in personal income taxes, but in fact charitable donations have declined steadily since the early 1990s. At a time when demand for their services and programs is at an all-time high, charities are being forced to cut staff and operations.[6] Just as the philanthropic sector benefited in many ways from the expansion of social services in the 1960s and 1970s, so too now are both public and charitable social programs being cut simultaneously.

Much of the academic research on the welfare state assumes a relatively uniform process that impacted on all sectors and regions in much the same way. This characterization is an oversimplification of a highly complex process that differed across time and space. The result has been to blind researchers to the nuances of state welfare and, in particular, to how voluntary organizations were restructured, transformed, and relocated in response to the post-1945 welfare state expansion. This expansion did not result in a near-eclipse of the voluntary sector, but rather, it reshaped and restructured it. For this reason, I have preferred to focus on the governance of welfarism. Such an approach draws analytical attention to how social welfare problems were managed. Thus, rather, than focusing strictly on the state or the voluntary sector, this approach foregrounds the multiple actors, practices, and techniques involved in the day-to-day operations of social welfare administration. It is a more micro-analytic approach, which opens up new possibilities for examining the enduring mixed social economy comprising the voluntary and state sectors.

Such an approach is necessary in order to understand the complexity of contemporary changes in social welfare. Today, we are not witnessing a decline in state welfare intervention. The state has not so much withdrawn from social welfare, as it has redefined its role to one of "encouraging" and "reconstructing" self-reliance in both recipients and non-governmental service providers. This approach constitutes a shift in the way that state welfare is rationalized and welfare recipients are governed. Government funding has been curtailed and services have been downloaded to the non-profit sector, but these changes have coincided with an intensification of government intervention in the lives of the poor and underprivileged. For example, the Ontario government has introduced workfare, established a province-wide fraud control database and "snitch line," expanded the investigative powers of welfare staff, and proposed the drug testing of all welfare recipients.[7]

In the voluntary sector, governments may be less involved in operating social services, but they continue to exert considerable influence. Governments often decide which charitable programs will be funded and by how much, and funding levels bear directly on the number and calibre of staff members and the quality of services provided. Given the overall decline in funding, charities are being forced to operate in a more competitive and efficient manner, vying with other organizations for scarce resources. Accordingly, governments are holding these private agencies more accountable by closely monitoring and evaluating their services. Despite rhetorical outpourings exalting diminished state intervention, governments continue to govern charities and their clients, even if now the governance of charities is being accomplished more by the stick of cutbacks than, as in earlier times, by the carrot of new grants.

While the new structure of public-private partnerships in social welfare affects all philanthropies and community groups, the Catholic agencies have some unique characteristics that may allow them to weather the crisis posed by neo-conservative policies better than other sectors. The principal such characteristic is the Catholic Church's ability to mobilize a vast pool of volunteer labour, not only from lay adults and from separate school secondary students but also from religious orders. Priests and nuns are much scarcer than they used to be, but nevertheless their highly skilled unpaid work enables church bodies to provide social services quite efficiently. It may be, therefore, that Catholic-run services will survive the current era of cutbacks better than agencies run by either professionals or community activists. To that extent, this book may turn out to be relevant in our thinking about the future as well as the past of Canada's mixed public-private system for governing moral, social, and political risks.

APPENDICES

APPENDIX ONE

Catholics in the Toronto Region, 1841–1960

Table A1.1
The Number and percentage of Catholics in Toronto, 1841–1911

Year	Toronto population	Catholic population	Catholic percentage
1841	14,249	2,400	16.8
1851	30,775	7,940	25.8
1861	44,821	12,135	27.8
1871	56,092	11,881	21.2
1881	86,415	15,716	18.2
1891	181,220	21,830	12.1
1901	208,040	23,699	11.4
1911	376,538	43,080	11.4

SOURCES: Census of Canada, 1851–1911; City of Toronto assessment, 1841.

Table A1.2
Population statistics for the Archdiocese of Toronto, 1920–1960

Year	Catholic population
1920	85,000
1930	128,000
1940	169,000
1950	196,000
1960	350,000

SOURCE: Newman Club of Toronto, *The Ontario Catholic Year Book and Directory*, 1920–1960.
NOTE: The Roman Catholic Archdiocese of Toronto extends far beyond the confines of Toronto. Its boundaries enclose Durham County in the east, Dufferin and Peel Counties in the west, the Niagara Peninsula in the south, and Georgian Bay in the north.

APPENDIX TWO

Catholic Charities in the Archdiocese of Toronto, 1849–1930s

1849   Roman Catholic Orphanage Asylum
The orphanage was initially run informally by lay volunteers. As the number of orphaned children grew, the archbishop in 1851 invited the Sisters of St Joseph to operate it.

1850   St Vincent de Paul Society
A society of men who operated parish outdoor relief programs to the poor and sick.

1856   House of Providence
A shelter run by the Sisters of St Joseph for the poor, elderly, chronically ill, abandoned women, widows, and prostitutes. It was torn down and the work transferred to Providence Villa in 1961.

1869   St Nicholas Home
A boarding home for homeless boys run by the Sisters of St Joseph. It was initially established to accommodate 55 waifs and strays. The house was closed in 1911, and the boys were transferred to Sunnyside Orphanage.

1871   Notre Dames des Anges
A boarding home for homeless girls run by the Sisters of St Joseph. The house opened with 30 beds, and by 1887 it housed 69 inmates.

1875   Good Shepherd Female Refuge for Fallen Women
An asylum run by the Sisters of the Good Shepherd for female prisoners and prostitutes. The refuge opened with 19 inmates.

1876   Sacred Heart Orphan Asylum
An orphanage operated by the Sisters of St Joseph for the care of infants under four years of age. In 1885 a new wing was built to house 149 orphaned boys from the Roman Catholic Orphanage Asylum, and in 1891 approximately 120 girls were placed under its care. In 1960 the asylum was transformed into a home for mentally challenged children, with approximately 47 beds.

1885   Catholic Ladies Hospital Visiting Society
An organization of lay women who visited the sick and female prisoners at the Mercer Reformatory and the Don Jail.

1892   St Michael's Hospital
Run by the Sisters of St Joseph.

1894   St Vincent de Paul Children's Aid Society
It supervised neglected and delinquent children made wards of the Society.

Its mandate was to save children from physical abuse, mental neglect, immoral surroundings, and other handicaps.

1895 St John's Industrial School
An industrial school for delinquent boys run by the Christian Brothers. The school opened with 60 beds. It was later relocated to Uxbridge, Ontario, and is still in operation.

1900 St Mary's Industrial School
An industrial school for delinquent girls run by the Sisters of the Good Shepherd. It was closed in the 1970s.

1906 St Vincent Home for Infants
A home for children aged four and under.

1908 St Elizabeth Visiting Nurses Association
It provided nursing care for the sick and poor in their homes.

1911 Camp Ozanam
A summer camp for underprivileged girls operated by the St Vincent de Paul Society.

1912 Catholic Charities
An umbrella organization providing central coordination for Catholic charitable agencies in Toronto; replaced by the Catholic Welfare Bureau in 1921.

1913 Carmelite Orphanage
Run by the Carmelite Sisters for girls of foreign nationality aged three to sixteen, it accommodated approximately 45 children.

1913 Camp Ozanam
A summer camp for boys run by the St Vincent de Paul Society. In 1920 the program was extended to girls and mothers with young infants. In that year 307 individuals were served by the camp.

1914 St Mary's Infant Home
Run by the Misericordia Sisters for unmarried mothers and their newborns. In 1956 it was renamed Rosalie Hall.

1918 Catholic Big Brothers
An organization of lay volunteers providing parole and probationary services to delinquent boys.

1919 Catholic Big Sisters
An organization of lay volunteers providing parole and probationary services to delinquent girls.

1919 St Mary's Hospital
A maternity hospital run by the Misericordia Sisters for unwed pregnant women, it accommodated 25 beds.

135 Catholic Charities in the Archdiocese of Toronto

1920 Catholic Women's League Hostel
Coordinated by the Sisters of Service for the care and protection of Catholic immigrant girls.

1921 Catholic Welfare Bureau
Formerly the Catholic Charities, this umbrella organization coordinated the work of Toronto's Catholic charity organizations and provided family casework. It consisted of two departments, the Family Welfare and the Child Caring Divisions.

1921 St Joseph's Hospital
Run by the Sisters of St Joseph.

1925 Our Lady of Mercy Hospital
Opened to care for incurable patients at the House of Providence.

1927 Federation of Catholic Charities
A central fundraising organization for Catholic agencies.

1929 Columbus Boy's Camp
Operated by the Knights of Columbus, it offered ten-day outings at Island Grove Camp for underprivileged boys.

1931 St Vincent de Paul Hostel
A hostel for 100 unemployed boys.

1934 St Francis Catholic Friendship House
A settlement house for the unemployed run by Catherine de Hueck.

1934 Mount St Francis Colony
A back-to-the-land project for poor families located north of Toronto in King Ridge.

1935 Bosco Hall
A residence for the homeless.

1936 Marylake Farm School
A back-to-the-land project for poor families located north of Toronto.

1937 Catholic Youth Organization
It provided recreational programs for juveniles and young adults.

APPENDIX THREE

Provincial and Municipal Grants to the Protestant House of Industry and the Catholic House of Providence in the City of Toronto for the Years 1870–1880

Year	Institution	No. of inmates	Provincial funding	Municipal funding	Total revenues
1870	H. Industry	247	2,900	3,000	9,361
	H. Providence	186	320	200	3,972
1871	H. Industry	317	2,900	4,000	11,095
	H. Providence	241	320	200	4,183
1872	H. Industry	236	2,900	4,000	12,314
	H. Providence	233	320	200	4,198
1873	H. Industry	252	2,900	4,000	9,327
	H. Providence	233	1,000	200	5,171
1874	H. Industry	205	2,900	–	9,720
	H. Providence	273	1,000	300	6,112
1875	H. Industry	176	2,900	–	11,625
	H. Providence	351	3,298	500	11,806
1876	H. Industry	179	2,900	5,000	11,775
	H. Providence	437	3,391	500	12,493
1877	H. Industry	159	2,900	6,000	12,942
	H. Providence	430	4,126	500	13,278
1878	H. Industry	169	2,900	2,000	9,515
	H. Providence	430	4,258	500	13,406
1879	H. Industry	139	2,900	6,000	12,539
	H. Providence	422	4,598	750	15,616
1880	H. Industry	136	2,188	4,000	9,530
	H. Providence	441	4,617	750	13,752

SOURCE: Archives of Ontario, *Report of the Inspector of Asylum, Prisons and Public Charities*, 1870–1880.

APPENDIX FOUR

Provincial and Municipal Grants to Protestant and Catholic Orphanages in the City of Toronto for the Years 1870–1880

Year	Institution	No. of inmates	Provincial funding	Total revenues
1870	Prot. orphanage	95	640	5,690
	Cath. orphanage	334	640	5,983
1871	Prot. orphanage	117	640	2,807
	Cath. orphanage	345	640	6,430
1872	Prot. orphanage	113	640	5,080
	Cath. orphanage	359	640	7,032
1873	Prot. orphanage	131	640	4,652
	Cath. orphanage	395	640	7,794
1874	Prot. orphanage	137	640	2,989
	Cath. orphanage	396	640	6,106
1875	Prot. orphanage	159	657	–
	Cath. orphanage	384	1,593	
1876	Prot. orphanage	154	698	–
	Cath. orphanage	412	1,251	
1877	Prot. orphanage	139	743	–
	Cath. orphanage	410	1,405	
1878	Prot. orphanage	134	733	4,521
	Cath. orphanage	423	1,625	9,426
1879	Prot. orphanage	153	729	–
	Cath. orphanage	471	1,764	
1880	Prot. orphanage	144	729	4,177
	Cath. orphanage	461	1,764	7,861

SOURCE: Archives of Ontario, *Report of the Inspector of Asylum, Prisons and Public Charities*, 1870–1880.
KEY: Prot. orphanage = the Protestant Orphans Home and Female Aid Society; Cath. orphanage = the Roman Catholic Orphanage Asylum.

APPENDIX FIVE

Catholic Welfare Bureau Year-End Report on Charitable Work with Single Unemployed Men, 1933–1939

Year	Registrations	New cases	Placed on farms	Placed in Toronto	Placed by other agency	Placed by city	Refused placement
1933	4,012	1,190	147	691	455	388	109
1934	3,128	927	124	1,071	576	245	55
1938	2,838	1,239	76	371	–	190	43
1939	1,672	1,131	186	288	28	184	105

APPENDIX SIX

Monthly Report of the Family Welfare Division, Catholic Welfare Bureau, on Charitable Work with Families on Poor Relief, 1932–1933

	March 1932	March 1933	February 1933
No. of families assisted	921	1,811	1,534
Adults	1,379	3,583	2,911
Children	2,270	4,977	4,024
New cases	11	207	166
Cases closed	3	21	21
Non-resident families	35	41	41
Office interviews	2,198	4,282	3,478
Visits	224	474	499
Letters written	823	1,653	1,539
Telephone calls received	3,677	6,779	6,180

SOURCE: "Catholic Charities Activities in the Archdiocese of Toronto," *Catholic Register*, 18 May 1933.

APPENDIX SEVEN

Casework Assessment Form Used by the Family Welfare Division, Catholic Welfare Bureau, with Poor Relief Applicants

Car'd Over	New	Re-op.	Re-curr.	1	2	3	4	5	6	7	8	9	10	11	12	DATE Opened Closed	Continued Service
Surname										Personal Application							Brief Service
Man's given names			Woman's given names					Parish		Referred by Individual						Re-opened	Veteran
Address										Referred by Agency							Active Service
Address										RELIGION				Country of Birth			War Bride
										MAN							Res. Non-Res.
Address										WOMAN							Cit. Non-Cit.

FAMILY STATUS

1. Single man
2. Single woman
3. Married couple
4. Widow
5. Widower
6. Deserted woman
7. Deserted man
8. Divorced woman
9. Divorced man
10. Woman sep. from husband
11. Man sep. from wife
12. Unmarried mother
13.
14. Unmarried couple
15. Orphans
16. Others

Adults

Children under 16

Between 16 and 21

Relief given by Agency	1	2	3		4	5	6		7	8	9	10	11	12
Emergency assistance	1	2	3		4	5	6		7	8	9	10	11	12
Loan	1	2	3		4	5	6		7	8	9	10	11	12
According to planned budget	1	2	3		4	5	6		7	8	9	10	11	12
Relating to case work plan												
To supplement public funds (e.g. D.P.W., M.A., O.A.P., Workmen's Comp., Unemp. Ins., Mil. pens.)	1	2	3		4	5	6		7	8	9	10	11	12
To supplement earnings or other private income	1	2	3		4	5	6		7	8	9	10	11	12
Where no public resource is available	1	2	3		4	5	6		7	8	9	10	11	12
Where need chiefly due to high cost of living, unemployment, low wages or other economic factors	1	2	3		4	5	6		7	8	9	10	11	12
Where need chiefly due to extra expenses for large family	1	2	3		4	5	6		7	8	9	10	11	12
Where need chiefly due to mismanagement, drinking, domestic trouble, or non-support	1	2	3		4	5	6		7	8	9	10	11	12
Where need chiefly due to illness	1	2	3		4	5	6		7	8	9	10	11	12
Request for child placement dealt with	1	2	3		4	5	6		7	8	9	10	11	12
Due to (a) Illness (mental or physical) or death of mother	1	2	3		4	5	6		7	8	9	10	11	12
(b) Separation of parents, domestic trouble, drinking, desertion, neglect, non-support	1	2	3		4	5	6		7	8	9	10	11	12
(c) Child parent relationship factors, or child behaviour problems	1	2	3		4	5	6		7	8	9	10	11	12
(d) Housing difficulties	1	2	3		4	5	6		7	8	9	10	11	12
(e) Mother's need to work outside home	1	2	3		4	5	6		7	8	9	10	11	12
(f) Inability to support	1	2	3		4	5	6		7	8	9	10	11	12
(g) Illegitimacy	1	2	3		4	5	6		7	8	9	10	11	12
Placement made	1	2	3		4	5	6		7	8	9	10	11	12
Housing problems affecting family life	1	2	3		4	5	6		7	8	9	10	11	12

PROBLEMS PRESENTED AND SERVICES RENDERED

1. Helped through discussion of family relationships..........................	1	2	3		4	5	6		7	8	9		10	11	12
2. Helped with conflicts or problems influenced by personality factors, emotional or mental disturbances.............................	1	2	3		4	5	6		7	8	9		10	11	12
3. Helped with problems arising out of alcoholism or excessive drinking......	1	2	3		4	5	6		7	8	9		10	11	12
4. Helped with problems caused by common-law union or illegitimacy.........	1	2	3		4	5	6		7	8	9		10	11	12
5. Helped to function more adequately in spite of low mentality..............	1	2	3		4	5	6		7	8	9		10	11	12
6. Helped with home management...	1	2	3		4	5	6		7	8	9		10	11	12
7. Helped with child training..	1	2	3		4	5	6		7	8	9		10	11	12
8. Helped to secure medical, surgical, dental, optical. orthopaedic, or nursing services....	1	2	3		4	5	6		7	8	9		10	11	12
9. Helped to secure admission to other than child-caring institution.........	1	2	3		4	5	6		7	8	9		10	11	12
10. Helped to use psychiatric resources.....................................	1	2	3		4	5	6		7	8	9		10	11	12
11. Helped with adjustments necessitated by illness...........................	1	2	3		4	5	6		7	8	9		10	11	12
12. Helped with nutritional standards.......................................	1	2	3		4	5	6		7	8	9		10	11	12
13. Helped to secure educational advantages, vocational training or guidance....	1	2	3		4	5	6		7	8	9		10	11	12
14. Helped to make use of employment opportunities........................	1	2	3		4	5	6		7	8	9		10	11	12
15. Helped to secure legal aid or naturalization..............................	1	2	3		4	5	6		7	8	9		10	11	12
16. Helped with adjustments at D.V.A......................................	1	2	3		4	5	6		7	8	9		10	11	12
17. Helped to use other special resources for ex-servicemen...................	1	2	3		4	5	6		7	8	9		10	11	12
18. Helped with adjustments at D.P.W......................................	1	2	3		4	5	6		7	8	9		10	11	12
19. Helped with adjustments at other Public agencies........................	1	2	3		4	5	6		7	8	9		10	11	12
20. Helped to make use of other community resources.......................	1	2	3		4	5	6		7	8	9		10	11	12
21. Helped with financial planning and budgetting..........................	1	2	3		4	5	6		7	8	9		10	11	12
22. Helped with adjustments necessitated by unemployment..................	1	2	3		4	5	6		7	8	9		10	11	12
23. Helped to secure better housing or improve home surroundings...........	1	2	3		4	5	6		7	8	9		10	11	12
24. Helped to secure support or interest from parents or relatives.............	1	2	3		4	5	6		7	8	9		10	11	12
25. Helped to secure camp outing or other vacation.........................	1	2	3		4	5	6		7	8	9		10	11	12
26. Helped to arrange for Christmas Cheer.................................	1	2	3		4	5	6		7	8	9		10	11	12
27. Helped to make contact with Church re spiritual or social problem.........	1	2	3		4	5	6		7	8	9		10	11	12
28. Helped New Immigrant to adjust.......................................	1	2	3		4	5	6		7	8	9		10	11	12
29. Helped with problems due to old age...................................	1	2	3		4	5	6		7	8	9		10	11	12

SOURCE: Marion Mo Bell, "The History of Catholic Welfare Bureau" (MSW thesis, University of Toronto, 1949), 122–3.

Notes

INTRODUCTION

1 Jacquelyn Thayer Scott, "Voluntary Sector in Crisis: Canada's Changing Public Philosophy of the State and Its Impact on Voluntary Charitable Organizations" (PhD dissertation, University of Colorado, 1992), 189–90.
2 Margaret Philip, "Ontarians Look for New Ways to Fight against Welfare Cuts," *Globe and Mail*, 29 September 1995, A12.
3 Government of Canada, "Partnering for the benefit of Canadians: Initiative Between the Government of Canada and the Voluntary Sector," December 2001 (www.vsi-isvc.ca).
4 At least since the late 1970s, governments have been downsizing social programs. Since 1984 the federal government has cut and capped the transfer of Established Program Financing to the provinces, reduced unemployment insurance, de-indexed family allowances, eliminated national standards in social programs, and replaced the Canada Assistance Plan with the weaker Canada Health and Social Transfer Plan, which substantially reduces payments to the provinces and territories. In Ontario the Harris government has slashed welfare benefits by 22 per cent, imposed workfare, increased user fees, and downloaded much of the cost of welfare to the municipalities. Ontario's municipalities are now expected to draw on property taxes to pay their 50 per cent share for family subsidies, child care, nursing homes, and social housing.
5 Canadian Centre for Philanthropy, "Facts on the Size and Scope of the Canadian Charitable and Voluntary Sector," 2001 (www.nonprofitscan.org/sizescop.html).

6 Scott, "Voluntary Sector in Crisis," 360.
7 Dennis Guest, *The Emergence of Social Security in Canada* (Vancouver: University of British Columbia Press, 1980); Richard Splane, *Social Welfare in Ontario, 1791–1893: A Study of Public Welfare Administration* (Toronto: University of Toronto Press, 1965); Allan Moscovitch and Jim Albert, eds., *The "Benevolent State": The Growth of Welfare in Canada* (Toronto: Garamond Press, 1987); Allan Moscovitch and Glenn Drover, eds., *Inequality: Essays on the Political Economy of Social Welfare* (Toronto: University of Toronto Press, 1991); James Pitsula, "The Relief of Poverty in Toronto" (PhD dissertation, York University, 1979); Gale Wills, *A Marriage of Convenience: Business and Social Work in Toronto, 1918–1957* (Toronto: University of Toronto Press, 1995).
8 Stephen Speisman, "Munificent Parsons and Municipal Parsimony: Voluntary vs Public Poor Relief in Nineteenth Century Toronto," *Ontario History* 65 (March 1973): 32.
9 Splane, *Social Welfare in Ontario*, 70.
10 Rainer Baehre, "Paupers and Poor Relief in Upper Canada," *Canadian Historical Association Historical Papers*, 1981.
11 Lynne Marks, "Indigent Communities and Ladies Benevolent Societies: Intersections of Public and Private Poor Relief in Late Nineteenth Century Small Town Ontario," *Studies in Political Economy* 47 (summer 1995): 61–87.
12 Jane Lewis, "The Boundary between Voluntary and Statutory Social Service in the late Nineteenth and Early Twentieth Centuries," *Historical Journal* 39 (1996): 159.
13 Nikolas Rose and Peter Miller, "Political Power beyond the State: Problematics of Government," *British Journal of Sociology* 43 (June 1992): 192.
14 For a discussion of Foucault's concept of governmentality, see the various articles in Graham Burchell, Colin Gordon, and Peter Miller, eds., *The Foucault Effect: Studies in Governmentality* (Chicago: University of Chicago Press, 1991); Andrew Barry, Thomas Osborne, and Nikolas Rose, eds., *Foucault and Political Reason: Liberalism, Neo-liberalism, and Rationalities of Government* (Chicago: University of Chicago Press, 1996); Nikolas Rose, *Powers of Freedom: Reframing Political Thought* (Cambridge: Cambridge University Press, 1999). See also chapters 9 and 10 in Mitchell Dean, *Critical and Effective Histories: Foucault's Methods and Historical Sociology* (London: Routledge, 1994).
15 Nikolas Rose, *Governing the Soul: The Shaping of the Private Self* (London: Routledge, 1989), 7–8.

16 Allan Irving, "The Scientific Imperative in Canadian Social Work: Social Work and Social Welfare Research in Canada, 1897–1945," *Canadian Social Work Review* 9 (winter 1992): 9–27; James Pitsula, "The Emergence of Social Work in Toronto," *Journal of Canadian Studies* 14 (spring 1979): 35–42; Wills, *A Marriage of Convenience*. Similar arguments are made by those who advance the secularization thesis. See, for example, chapter 18 in Richard Allen, *The Social Passion: Religion and Social Reform in Canada, 1914–1928* (Toronto: University of Toronto Press, 1973); Ramsay Cook, *The Regenerators: Social Criticism in Late Victorian Canada* (Toronto: University of Toronto Press, 1985); David B. Marshall, *Secularizing the Faith: Canadian Protestant Clergy and the Crisis of Belief, 1850–1940* (Toronto: University of Toronto Press, 1992).

17 Nancy Christie and Michael Gauvreau, *A Full-Orbed Christianity: The Protestant Churches and Social Welfare in Canada, 1900–1940* (Montreal: McGill-Queen's University Press, 1996), 246.

18 Ibid., 247.

19 For works on Catholic charities in Canada, see Marion M. Bell, "The History of the Catholic Welfare Bureau" (MSW thesis, University of Toronto, 1949); Mary Alvan Bouchard, "Pioneers Forever: The Community of St. Joseph in Toronto and Their Ventures in Social Welfare and Health Care," in Mark McGowan and Brian Clarke, eds., *Catholics at the "Gathering Place": Historical Essays on the Archdiocese of Toronto, 1841–1991* (Toronto: The Canadian Catholic Historical Association, 1993); Brian Clarke, *Piety and Nationalism: Lay Voluntary Associations and the Creation of an Irish-Catholic Community in Toronto, 1850–1895* (Montreal: McGill-Queen's University Press, 1993); Marta Danylewycz, *Taking the Veil: An Alternative to Marriage, Motherhood, and Spinsterhood in Quebec, 1840–1920* (Toronto: McClelland and Stewart, 1987); Murray W. Nicholson, "The Catholic Church and the Irish in Victorian Toronto," (PhD dissertation, University of Guelph, 1981); Mary Lassance Parthun, "Origins of Anglophone Catholic Social Services in Ontario, 1826–1860" (Working Papers on Social Welfare in Canada, University of Toronto, Faculty of Social Work, 1988).

20 Notable exceptions include Denyse Baillargeon, "Les rapports médicins-infirmières et l'implication de la Métropolitaine dans la lutte contre la mortalité infantile, 1909–53," *Canadian Historical Review* 77 (March 1996): 33–61; Jean-Marie Facteau, "La construction d'un espace social: Les rapports de l'Église et de l'État et la question de l'assistance publique au Québec dans la seconde moitié du XIXe siècle," *Milanges Galarneau*, 1995.

21 See the following articles in *Studies in Political Economy* 47 (summer 1995): Mariana Valverde, "The Mixed Social Economy as a Canadian Tradition," 33–60; Lynne Marks, "Indigent Committees and Ladies Benevolent Societies,"61–87; Margaret Little,"The Blurring of Boundaries: Private and Public Welfare for Single Mothers in Ontario,"89–110.
22 Valverde, "The Mixed Social Economy," 54.
23 Josephine Rekart, *Public Funds, Private Provisions: The Role of the Voluntary Sector* (Vancouver: University of British Columbia Press, 1993).
24 James Struthers, "Reluctant Partners: State Regulation of Private Nursing Homes in Ontario, 1941–72," in Raymond B. Blake, Penny E. Bryden, and J. Frank Strain, eds., *The Welfare State in Canada: Past, Present and Future* (Concord: Irwin Publishing, 1997), 171–92.
25 For an analysis of privatization in criminal justice, see Alexis M. Durham III, "Origins of Interest in the Privatization of Punishment: The Nineteenth and Twentieth Century American Experience," *Criminology* 27 (1989): 107–39.
26 Phillip Corrigan and Derek Sayer, *The Great Arch: English State Formation as Cultural Revolution* (Oxford: Basil Blackwell, 1985); Bruce Curtis, *Building the Educational State: Canada West, 1836–1871* (London: The Althouse Press, 1988).
27 Peter Miller and Nikolas Rose, "Governing Economic Life," *Economy and Society* 19 (February 1990): 10.

CHAPTER ONE

1 Rainer Baehre, "Paupers and Poor Relief in Upper Canada," *Canadian Historical Association Historical Papers*, 1981, 57–80.
2 Richard Splane, *Social Welfare in Ontario, 1791–1893: A Study of Public Welfare Administration* (Toronto: University of Toronto Press, 1965); Michael B. Katz, Michael J. Doucet, and Mark J. Stern, *The Social Organization of Early Industrial Capitalism* (Cambridge: Harvard University Press, 1982).
3 Jacques Donzelot, *The Policing of Families* (New York: Random House, 1979); Mary Poovey, *Making a Social Body: British Cultural Formation, 1830–1864* (Chicago: University of Chicago Press, 1995).
4 Poovey, *Making a Social Body*, 9.
5 Baehre, "Paupers and Poor Relief in Upper Canada," 65–79.
6 In addition to legislation affecting municipalities, Canada West passed an act in 1847 forcing shipping companies to provide a bond with sureties for any immigrant they brought over who became destitute within the first

year. The act was amended in 1851 to allow the collection from bonds to be given directly to charities working with immigrants. See Splane, *Social Welfare in Ontario*, 78.
7 Susan Elizabeth Houston, "The Impetus to Reform: Urban Crime, Poverty and Ignorance in Ontario, 1850–1875" (PhD dissertation, University of Toronto, 1974), 187.
8 Splane, *Social Welfare in Ontario*, 68.
9 Murray W. Nicolson, "Michael Power: First Bishop of Toronto," *Canadian Catholic Historical Association Historical Papers*, 54 (1987): 27–38; Mary Lassance Parthun, "Origins of Anglophone Catholic Social Services in Ontario, 1826–1860" (Working Papers on Social Welfare in Canada, University of Toronto, Faculty of Social Work, 1988), 29; Roberto Perin, *Rome in Canada: The Vatican and Canadian Affairs in the Late Victorian Age* (Toronto: University of Toronto Press, 1990), 18–19.
10 *Journal of the Legislative Assembly of Canada*, 1842, appendix M; *Census of Canada*, 1851–52, 52.
11 Prior to the wave of Irish immigrants, the Catholic Church in Toronto had been predominantly Scottish. See Terrence Murphy, "Introduction," in Terrence Murphy and Gerald Stortz, eds., *Creed and Culture: The Place of English-Speaking Catholics in Canadian Society, 1750–1930* (Montreal: McGill-Queen's University Press, 1993), xxviii.
12 Archives of Ontario (AO), *Report of the Inspector of Asylums, Prisons and Public Charities*, 1874.
13 Brian P. Clarke, *Piety and Nationalism: Lay Voluntary Associations and the Creation of an Irish-Catholic Community in Toronto, 1850–1895* (Montreal: McGill-Queen's University Press, 1993); Houston, "The Impetus to Reform," 18; Murray Nicolson, "The Irish Catholics and Social Action in Toronto, 1850–1900," *Studies in History and Politics* 1 (1980): 30, 60; Parthun, "Origins of Anglophone Catholic Social Services," 61.
14 Both organizations were administered by Protestant groups, although the latter did have Catholic representation on its board.
15 Nicolson, "The Irish Catholics and Social Action," 31.
16 Houston, "The Impetus to Reform," 201; Murray W. Nicolson, "John Elmsley and the Rise of Irish Catholic Social Action in Victorian Toronto," *Canadian Catholic Historical Association Historical Studies* 51 (1984): 47–66; Nicolson, "The Irish Catholics and Social Action"; Parthun, "Origins of Anglophone Catholic and Social Services," 32, 58.
17 Brian Clarke, "English-Speaking Canada from 1854," in Terrence Murphy and Roberto Perin, eds., *A Concise History of Christianity in Canada* (Toronto: Oxford University Press, 1996), 297.

18 Robert Choquette, "English-French Relations in the Canadian Catholic Community," in Murphy and Stortz, eds., *Creed and Culture*, 3–24; John S. Moir, "Toronto's Protestants and Their Perceptions of Their Roman Catholic Neighbours," in Mark McGowan and Brian Clarke, eds., *Catholics at the "Gathering Place": Historical Essays on the Archdiocese of Toronto, 1841–1991* (Toronto: The Canadian Catholic Historical Association, 1993).

19 Clarke, *Piety and Nationalism*, 43.

20 In many ways, Catholic social action, which took on a distinctly Irish character in Toronto, was similar to the Protestant social gospel movement of the 1880s. However, it tended to be more unified and extensive, in that the church was to be involved in all aspects of cultural, educational, and welfare provisions for the community. See Clarke, *Piety and Nationalism*, 40; Murray W. Nicolson, "Bishop Charbonnel: The Beggar Bishop and the Origins of Catholic Social Action," *Canadian Catholic Historical Association Historical Studies* 52 (1985): 51–66; Murray Nicolson, "The Growth of Roman Catholic Institutions in the Archdiocese of Toronto, 1841–1890," in Murphy and Stortz, eds., *Creed and Culture*; John E. Zucchi, "The Catholic Church and the Italian Immigrant in Canada 1880–1920: A Comparison between Ultramontane Montréal and Hibernian Toronto," in Gianfausto Rosoli and Gabriele De Rosa, eds., *Scalabrini tra Vecchio e Nuovo Mondo* (Roma: Centro Studi Emigrazione, 1989), 492.

21 Clarke, "English-Speaking Canada," 293.

22 Franklin A. Walker, *Catholic Education and Politics in Upper Canada* (Toronto: J.M. Dent & Sons, 1955), 114, 121.

23 Houston, "The Impetus to Reform," 205–8; Susan E. Houston and Alison Prentice, *Schooling and Scholars in Nineteenth-Century Ontario* (Toronto: University of Toronto Press, 1988), 279–96. For an analysis that explores the French-language separate school question in terms of social and cultural identity, see Chad Gaffield, *Language, Schooling, and Cultural Conflict: The Origins of the French-Language Controversy in Ontario* (Kingston: McGill-Queen's University Press, 1987).

24 Sister Mary Agnes, *The Congregation of the Sisters of St. Joseph* (Toronto: University of Toronto Press, 1951); Mary Alban Bouchard, "Pioneers Forever: The Community of St. Joseph in Toronto and Their Ventures in Social Welfare and Health Care," in McGowan and Clarke, eds., *Catholics at the "Gathering Place,"* 105–118; "Dinan, Ellen," *Dictionary of Canadian Biography*, vol. 13 (Toronto: University of Toronto Press, 1994); Elizabeth Smyth, "Christian Perfection and Service to Neighbours: The Congregation of the Sisters of St. Joseph, Toronto,

1851–1920," in Elizabeth Gillan Muir and Marilyn Färdig Whiteley, eds., *Changing Roles of Women within the Christian Church in Canada* (Toronto: University of Toronto Press, 1995), 38–54; Archives of the Sisters of St. Joseph, Toronto (ACSJ), *Historical Sketch*; ACSJ, Mary Bird and Pat Bird, "Welfare in the Nineteenth Century: The Private Response: A Study of the Work of the Sisters of St. Joseph of Toronto" (unpublished manuscript); ACSJ, *Community Annals, Sister of St. Joseph of Toronto*, vol. 1 (1851–1914).

25 Parthun, "Origins of Anglophone Catholic Social Services," 7, 53.
26 For a detailed discussion of the work of the St Vincent de Paul Society and women's confraternities, see Clarke, *Piety and Nationalism*, chapters 4–5.
27 Smyth, "Christian Perfection."
28 Choquette, "English-French Relations," 11.
29 Smyth, "Christian Perfection," 39.
30 Bouchard, "Pioneers Forever," 110.
31 For example, see Mary J. Oates, *The Catholic Philanthropic Tradition in America* (Bloomington: Indiana University Press, 1995), 19–45
32 Nicolson, "Bishop Charbonnel," 55.
33 Ibid., 55–6.
34 The Sisters of St Joseph were not paid for their service. They subsisted on the money allotted to the community. Hence Catholic institutions were often far more "efficient" than non-Catholic charities.
35 AO, *Report of the Inspector of Asylums, Prisons and Public Charities*, 1874–1920; Oates, *The Catholic Philanthropic Tradition in America*, 48–9.
36 Splane, *Social Welfare in Ontario*, 40.
37 Clarke, "English-Speaking Canada," 271.
38 Gordon Darroch and Michael Ornstein, "Ethnicity and Occupational Structure in Canada in 1871: The Vertical Mosaic in Historical Perspective," *Canadian Historical Review* 61 (September 1980): 305–3.
39 Mark G. McGowan, *The Waning of the Green: Catholics, the Irish, and Identity in Toronto, 1887–1922* (Montreal & Kingston: McGill-Queen's University Press, 1999).
40 John S. Moir, *Church and Society: Documents on the Religious and Social History of the Roman Catholic Archdiocese of Toronto* (Toronto: Archdiocese of Toronto, 1991), 171, 177–80.
41 McGowan, *The Waning of the Green*, 12.
42 See Anne Freemantle, *The Papal Encyclicals in Their Historical Context: The Teachings of the Popes from Peter to John XXIII* (New York: The New American Library, 1963).

43 Clarke, "English-Speaking Canada," 352.
44 Paula Kane, *Separatism and Subculture: Boston Catholicism, 1900–1920* (Chapel Hill: University of North Carolina Press, 1994), 11.
45 Giovanna Procacci, "Social Economy and the Government of Poverty," in Graham Burchell, Colin Gordon, and Peter Miller, eds., *The Foucault Effect: Studies in Governmentality* (Chicago: University of Chicago Press, 1991). See also Nancy Fraser and Linda Gordon, "A Genealogy of Dependency: Tracing a Keyword of the U.S. Welfare State," *Signs* 19 (winter 1994): 309–36.
46 Donzelot, *The Policing of Families*, 68.
47 Mariana Valverde, *The Age of Light, Soap and Water: Moral Reform in English Canada, 1885–1925* (Toronto: McClelland and Stewart, 1991), 20.
48 David J. O'Brien, "Social Teaching, Social Action, Social Gospel," *U.S. Catholic Historian* 5 (1986): 195–224.
49 Jean-Yves Calvez and Jacques Perrin, *The Church and Social Justice: The Social Teaching of the Popes from Leo XIII to Pius XII (1878–1958)* (Chicago: Henry Regnery Company, 1961), 163.
50 Rudolph Villeneuve, *Catholic Social Work* (Montreal: Grand Seminary of Montreal, 1955), 8.
51 Clarke, *Piety and Nationalism*, 118.

CHAPTER TWO

1 J.E. Hodgetts, *From Arm's Length to Hands On: The Formative Years of Ontario's Public Service, 1867–1940* (Toronto: University of Toronto Press, 1995), 8.
2 Archives of Ontario (AO), *Report of the Inspector of Asylums, Prisons and Public Charities*, 1870, 1876, 1890.
3 Hodgetts, *From Arm's Length*, 31.
4 Bruce Curtis, *True Government by Choice Men? Inspection, Education, and State Formation in Canada West* (Toronto: University of Toronto Press), 30.
5 Ibid., 11; Bruce Curtis, "Class Culture and Administration: Educational Inspection in Canada West," in Allan Greer and Ian Radforth, eds., *Colonial Leviathan: State Formation in Mid-Nineteenth-Century Canada* (Toronto: University of Toronto Press, 1992); Michel Foucault, *Discipline and Punish: The Birth of the Prison*, translated by Alan Sheridan (New York: Vintage Books, 1979); Hodgetts, *From Arm's Length*; Peter Miller and Nikolas Rose, "Political Power beyond the State: Problematics of Government," *British Journal of Sociology* 43 (1992): 173–205; John C. Weaver,

"The Modern City Realized: Toronto Civic Affairs, 1880–1915," in Alan F. J. Artibise and Gilbert A. Stelter, eds., *The Usable Urban Past: Planning and Politics in the Modern Canadian City* (Toronto: Macmillan, 1979), 39.

6 The rise of inspectors dates back to the 1830s in England. In Canada, other domains in which inspection became a regulatory practice included public health (1849), prisons (1857), insurance companies (1879), registry offices (1879), factories (1887), and child protection (1893). See Curtis, *True Government by Choice Men?*, 4; Weaver, "The Modern City Realized."

7 A Board of Inspectors of Prisons, Asylums and Public Charities had been established earlier in 1859, but it did little in the way of inspecting private charities.

8 Curtis, "Class Culture and Administration;" Hodgetts, *From Arm's Length*; Ian Hacking, "How Should We Do the History of Statistics?," in Andrew Barry, Thomas Osborne, and Nikolas Rose, eds., *Foucault and Political Reason: Liberalism, Neo-liberalism, and Rationalities of Government* (Chicago: University of Chicago Press, 1996); Nikolas Rose, "Governing 'Advanced' Liberal Democracies," in Barry, Osborne, and Rose, eds., *Foucault and Political Reason*; Nikolas Rose, *Governing the Soul: The Shaping of the Private Self* (London: Routledge, 1989), 6–7.

9 Peter Miller, "Accounting as Social and Institutional Practice: An Introduction," in Anthony G. Hopwood and Peter Miller, eds., *Accounting as Social and Institutional Practice* (New York: Cambridge University Press, 1994), 3.

10 AO, *Report of the Inspector of Asylums, Prisons and Public Charities*, 1874.

11 Richard Splane, *Social Welfare in Ontario, 1791–1893: A Study of Public Welfare Administration* (Toronto: University of Toronto Press, 1965), 80–8.

12 Initially, only the Roman Catholic Orphanage Asylum and the House of Providence were awarded government aid in Toronto, but later other Catholic organizations were included under the Charity Aid Act.

13 AO, *Report of the Inspector of Asylums, Prisons and Public Charities*, 1874–75.

14 Mariana Valverde, "The Mixed Social Economy as a Canadian Tradition," *Studies in Political Economy* 47 (summer 1995): 49.

15 AO, *Report of the Inspector of Asylums, Prisons and Public Charities*, 1875.

16 Paul Adolphus Bator, "'The Struggle to Raise the Lower Classes': Public Health Reform and the Problem of Poverty in Toronto, 1910–1921," *Journal of Canadian Studies* 14 (spring 1979): 43.

17 Ibid.
18 The development of this movement paralleled the rise of the Progressive era in the Untied States.
19 John C. Weaver, "Order and Efficiency: Samuel Morley Wickett and the Urban Progressive Movement in Toronto, 1900–1915," *Ontario History* 69 (December 1977): 218–34. See also Doug Owram, *The Government Generation: Canadian Intellectuals and the State, 1900–1945* (Toronto: University of Toronto Press, 1986), 50–79; Graham S. Lowe, "Mechanization, Feminization, and Managerial Control in the Early Twentieth-Century Canadian Office," in Craig Heron and Robert Storey, eds., *On the Job: Confronting the Labour Process in Canada* (Montreal: McGill-Queen's University Press, 1986); Paul Rutherford, "The Reform of Municipal Government," in *Saving the Canadian City: The First Phase, 1880–1920* (Toronto: University of Toronto Press, 1974).
20 Frederick Winslow Taylor, *The Principles of Scientific Management* (New York: Harper, 1911). For a detailed discussion of Taylor's ideas, see S. Haber, *Efficiency and Uplift: Scientific Management in the Progressive Era, 1890–1920* (Chicago: University of Chicago Press, 1964).
21 Taylor, *The Principles of Scientific Management*, 8.
22 Paul Rutherford, "Tomorrow's Metropolis: The Urban Reform Movement in Canada, 1880–1920," in Gilbert A. Stelter and Alan F.J. Artibise, eds., *The Canadian City: Essays in Urban and Social History* (Ottawa: Carleton University Press, 1984); John C. Weaver, "Tomorrow's Metropolis: The Urban Reform Movement in Canada, 1890–1920," ibid.
23 Valverde, "Moral Capital," *Canadian Journal of Law and Society* 9 (1994): 215.
24 James Michael Pitsula, "The Emergence of Social Work in Toronto," *Journal of Canadian Studies* 14 (spring 1979): 40.
25 Peter Miller and Ted O'Leary, "Governing the Calculable Person," in Hopwood and Miller, eds., *Accounting as Social and Institutional Practice*, 103.
26 James Michael Pitsula, "The Relief of Poverty in Toronto, 1880–1930" (PhD dissertation, York University, 1979); Pitsula, "The Emergence of Social Work in Toronto"; Gale Wills, *A Marriage of Convenience: Business and Social Work in Toronto, 1918–1957* (Toronto: University of Toronto Press, 1995).
27 Pitsula, "The Relief of Poverty in Toronto," 225, 227, 233.
28 By 1919, eleven individual agencies were coordinated under the Catholic Charities organization: Carmelite Orphanage, Catholic Big Brothers and Big Sisters, Good Shepherd Refuge, House of Providence, Sacred Heart Orphanage, St Elizabeth Visiting Nurses, St Mary's Home and Hospital, St Michael's Hospital and the St Vincent de Paul Children's Aid Society.

29 In 1914 the Neighbourhood Workers Association was established at the request of the city; it was initially under the control of the Social Service Commission. In 1918 it severed its ties with the commission and was restructured as an independent body administered by local charity leaders. For works on the Neighbourhood Workers Association see F.N. Stapleford, *After Twenty Years: A Short History of the Neighbourhood Workers Association* (Toronto: Neighbourhood Workers Association, 1938); Pitsula, "The Relief of Poverty in Toronto," chapter 6; Wills, *A Marriage of Convenience*, 46–9.

30 Marion M. Bell, "The History of the Catholic Welfare Bureau" (MSW thesis, University of Toronto, 1949), 19–23; 38; Archives of the Roman Catholic Archdiocese of Toronto (ARCAT), Archbishop Neil McNeil Papers, file WL03.05, McNeil to Taylor, 20 November 1919. For similar developments in the United States, see Mary J. Oates, *The Catholic Philanthropic Tradition in America* (Bloomington: Indiana University Press, 1995), chapter 4.

31 Dorothy M. Brown and Elizabeth McKeown, *The Poor Belong to Us: Catholic Charities and American Welfare* (Cambridge: Harvard University Press, 1997); Leslie Woodcock Tentler, *Seasons of Grace: A History of the Catholic Archdiocese of Detroit* (Detroit: Wayne State University Press, 1990.

32 Brown and McKeown, *The Poor Belong to Us*, 51.

33 Wills, *A Marriage of Convenience*.

34 AO, *Report of the Inspector of Prisons, Asylums and Charities*, 1915.

35 Bell, "The History of the Catholic Welfare Bureau."

36 Wills, *A Marriage of Convenience*, 53–5.

37 ARCAT, McNeil Papers, file WL03.13, Stanton to McNeil, May 1934.

38 ARCAT, McNeil Papers, file WL04.108, Federation of Catholic Charities to McNeil, 28 April 1930.

39 Alan Hunt, "Regulating the Social," in Mariana Valverde, ed., *Radically Rethinking Regulation: Workshop Report* (Toronto: Centre for Criminology, University of Toronto, 1994), 50. For other discussions on the concept of governance, see the articles in Graham Burchell, Colin Gordon, and Peter Miller, eds., *The Foucault Effect: Studies in Governmentality* (Chicago: University of Chicago Press, 1991).

CHAPTER THREE

1 Archives of the Roman Catholic Archdiocese of Toronto (ARCAT), Catholic Charities Papers, file OC06 FA03, Archbishop McNeil, circular letter, 1930.

2 Gale Wills, *A Marriage of Convenience: Business and Social Work in Toronto, 1918–1957* (Toronto: University of Toronto Press, 1995), 8.
3 Allan Irving, "The Scientific Imperative in Canadian Social Work: Social Work and Social Welfare Research in Canada, 1897–1945," *Canadian Social Work Review* 9 (winter 1992): 16.
4 Sara Z. Burke, *Seeking the Highest Good: Social Service and Gender at the University of Toronto, 1888–1937* (Toronto: University of Toronto Press, 1996).
5 Richard Allen, *The Social Passion: Religion and Social Reform in Canada, 1914–1928* (Toronto: University of Toronto Press, 1973); Ramsay Cook, *The Regenerators: Social Criticism in Late Victorian Canada* (Toronto: University of Toronto Press, 1985); David B. Marshall, *Secularizing the Faith: Canadian Protestant Clergy and the Crisis of Belief, 1850–1940* (Toronto: University of Toronto Press, 1992).
6 Thomas Haskell, *The Emergence of Professional Social Science* (Urbana: University of Illinois Press, 1977).
7 Doug Owram, *The Government Generation: Canadian Intellectuals and the State, 1900–1945* (Toronto: University of Toronto Press, 1986); Marlene Shore, *The Science of Social Redemption: McGill, the Chicago School, and the Origins of Social Research in Canada* (Toronto: University of Toronto Press, 1987); Allen, *The Social Passion*; Cook, *The Regenerators*; Marshall, *Secularizing the Faith*.
8 David Howe, "Modernity, Postmodernity and Social Work," *British Journal of Social Work* 24 (1994): 513–32; Nigel Parton, ed., *Social Theory, Social Change and Social Work* (London: Routledge, 1996); Nigel Parton, "Problematics of Government, (Post) Modernity and Social Work" *British Journal of Social Work*, 24 (1994) 9–32; Nigel Parton, *Governing the Family: Child Care, Child Protection and the State* (London: MacMillan Education, 1991); Nikolas Rose and Peter Miller, "Political Power beyond the State: Problematics of Government," *British Journal of Sociology* 43 (June 1992): 173–205.
9 James Michael Pitsula, "The Emergence of Social Work in Toronto," *Journal of Canadian Studies*, 14 (spring 1979): 37; Roy Lubove, *The Professional Altruist: The Emergence of Social Work as a Career, 1880–1930* (New York: Atheneum, 1977).
10 Irving, "The Scientific Imperative," 9–16.
11 See Paul Adolphus Bator, " 'The Struggle to Raise the Lower Classes': Public Health Reform and the Problem of Poverty in Toronto, 1910–1921," *Journal of Canadian Studies* 14 (spring 1979): 43–9; J.S. Woodsworth, *My Neighbour: A Study of City Conditions, a Plea for Social Service* (1911;

Toronto: University of Toronto Press, 1972); Herbert Brown Ames, *The City below the Hill: A Sociological Study of a Portion of the City of Montreal, Canada* (1897; Toronto: University of Toronto Press, 1972).

12 Allen, *The Social Passion*; Cook, *The Regenerators*; Marshall *Secularizing the Faith*.

13 Nancy Christie and Michael Gauvreau, *A Full-Orbed Christianity: The Protestant Churches and Social Welfare in Canada, 1900–1940* (Montreal: McGill-Queen's University Press, 1996); Mariana Valverde, *The Age of Light, Soap and Water: Moral Reform in English Canada, 1885–1925* (Toronto: McClelland and Stewart, 1991).

14 Mark G. McGowan, "Coming Out of the Cloister: Some Reflections on Developments in the Study of Religion in Canada, 1980–1990" *International Journal of Canadian Studies*, spring-fall 1990, 175–202.

15 Some exceptions include Valverde, *The Age of Light*; A.J.B. Johnston, *Religion and Life at Louisbourg, 1713–1758* (Montreal: McGill-Queen's University Press, 1984); Brian P. Clarke, *Piety and Nationalism: Lay Voluntary Associations and the Creation of an Irish-Catholic Community in Toronto, 1850–1895* (Montreal: McGill-Queen's University Press, 1993).

16 Christie and Gauvreau, *A Full-Orbed Christianity*, xiv.

17 Ibid., xi.

18 Ramsay Cook, "Salvation, Sociology and Secularism," *Literary Review of Canada* 6 (April 1997): 11; Cook, *The Regenerators*.

19 Peter L. Berger, *Facing Up to Modernity: Excursions in Society, Politics, and Religion* (New York: Basic Books, 1977); David Lyon, "Introduction," in David Lyon and Marguerite Van Die, eds., *Rethinking Church, State, and Modernity: Canada between Europe and America* (Toronto: University of Toronto Press, 2000); David Martin, *The Religious and the Secular: Studies in Secularization* (London: Routledge and Kegan Paul, 1969); Bryan R. Wilson, "Reflections on a Many Sided Controversy," in Steve Bruce, ed., *Religion and Modernization: Sociologists and Historians Debate the Secularization Thesis* (Oxford: Clarendon Press, 1992).

20 Martin, *The Religious and the Secular*, 22.

21 Lyon and Van Die, *Rethinking Church, State, and Modernity*, 13.

22 Lyon, "Introduction," 10.

23 ARCAT, "Parishes of the Archdiocese of Toronto," in *Directory of the Roman Catholic Archdiocese of Toronto* (Toronto: Roman Catholic Archdiocese of Toronto, December 1993), 111–12.

24 Roman Catholic Archdiocese of Toronto, *Walking the Less Travelled Road: A History of the Religious Communities within the Archdiocese of Toronto, 1841–1991* (Toronto: Mission Press, 1993), 201–2.

25 See, for instance, Murray W. Nicolson, "Bishop Charbonnel: The Beggar Bishop and the Origins of Catholic Social Action," *Canadian Catholic Historical Association Historical Studies* 52 (1985): 51–66; Murray W. Nicolson, "The Irish Catholics and Social Action in Toronto, 1850–1900," *Studies in History and Politics* 1 (1980): 30–54.

26 Brian F. Hogan, "Salted with Fire: Studies in Catholic Social Thought and Action in Ontario, 1931–1961" (PhD dissertation, University of Toronto, 1986).

27 Donal Dorr, *Option for the Poor: A Hundred Years of Vatican Social Teaching* (Dublin: Gill and MacMillan, 1983), 58.

28 Henry Somerville, *Studies in the Catholic Social Movement* (London: Burns Oates & Washbourne, 1933).

29 Hogan, "Salted with Fire," 6.

30 David J. O'Brien, "Social Teaching, Social Action, Social Gospel," *U.S. Catholic Historian* 5 (1986): 199. See also Elizabeth McKeown, *War and Welfare: American Catholics and World War 1* (New York: Garland Publishing, 1988.

31 See Jacques Donzelot, *The Policing of Families* (New York: Random House, 1979).

32 Brian F. Hogan, "Ivory Tower and Grass Roots: The Intellectual Life and Social Action in the Congregation of St. Basil, Archdiocese of Toronto, 1930–1960," in Mark McGowan and Brian Clarke, eds., *Catholics at the "Gathering Place": Historical Essays on the Archdiocese of Toronto, 1841–1991* (Toronto: The Canadian Catholic Historical Association, 1993), 270.

33 The "Life and Labour" column was initiated by Somerville in 1916, but it ended three years later, when because of family obligations, he returned to England. In September 1933 he resumed his post in Toronto. See Jeanne R. Beck, "Contrasting Approaches to Catholic Social Action during the Depression: Henry Somerville the Educator and Catherine de Hueck the Activist," in McGowan and Clarke, eds., *Catholics at the "Gathering Place."*

34 Jeanne R. Beck, "Henry Somerville and the Development of Catholic Social Thought in Canada: Somerville's Role in the Archdiocese of Toronto, 1913–1943" (PhD dissertation, McMaster University, 1977), 326.

35 Henry Somerville, "30,000 Laid Off," *Catholic Register*, 6 January 1938.

36 Henry Somerville, "Family Allowances," *Catholic Register*, 18 August 1938; Henry Somerville, "Call for Housing Campaign," *Catholic Register*, 22 July 1937; Henry Somerville, "Homes for the Workers," *Catholic Register*, 2 December 1937; Beck, "Henry Somerville," 321–5.

37 Hogan, "Salted with Fire," 33.
38 M.M. Coady, *Masters of Their Own Destiny: The Story of the Antigonish Movement of Adult Education through Economic Cooperation* (New York: Harper & Brothers, 1939).
39 Hogan, "Ivory Tower," 257.
40 Hogan, "Salted with Fire," 33.
41 Ibid., 56.
42 Ibid., 31.
43 James Struthers, *No Fault of Their Own: Unemployment and the Canadian Welfare State, 1914–1941* (Toronto: University of Toronto Press, 1983).
44 Quoted in Hogan, "Salted with Fire," 66.
45 Ibid, 257.
46 Rudolph Villeneuve, *Catholic Social Work* (Montreal: Grand Seminary of Montreal, 1955), 79.
47 Michael Behiels, "Le Père Georges-Henri Lévesque et l'établissement de sciences sociales à Laval, 1938–1955," *University of Ottawa Quarterly* 52 (1982): 355–76.
48 See collection of articles in Peter C. McCabe and Francis J. Turner, eds., *Catholic Social Work: A Contemporary Overview* (Ottawa: Catholic Charities of Canada, 1965).
49 Mary J. Oates, *The Catholic Philanthropic Tradition in America* (Bloomington: Indiana University Press, 1995), 91.
50 James Michael Pitsula, "The Relief of Poverty in Toronto, 1880–1930" (PhD dissertation, York University, 1979), 261.
51 Noel Parry and Jose Parry, "Social Work, Professionalism and the State," in Noel Parry, Michael Rustin, and Carole Satyamurti, eds., *Social Work, Welfare and the State* (Beverly Hills: Sage Publications, 1979), 33; David Howe, "Surface and Depth in Social Work Practice," in Nigel Parton, eds., *Social Theory, Social Change and Social Work* (London: Routledge, 1996), 80.
52 John O'Grady, *Catholic Charities in the United States* (New York: Arno Press, 1930, 1971), 430.
53 Oates, *The Catholic Philanthropic Tradition*, 196, fn. 91; O'Grady, *Catholic Charities in the United States*, 434.
54 ARCAT, Catholic Charities Papers, *Catholic Charities: The First 75 Years: An Informal History, 1913–1988* (Toronto: Catholic Charities of the Archdiocese of Toronto, 1988).
55 Canada has three Catholic schools of social work, but the first, l'École de service social at the Université de Montréal, was not created until 1939. The others are L'École de service social at Université Laval and St Patrick's School of Social Welfare at the University of Ottawa. See Villeneuve,

Catholic Social Work, 25n38; James Gripton and Allan Irving, "Social Work and Social Welfare Research in Canada in the Post-War Years, 1945–1960" *Canadian Social Work Review* 13 (summer 1996): 211.

56 ARCAT, Catholic Charities Papers, Federation of Catholic Charities, Budget Committee minutes, 16 June 1932.

57 Rosemary Howorth, *For the Love of Children: A History of the Catholic Children's Aid Society of Metropolitan Toronto, 1894–1994* (Toronto: The Catholic Children's Aid Society, 1994).

58 James Struthers, "'Lord Give Us Men': Women and Social Work in English Canada, 1918 to 1953," in A. Moscovitch and J. Albert, eds., *The "Benevolent" State: The Growth of Welfare in Canada* (Toronto: Garamond Press, 1987), 132; See also Wills, *A Marriage of Convenience*.

59 ARCAT, Catholic Charities Papers, Federation of Catholic Charities, Budget Committee minutes, 24 February 1933.

60 The Carmelite Orphanage, the Sacred Heart Orphanage, the St Mary's Infant Home, and the Catholic Women's League Hostel were administered by nuns. The Catholic Big Sisters and the St Elizabeth Visiting Nurses were directed by laywomen.

61 Marta Danylewycz, *Taking the Veil: An Alternative to Marriage, Motherhood, and Spinsterhood in Quebec, 1840–1920* (Toronto: McClelland and Stewart, 1987), 133.

62 Catholic Welfare Bureau, "Sisters Graduate," *Catholic Register*, 6 June 1935.

63 ARCAT, Catholic Charities Papers, Federation of Catholic Charities to McNeil, 26 September 1929; Archbishop Neil McNeil Papers, file, AE04.40, Brother Barnabus, "Proposed Five-Year Program for Knights of Columbus Boy Life Bureau," 1927.

64 ARCAT, Catholic Charities Papers, file OC06 FS03, "Catholic Welfare Head Dies after Long Illness from Heart Condition," 21 March 1931.

65 Marion M. Bell, "The History of the Catholic Welfare Bureau" (MSW thesis, University of Toronto, 1949), 39.

66 Archives of Ontario (AO), Ministry of Community and Social Services, Deputy Minister's Correspondence, RG 29-01-1, file 770, "Suggested Plans for Canadian Conference on Social Work," 4 January 1940.

67 Catholic Welfare Bureau, "Canadian Conference on Social Work," *Catholic Register*, 10 May 1928; ARCAT, Catholic Charities Papers, "Report of the First Ontario Conference on Social Welfare: Partnership for Social Welfare," 12–14 June 1947.

68 ARCAT, Catholic Charities Papers, file OC06 C002, Bishop of Los Angeles and San Diego to McNeil, 3 March 1927.

69 "Catholic Charities' Activities in the Archdiocese of Toronto," *Catholic Register*, 20 September 1928.
70 Such surveys were not exclusive to the Catholic Church. They were popularly used in Toronto to gauge the efficiency and effectiveness of social services. See Wills, *A Marriage of Convenience*, 50.
71 ARCAT, Catholic Charities Papers, file OC06 SU04, Dr John Lapp, "Social Welfare Survey of the Archdiocese of Toronto," 1922; Bell, "The History of the Catholic Welfare Bureau."
72 ARCAT, Lapp, "Social Welfare Survey"; Bell, "The History of the Catholic Welfare Bureau."
73 ARCAT, Catholic Charities Papers, file OC06 COBB, McNeil to Rev. J. Haley, 5 September 1922.
74 ARCAT, Lapp, "Social Welfare Survey."
75 Rose and Miller, "Political Power beyond the State."
76 Alan Hunt and Gary Wickham, *Foucault and Law: Towards a Sociology of Law as Governance* (London: Pluto Press, 1994), 54.
77 Parton, *Social Theory*, 8.
78 Donzelot, *The Policing of Families*; Parton, *Governing the Family*.
79 Catholic Welfare Bureau, "Behaviour Problems as Related to Family Rehabilitation," *Catholic Register*, 28 June 1928.
80 David Howe, "The Family and the Therapist: Towards a Sociology of Social Work Method," in Martin Davies, eds., *The Sociology of Social Work* (London: Routledge, 1991), 150–1; Nikolas Rose, "Government, Authority and Expertise in Advanced Liberalism," *Economy and Society* 22 (1993): 293–4.
81 See, for example, Donzelot, *The Policing of Families*; E. Zaretsky, "The Place of the Family in the Origins of the Welfare State," in B. Thorne and M. Yalom, eds., *Rethinking the Family* (New York: Longman, 1982).
82 Ernest J. MacDonald, "The Role of the Catholic Social Agency in the Total Community," in Peter C. McCabe and Francis J. Turner, eds., *Catholic Social Work: A Contemporary Overview* (Ottawa: Catholic Charities of Canada, 1965), 45.
83 Dr Paul Hanley Furfey, "Heredity and Social Work," *Catholic Register*, 28 November 1929.
84 Mary E. Richmond, *Social Diagnosis* (New York: Russell Sage Foundation, 1917); Mary E. Richmond, *What Is Social Case Work?: An Introductory Description* (New York: Russell Sage Foundation, 1922).
85 William C. Berleman, "Mary Richmond's Social Diagnosis in Retrospect," *Social Casework* 49 (July 1968): 397.
86 Catholic Welfare Bureau, "The Social Worker," *Catholic Register*, 6 May 1926.

87 Father Haley, "The Art of Interviewing," *Catholic Register*, 24 and 31 May 1928.
88 Richmond, *What Is Social Case Work?*, 238.
89 Howe, "Surface and Depth in Social Work Practice," 81.
90 Dorothy M. Brown and Elizabeth McKeown, *The Poor Belong to Us: Catholic Charities and American Welfare* (Cambridge: Harvard University Press, 1997), 79.
91 "A Plea for the Homeless Child," *Catholic Register*, 22 April 1926.
92 Howorth, *For the Love of Children*; "Adopt a Child Campaign Successful," *Catholic Register*, 18 July 1935; "The Care of Children in Their Own Homes," *Catholic Register*, 26 February 1926; "Institutions vs. Foster Homes in Caring for Dependent and Neglected Children," *Catholic Register*, 17 November 1927; "Catholic Agencies Seek Adoptive Homes," *Catholic Register*, 20 December 1934.
93 ARCAT, Lapp, "Social Welfare Survey."
94 "The Problem of Illegitimacy," *Catholic Register*, 19 March 1925.
95 Bell, "The History of the Catholic Welfare Bureau," 105.

CHAPTER FOUR

1 Harry M. Cassidy, *Unemployment and Relief in Ontario, 1929–1932* (Toronto: J.M. Dent & Sons, 1932), 121.
2 Alvin Finkel, *Business and Social Reform in the Thirties* (Toronto: J. Lorimer, 1979); John R. Graham, "Lessons for Today: Canadian Municipalities and Unemployment Relief during the 1930s Great Depression," *Canadian Review of Social Policy* 35 (spring 1995): 1–18; Dennis Guest, *The Emergence of Social Security in Canada* (Vancouver: University of British Columbia Press, 1980); Roger E. Riendeau, "A Clash of Interests: Dependency and the Municipal Problem in the Great Depression," *Journal of Canadian Studies* 14 (spring 1979): 50–8; James Struthers, *The Limits of Affluence: Welfare in Ontario, 1920–1970* (Toronto: University of Toronto Press, 1994); James Struthers, *No Fault of Their Own: Unemployment and the Canadian Welfare State, 1914–1941* (Toronto: University of Toronto Press, 1983); James Struthers, "Two Depressions: Bennett, Trudeau and the Unemployed," *Journal of Canadian Studies* 14 (spring 1979): 70–80; John H. Taylor, "'Relief from Relief': The Cities' Answer to Depression Dependency," *Journal of Canadian Studies* 14 (spring 1979): 16–23; Jane Ursel, *Private Lives, Public Policy: 100 Years of State Intervention in the Family* (Toronto: Women's Press, 1992).

3 John Douglas Belshaw, "Two Christian Denominations and the Administration of Relief to Vancouver's Unemployed, 1929–1939," *British Journal of Canadian Studies* 2 (December 1987): 289.
4 See Nikolas Rose and Peter Miller, "Political Power beyond the State: Problematics of Government," *British Journal of Sociology* 43 (June 1992): 180.
5 Nancy Fraser and Linda Gordon, "A Genealogy of Dependency: Tracing a Keyword of the U.S. Welfare State," *Signs* 19 (winter 1994): 309–36; Nancy Fraser and Linda Gordon, "Contract versus Charity: Why Is There No Social Citizenship in the United States?," *Socialist Review* 22 (July-September 1992): 45–67. See also Nancy Fraser, *Unruly Practices: Power, Discourse, and Gender in Contemporary Social Theory* (Minneapolis: University of Minnesota Press, 1989); Linda Gordon, "What Does Welfare Regulate?" *Social Research* 55 (winter 1988): 610–30. For a critique of Gordon's work, see Frances Fox Piven and Richard A. Cloward, "Welfare Doesn't Shore Up Traditional Family Role: A Reply to Linda Gordon," *Social Research* 55 (winter 1988), 631–47.
6 For a description of the interrelation between Catholic charities and the municipal government in Vancouver and Montreal, see respectively Belshaw, "Two Christian Denominations," and Terry Copp, "Montreal's Municipal Government and the Crisis of the 1930s," in Alan F.J. Artibise and Gilbert A. Stelter, eds., *The Usable Urban Past: Planning and Politics in the Modern Canadian City* (Toronto: Macmillan, 1979). For American examples, see Mary J. Oates, *The Catholic Philanthropic Tradition in America* (Bloomington: Indiana University Press, 1995), 111–15.
7 Archives of the Roman Catholic Archdiocese of Toronto (ARCAT), Archbishop James McGuigan Papers, file MG S006.131, Rev. Michael J. McGrath to Toronto pastors, 7 March 1940.
8 The population of the Roman Catholic Archdiocese of Toronto increased from 85,000 in 1925 to 128,000 by 1930; it further expanded during the Depression to 164,000 by 1935. Many of these recent arrivals were immigrants. See "Catholic Charities: Activities in the Archdiocese of Toronto," *Catholic Register*, 19 May 1932.
9 ARCAT, McGuigan Papers, file MG S006.121, Catholic Adjustment Bureau, Memorandum on municipal welfare agencies, October 1936.
10 "Catholic Charities' Activities in the Archdiocese of Toronto," *Catholic Register*, 8 June 1933.
11 At the provincial level, mother's allowances and means-tested old age pensions were implemented in Ontario in 1920 and 1929 respectively. See

Struthers, *The Limits of Affluence*, 25, 63; City of Toronto Archives (CTA), Alan Bass, "A Properly Socialized Service: Unemployment Relief and the Formation of Toronto's Civic Department of Welfare" (MA research paper, York University, 1989).
12 See Struthers, *No Fault of Their Own*, 12–43.
13 "Division of Social Welfare" *Social Welfare*, 11 (May 1929): 188, 191.
14 Ibid.
15 Gale Wills, *A Marriage of Convenience: Business and Social Work in Toronto, 1918–1957* (Toronto: University of Toronto Press, 1995), 48, 65.
16 ARCAT, Archbishop Neil McNeil Papers, file MN WL04.89, Rev. J. Haley, director of the Catholic Welfare Bureau, to Mr J.P. Haynes, 9 September 1929.
17 "Report on Increased Control by the Division of Social Welfare on the Use Made of Public Relief by the Private Agencies," undated, vol. 4, Division of Social Welfare, 1921–31; cited in Marion M. Bell, "The History of the Catholic Welfare Bureau" (MSW thesis, University of Toronto, 1949), 82.
18 Sara Z. Burke, *Seeking the Highest Good: Social Service and Gender at the University of Toronto, 1888–1937* (Toronto: University of Toronto Press, 1996), 123.
19 Ibid.
20 Differential casework sought to define the individual and social circumstances underlying pauperism. Diagnostic casework was informed by a Freudian perspective in which social problems reflected a psychopathology. See Roy Lubove, *The Professional Altruist: The Emergence of Social Work as a Career, 1880–1930* (Cambridge: Harvard University Press, 1965), 114–16.
21 ARCAT, McNeil Papers, file MN WL01.23, Mr F.D. Tolchard to Mr Hardie, 29 October 1930.
22 CTA, Bass, "A Properly Socialized Service," 27.
23 Struthers, *The Limits of Affluence*, 79–81; CTA, Bass, "A Properly Socialized Service," 16; Cassidy, *Unemployment and Relief*, 204–5.
24 Cassidy, *Unemployment and Relief*, 231.
25 Frances Fox Piven and Richard A. Cloward, *Regulating the Poor: The Functions of Public Welfare* (New York: Pantheon Books, 1971).
26 Catholics numbered approximately 14 per cent of Toronto's population, while comprising roughly one-quarter of the relief population. See ARCAT, McNeil Papers, file MN WL01.25, H.S. Rupert, Civic Unemployment Relief Committee, to Archbishop McNeil, 5 December 1930.
27 "St Vincent de Paul Hostel for Unemployed Men," *Catholic Register*, 29 January 1931.
28 Cassidy, *Unemployment and Relief*, 205.

163 Notes to pages 74–8

29 CTA, Bass, "A Properly Socialized Service," 42.
30 "Catholic Charities: Change of Function at C.W.L. Hostel," *Catholic Register*, 24 May 1934.
31 Multicultural History Society of Ontario Archives, C-7374, file 115272, Catholic Women's League Hostel, 1932–35.
32 ARCAT, McNeil Papers, file MN WL01.127, Mr F.D. Tolchard to Mr Hardie, 29 October 1930; McNeil Papers, file WL01.23, F.D. Tolchard to Archbishop McNeil, 1 December 1930.
33 Financing for all Catholic charities, including the Catholic Welfare Bureau, was organized by the Federation of Catholic Charities.
34 "City Grants $160,000 for Charity's Sake," *Toronto Star*, 18 November 1930.
35 Albert W. Laver, *Department of Public Welfare, Annual Report, 1942* (City of Toronto, 1942), 10.
36 ARCAT, McNeil Papers, file MN WL02.03, Charlotte Whitton to Archbishop McNeil, 25 March 1931.
37 Ibid.
38 Laver, *Department of Public Welfare*, 20–1.
39 "Catholic Charities Activities in the Archdiocese of Toronto," *Catholic Register*, 8 June 1933.
40 Laver, *Department of Public Welfare*, 21.
41 "Catholic Welfare Bureau Shows Definite Success in Social Adjustments," *Catholic Register*, 1 October 1931; "Catholic Charities' Activities in the Archdiocese of Toronto," *Catholic Register*, 4 February 1932.
42 Jeanne R. Beck, "Henry Somerville and the Development of Catholic Social Thought in Canada: Somerville's Role in the Archdiocese of Toronto, 1913–1943" (PhD dissertation, McMaster University, 1977), 265.
43 "Catholic Charities Activities in the Archdiocese of Toronto," *Catholic Register*, 1 June 1933.
44 In December 1932 the provincial government established ceilings for food, shelter, and other necessities, and food vouchers were issued to all the municipalities. See Struthers, *The Limits of Affluence*, 89.
45 The Liberal platform proposed a welfare structure sympathetic to the plight of the unemployed, but Premier Hepburn reneged on this promise in July 1935 when he terminated relief for all single men. Public denunciation and fears of civil unrest persuaded him to restrict the measure to hostel residents. Those living with families on relief would retain their entitlement. From 1932 to 1936 the federal government operated relief camps for single men. See CTA, Bass, "A Properly Socialized Service," 57–9; Struthers, *The Limits of Affluence*.

46 F.N. Stapleford, *After Twenty Years: A Short History of the Neighborhood Workers Association* (Toronto: Neighborhood Workers Association, 1938). See also Bell, "The History of the Catholic Welfare Bureau," 86.
47 The caseload of the Neighbourhood Workers Association was reduced to 3,000 families.
48 "Catholic Charities: Catholic Family Work," *Catholic Register,* 10 June 1935.
49 Bell, "The History of the Catholic Welfare Bureau."
50 Archives of Ontario, Department of Public Welfare Papers, "Annual Report of the Minister of Public Welfare," 1943–44, 39.
51 Toronto *Mail,* 15 September 1936, cited in Angus McLaren, *Our Own Master Race: Eugenics in Canada, 1885–1945* (Toronto: McClelland and Stewart, 1990), 123.
52 McLaren, *Our Own Master Race,* 150.
53 See Giovanna Procacci, "Social Economy and the Government of Poverty," in Graham Burchell, Colin Gordon, and Peter Miller, eds., *The Foucault Effect: Studies in Governmentality* (Chicago: University of Chicago Press, 1991); and her article "Governing Poverty: Sources of the Social Question in Nineteenth-Century France," in Jan Gouldstein, ed., *Foucault and the Writing of History* (Cambridge, Mass.: Blackwell, 1994).
54 Publicly funded old age pensions and mother's allowances did exist prior to the 1930s, but these groups did not require character reform and did not figure in concerns over a work ethic. See Struthers, *The Limits of Affluence.*
55 Struthers, *No Fault of Their Own,* 3.
56 Cassidy, *Unemployment and Relief,* 164.
57 William Walters, "The Fate of Unemployment: A Study in Governmentality" (PhD dissertation, York University, 1996), 123–4.
58 Walters, "The Fate of Unemployment, 130.
59 Margaret Little, "No Car, No Radio, No Liquor Permit": The Moral Regulation of Single Mothers in Ontario, 1920–1993" (PhD dissertation, York University, 1994).

CHAPTER FIVE

1 Archives of the Roman Catholic Archdiocese of Toronto (ARCAT), Archbishop James McGuigan Papers, file FA03.29A, McGuigan to Archbishop H.J. O'Leary, Toronto, 1 June 1937.
2 The term "English-speaking Catholics" is used to differentiate the established hierarchy of the church, those who arrived from Ireland and Scot-

land in the 1800s, from Catholics who emigrated from eastern and central Europe after World War 1.

3 At the time, the church equated socialism with communism. See Gregory Baum, *Catholics and Canadian Socialism: Political Thought in the Thirties and Forties* (Toronto: James Lorimer, 1980).

4 Ontario, in particular, Toronto, was deemed by the archdiocese a spawning ground for Bolshevik organizing: the Communist Party of Canada was secretly founded in Guelph in 1921, and the Social Democratic Party of Canada and the Socialist Party of North America were gaining momentum in the province. Moreover, by the 1930s the CCF was achieving a stronghold within the province.

5 Gregory S. Kealey, "State Repression of Labour and the Left in Canada, 1914–1920: The Impact of the First World War," *Canadian Historical Review* 73 (September 1992): 281–314; Reg Whitaker and Gary Marcuse, *Cold War Canada: The Making of a National Insecurity State, 1945–1957* (Toronto: University of Toronto Press, 1994); Reg Whitaker, "Origins of the Canadian Government's Internal Security System, 1946–1952," *Canadian Historical Review* 65 (June 1984): 154–83.

6 According to Clifford D. Shearing, the creation of the new London police in 1829 marks the "symbolic turning point in a gradual but steady transfer of responsibility for policing from private to public hands." See his article "The Relation between Public and Private Policing," in Michael Tonry and Norval Morris, eds., *Modern Policing* (Chicago: University of Chicago Press, 1992), 403.

7 According to Clifford Shearing and Philip Stenning, private policing also includes private forms of surveillance such as electronic monitors and video cameras, as well as amusement park attendants dressed as Disney characters or the arrangement of flower beds in parks. See their articles "Snowflakes or Good Pinches? – Private Security's Contribution to Modern Policing," in Rita Donelan, ed., *The Maintenance of Order in Society* (Ottawa: Canadian Police College, 1982); "From the Panopticon to Disney World: the Development of Discipline," in Anthony N. Doob and Edward L. Greenspan, eds., *Perspectives in Criminal Law* (Aurora: Canada Law Book, 1985).

8 A new approach has emerged within the criminology literature – the pluralist perspective – which does question the centrality of the state; however, it continues to identify private policing as a corporate agenda. See Shearing, "The Relation between Public and Private Policing."

9 For works on moral regulation, see the special issue of the *Canadian Journal of Sociology* 19 (spring 1994).

10 Clifford D. Shearing, Philip C. Stenning, and Susan M. Addario, "Public Perception of Private Security," *Canadian Police College Journal* 9 (1985): 367–90.
11 Mariana Valverde, *The Age of Light, Soap and Water: Moral Reform in English Canada, 1885–1925* (Toronto: McClelland and Stewart, 1991).
12 Ibid.; Nikolas Rose, "Beyond the Public/Private Division: Law, Power and the Family," *Journal of Law and Society* 14 (spring 1987): 61–76.
13 Mariana Valverde, "The Mixed Social Economy as a Canadian Tradition," *Studies in Political Economy* 47 (summer 1995): 33–60.
14 Archbishop James McGuigan was made a cardinal in 1946.
15 In the 1930s the Archdiocese of Toronto extended from the Niagara Peninsula to Georgian Bay in the north and from Long Beach in the west as far as Oshawa in the east. See Newman Club of Toronto, *The Ontario Catholic Year Book and Directory* (Toronto, 1920, 1935); *Census of Canada, 1941*, 98.
16 Mark McGowan, "Toronto's English-Speaking Catholics, Immigration, and the Making of a Canadian Catholic Identify," in Terrance Murphy and Gerald Stortz, eds., *Creed and Culture: The Place of English-Speaking Catholics in Canadian Society, 1750–1930* (Montreal: McGill-Queen's University Press, 1993).
17 Jeanne R. Beck, "Henry Somerville and the Development of Catholic Social Thought in Canada: Somerville's Role in the Archdiocese of Toronto, 1913–1943" (PhD dissertation, McMaster University, 1977); Brian F. Hogan, "Salted with Fire: Studies in Catholic Social Thought and Action in Ontario, 1931–1961" (PhD dissertation, University of Toronto, 1986); McGowan, "Toronto's English-Speaking Catholics."
18 Report of the Sixth National Convention of the Communist Party in Canada (May-June 1929),12; cited in Watson Kirkconnell, "Communism in Canada and the U.S.A.," *Canadian Catholic Historical Association, Historical Studies*, 1948, 41–51. The failure of the Finnish revolution forced many socialists to leave the country after World War I, a number of whom came to Canada. The Ukrainian community in Canada was composed of two groups: those who emigrated during the tsarist regime were predominantly pro-communist, while those who arrived in the twenties were typically anti-communist. The latter group had experienced the failure of an independent socialist Ukraine. See Lita-Rose Betcherman, *The Little Band: The Clashes Between the Communists and the Political and Legal Establishment in Canada, 1928–1932* (Ottawa: Deneau Publishers, 1982), 10. For other works on the Communist Party in Canada, see Irving Martin

Abella, *Nationalism, Communism, and Canadian Labour: The CIO, the Communist Party and the Canadian Congress of Labour, 1935–1956* (Toronto: University of Toronto Press, 1973); Ivan Avakumovic, *The Communist Party in Canada: A History* (Toronto: McClelland and Stewart, 1975); Norman Penner, *The Canadian Left: A Critical Analysis* (Scarborough: Prentice-Hall, 1977); William Rodney, *Soldiers of the International: A History of the Communist Party of Canada, 1919–1929* (Toronto: University of Toronto Press, 1968).

19 Avakumovic, *The Communist Party*; Betcherman, *The Little Band*, 11, 75.
20 Watson Kirkconnell, *The Seven Pillars of Freedom* (London: Oxford University Press, 1944).
21 Avakumovic, *The Communist Party*, 37, 115.
22 ARCAT, Archbishop Neil McNeil Papers, file MN WL04, Annual Activity Report of the Catholic Big Brothers Association, Toronto, circa early 1930s.
23 Luigi G. Pennacchio, "The Torrid Trinity: Toronto's Fascists, Italian Priests and Archbishops during the Fascist Era, 1929–1940," in Mark McGowan and Brian Clarke, eds., *Catholics at the "Gathering Place": Historical Essays on the Archdiocese of Toronto, 1841–1991* (Toronto: Canadian Catholic Historical Association, 1993), 234.
24 In response to rumours that Prime Minister Mackenzie King had considered disbanding the RCMP in 1926, several members of the Catholic Church, wrote to Hon. Col. George E. Amyot arguing the necessity of such a force for the security of the country. One letter went as far as to suggest that the RCMP and the Catholic Church were the "two stabilizing institutions in this country." See ARCAT, McNeil Papers, file MN AS01.04, J.B. Maclean to McNeil, Toronto, 6 August 1926.
25 Betcherman, *The Little Band*; Suzanne Michelle Skebo, "Liberty and Authority: Civil Liberties in Toronto, 1929–1935" (MA thesis, University of British Columbia, 1968).
26 *Globe*, 19 August 1929; cited in Betcherman, *The Little Band*, 64.
27 ARCAT, McNeil Papers, file MN AS01.06, Abbé Philipe Casgrain to McNeil, Toronto, 7 March 1927.
28 ARCAT, Ruthenian Catholics, General Correspondence, 1920–28, box 2, no. 210, "Notes Respecting Revolutionary Organizations and Agitators in Canada," Toronto, 31 January 1923.
29 ARCAT, McNeil Papers, file MN AS01.08, Inspector Marshall's Reports, Toronto, 21 April 1932, 30 May 1932; McNeil Papers, file MN AS01.10, Draper to McNeil, Toronto, 7 June 1932.

30 Eddie Doherty, *Tumbleweed: A Biography* (Milwaukee: Bruce, 1948), 149.
31 For works on Catherine de Hueck, see Jeanne R. Beck, "Contrasting Approaches to Catholic Social Action during the Depression: Henry Somerville the Educator and Catherine de Hueck the Activist," in McGowan and Clarke, eds., *Catholics at the "Gathering Place"*; Shane P. Carmody, "Catherine de Hueck and Catholic Action in Toronto 1930–1936" (unpublished paper, May 1985); Catherine de Hueck Doherty, *Fragments of My Life* (Notre Dame, Ind.: Ave Maria Press, 1979); Doherty, *Tumbleweed*; Lorene Hanley Duquin, *They Called Her the Baroness: The Life of Catherine de Hueck Doherty* (New York: Alba House, 1995); Hogan, "Salted with Fire"; Elizabeth Sharum, "A Strange Fire Burning: A History of the Friendship House Movement" (PhD dissertation, Texas Technical University, 1977).
32 Doherty, *Tumbleweed*, 150.
33 Catherine Doherty, "Little Mandate"; cited in Sharum, "A Strange Fire Burning," 40; Doherty, *Tumbleweed*, 150.
34 Sharum, "A Strange Fire Burning," 42–7; Doherty, *Tumbleweed*, 150; "Baroness de Hueck Tells of Her Fight against Communism," *Social Forum* 1 (March 1936): 1; Gustave Sauve, "Moscow in Canada," *Social Forum* 1 (March 1936): 2.
35 ARCAT, McNeil Papers, file MN AS01.16, Communist Activities in St Patrick's Parish, Toronto, (de Hueck's map) circa early 1930s. St Patrick's Parish was encompassed by College Street at the north end and went as far south as Front Street; it began at Spadina Avenue and extended east to Elizabeth Street.
36 For an analysis of social mapping, see Charles Booth, *Labour and Life of the People in London* (London: Williams and Norgate, 1891); Martin Bulmer, Kevin Bales, and Kathryn Kish Sklar, *The Social Survey in Historical Perspective, 1880–1940* (Cambridge: Cambridge University Press, 1991).
37 The Vatican issued two papal encyclicals, *Rerum novarum* (1891) and *Quadragesimo anno* (1931), that denounced communism as an enemy of the church. The encyclicals called upon all Catholics to work towards the eradication of communism. For an analysis of the impact of the encyclicals on the Catholic Church in Ontario, see Hogan, "Salted with Fire," 1–45.
38 ARCAT, McNeil Papers, file MN AS01.12, McNeil, "The Papal Solution," *The Red Menace* (Toronto), 8 September 1933.
39 ARCAT, McNeil Papers, file MN AS01.07, Pope Pius XI to pastors in Toronto, 3 November 1930; McGuigan Papers, file MG SU03.03, Mr G. Murray, general manager, Canadian Broadcasting Corporation, to McGuigan, Toronto, 4 January 1939.

40 Joseph H. O'Neill, "Archbishop McGuigan of Toronto and the Holy Name Society: Its Role as a Force against Canadian Communism," *Canadian Catholic Historical Association Historical Studies*, 1988, 61–77.
41 ARCAT, McGuigan Papers, file MG S006.124, Rev. Michael J. McGrath to McGuigan, Toronto, 17 May 1939; McGuigan Papers, file MG SU03.03, Financial Reports of the Catholic Adjustment Bureau, Toronto, 1939.
42 Hogan, "Salted with Fire."
43 Sharum, "A Strange Fire Burning," 81.
44 ARCAT, McNeil Papers, MN AS01.11, Mrs Harris McPhedran to the Honourable J.H. Robb, minister of health, Toronto, 13 April 1933.
45 Ibid.
46 Baroness's Clippings, Combermere, 1930–37, Madonna House Files; cited in Sharum, "A Strange Fire Burning."
47 The encyclicals supported the right to private property as the basis of individual and social rights, even though they called for a restructuring of the excesses of capitalist economics and individualism. Socialism was equated with communism and vehemently repudiated for promoting the use of violence and the overthrow of the natural order, and for restricting religious freedoms. See Anne Freemantle, *The Papal Encyclicals in Their Historical Context: The Teachings of the Popes from Peter to John XXIII* (New York: The New American Library, 1963); Virgil Michel, *Christian Social Reconstruction: Some Fundamentals of "Quadragesimo Anno"* (Milwaukee: Bruce, 1937).
48 ARCAT, McNeil Papers, file MN AE14.01, Anonymous letter to McNeil, Toronto, circa 1934.
49 Baum, *Catholics and Canadian Socialism*. For other works on the Catholics reaction to the CCF, see Beck, "Henry Somerville"; Murry G. Ballantyne, "The Catholic Church and the CCF," *Canadian Catholic Historical Association*, 1963, 33–45; Walter D. Young, *The Anatomy of a Party: The National CCF, 1932–61* (Toronto: University of Toronto Press, 1969), 210–15.
50 Ballantyne, "The Catholic Church and the CCF."
51 Ibid., 36.
52 Beck, "Henry Somerville," 394.
53 The Seventh National Convention in 1942 marked a change in direction for the CCF. The ideology of social ownership and cooperative production advanced in the Regina Manifesto was abandoned for a more open system that promoted "personal property for more people"; the party's initial doctrinaire opposition to the war turned to support for the war effort in 1940 and for conscription by 1942; and the new party policy adopted less

of a militant approach, focusing instead on post-war, peacetime solutions that advocated reconstruction, stability, and welfare socialism. See Young, *The Anatomy of a Party*, 106–9; Baum, *Catholics and Canadian Socialism*, 127.
54 ARCAT, McNeil Papers, file MN AE14.02, "The Church and the CCF," Toronto, circa 1943.
55 Young, *The Anatomy of a Party*, 211.
56 Ballantyne, "The Catholic Church and the CCF," 42; Baum, *Catholics and Canadian Socialism*, 131.
57 Tensions between the Vatican and Mussolini were exacerbated after the conquest of Abyssinia in 1936, when the Italian government, instead of privileging Catholicism as the state religion in the empire, merely adopted a policy of religious toleration. The publication of the government's 1938 manifesto on racial purity and the subsequent anti-Semitic legislation elicited a denunciation from the pope. See Peter S. Kent, "The Catholic Church in the Italian Empire, 1936–38," *Canadian Historical Association Historical Papers*, 1984, 138–50.
58 For the church's opposition to the persecution of Jews in Germany, see John S. Moir, *Church and Society: Documents on the Religious and Social History of the Roman Catholic Archdiocese in Toronto from the Archives of the Archdiocese* (Toronto: Archdiocese of Toronto, 1991), 226–30.
59 ARCAT, McGuigan Papers, file MG SO14.02a, Fr Daniel Ehamn to McGuigan, Toronto, 10 June 1938.
60 ARCAT, McGuigan Papers, file MG SO14.02c, McGuigan to Revs. Sanson, Pellicelita, Balo, and Ehman, Toronto, 11 June 1938.
61 Pennacchio, "The Torrid Trinity."
62 For a discussion of relief in Ontario during the Depression, see James Struthers, *The Limits of Affluence: Welfare in Ontario, 1920–1970* (Toronto: University of Toronto Press, 1994); Roger E. Riendeau, "A Clash of Interests: Dependency and the Municipal Problem in the Great Depression," *Journal of Canadian Studies* 14 (spring 1979): 50–8.
63 Marion M. Bell, "The History of the Catholic Welfare Bureau" (MSW thesis, University of Toronto, 1949).
64 ARCAT, McGuigan Papers, file MG SO06.122, McGrath to McGuigan, October 1938.
65 Ibid., Rev. M.J. McGrath to McGuigan, Toronto, circa October 1938.
66 ARCAT, McGuigan Papers, file MG SO06.123, McGrath to McGuigan, Toronto, circa January 1939.
67 ARCAT, McNeil Papers, file MN AP02.01, de Hueck to McNeil, Toronto, 1 July 1934.

68 Ibid., John Fitzgerald, retiring editor of the Montreal *Beacon*, Toronto, circa 1934.
69 Sharum, "A Strange Fire Burning," 68–70.
70 Ibid.; Hogan, "Salted with Fire."
71 ARCAT, McGuigan Papers, file MG SP05.06, Rev. Francis to McGuigan, Toronto, 18 December 1936.
72 Hogan, "Salted with Fire."
73 For an analysis of how the private family sphere was involved in promoting "domestic containment" in the United States, see Elaine Tyler May, *Homeward Bound: American Families in the Cold War Era* (New York: Basic Books, 1988).
74 Whitaker and Marcuse, *Cold War Canada*.
75 Ibid., 276. See also Reg Whitaker's article "Fighting the Cold War on the Home Front: America, Britain, Australia and Canada," *Socialist Register*, 1984, 23–67. In this article, Whitaker does present an analytical distinction between "state repression" and "political repression," the latter referring to a wider "political system" outside the state, typified by "McCarthyism" in the United States. This political system, however, is still characterized as an extension of or propelled by the state.
76 ARCAT, McGuigan Papers, file MG P008.04, J. Bacon to McGuigan, Toronto, 22 August 1949.
77 R.D. Cuff and J.L. Granatstein, *Ties That Bind: Canadian-American Relations in Wartime, from the Great War to the Cold War* (Toronto: Hakkert, 1977),149.
78 Whitaker and Marcuse, *Cold War Canada*, 266.
79 Premier Drew, notorious for his red-baiting ideology, had been maintaining a secret Special Branch of the Ontario Provincial Police, a "Gestapo" based on the old Red Squad. See Gerald L. Caplan, *The Dilemma of Canadian Socialism: The CCF in Ontario* (Toronto: McClelland and Stewart, 1973), 168–90.
80 ARCAT, McGuigan Papers, file MG P003.08, Ontario premier George A. Drew to McGuigan, Toronto, 31 May 1945, 14 June 1945. In the 1940s, two members of the Communist Party were elected the Ontario legislature: Joe Salsberg in the predominantly Jewish Spadina district (1943–55) and Alex MacLeod in the Bellwoods riding (1943–51). Also, a number of communists had been elected to the Toronto Board of Education.
81 ARCAT, McGuigan Papers, file MG EN13.04, Report on the Religious Conditions among New Canadians of Slovenian Descent, Toronto, circa 1949.
82 See O'Neill, "Archbishop McGuigan of Toronto and the Holy Name Society."

83 ARCAT, McGuigan Papers, file MG EN13.10, Fr Jakob Kolaric to McGuigan, Toronto, 31 July 1952; McGuigan Papers, file MG EN13.08, Confidential correspondence to McGuigan, Toronto, 14 July 1951; McGuigan Papers, file MG EN13.17, F. Turk to McGuigan, Toronto, 5 April 1955; McGuigan Papers, file MG EN13.16, Rudolf Cujs to McGuigan, Toronto, 6 March 1955.
84 ARCAT, McGuigan Papers, file MG SO31.11b, McGuigan to Robert Lindsay, CFNC president, Toronto, 16 January 1947; McGuigan Papers, file MG SO31.35, Toronto Newman Club to McGuigan, Toronto, 22 November 1948.
85 ARCAT, McGuigan Papers, file MG P003.16, E. Dubois to McGuigan, Toronto, 8 December 1947.
86 For information on the communist infiltration of university campuses, see Paul Axelrod, "Spying on the Young in Depression and War: Students, Youth Groups and the RCMP, 1935–1942," *Labour/Le Travail* 35 (spring 1995): 43–63.
87 ARCAT, McGuigan Papers, file MG SO31.11b, McGuigan to Robert Lindsay, CFNC president, Toronto, 16 January 1947; McGuigan Papers, file MG SO31.35, Toronto Newman Club to McGuigan, Toronto, 22 November 1948.
88 ARCAT, McGuigan Papers, file MG P003.16, Catherine D. McLean, CFNC external affairs chairman, to McGuigan, Toronto, 30 January 1947.
89 "She's Redhead Who's Out to Beat the Reds," *Toronto Telegram*, 30 January 1959.
90 Marjorie Lamb, *Communism in Canada* (Toronto: Alert Service, 1958), 2.
91 Marjorie Lamb, "Opportunities Unlimited: A Time of Choice," *Vital Speeches of the Day*, 26, no. 11 (New York: City News Publishing, 15 March 1960).
92 ARCAT, McGuigan Papers, file MG P008.51, Lamb to Wall, Archdiocese of Toronto chancellor, Toronto, 1949–58; McGuigan Papers, file MG P008.52, Lamb to McGuigan, Toronto, 1958–60; Marjorie Lamb, *Communism and You* (Toronto: Alert Service, 1962).
93 "'Atheistic Communism' Study Clubs," *Catholic Register*, 18 October 1947; "HNS Central Study Club on Atheistic Communism," *Catholic Register*, 1 November, 1947.
94 *Catholic Register*, 8 July 1950.
95 Kirkconnell, "Communism in Canada and the U.S.A."
96 See Whitaker and Marcuse, *Cold War Canada*, 277–9.
97 ARCAT, McGuigan Papers, file MG P008.58, Article by McGuigan, Toronto, circa 1961.

98 For a discussion of the union movement in Quebec, see Fraser Isbester, "A History of the National, Catholic Unions in Canada, 1901–1965" (PhD dissertation, Cornell University, 1968).
99 "Toronto Labour Schools Noted for Unmasking Communism," *Catholic Register*, 31 August 1957.
100 Hogan, "Salted with Fire"; Beck, "Henry Somerville."
101 Whitaker and Marcuse, *Cold War Canada*, 22.
102 See, for example, Kelly Hannah-Moffat and Mariana Valverde, "Saving the Prisoner or Saving the Prison? Private Philanthropy and State Punishment in the Turn-of-the-Century Ontario," *Canadian Journal of Law and Society*, forthcoming; Margaret Little, "The Blurring of Boundaries: Private and Public Welfare for Single Mothers in Ontario," *Studies in Political Economy* 47 (summer 1995): 89–109.
103 Michel Foucault, *Discipline and Punish: The Birth of the Prison*, translated by Alan Sheridan (New York: Vintage Books, 1979).

CHAPTER SIX

1 J.T.L. James, *A Living Tradition: Penitentiary Chaplaincy* (Ottawa: Chaplaincy Division, Correctional Service of Canada, 1990), 19, 115–18.
2 Ibid., 26.
3 St Mary's was later renamed St Euphrasia and for a few years was administered by the Sisters of Our Lady of Charity.
4 The first Catholic industrial school in Canada, the St Patrick's Industrial School for Roman Catholic boys, was built in Halifax in 1865. Others were opened in Saint John's, New Brunswick, and in Montreal. Later, in 1933, St Joseph's Industrial School, also run by the Christian Brothers, was opened in Alfred, Ontario, adjacent to the Ottawa-Montreal highway. This school was designed primarily to cater to the French-speaking community and to those from the Ottawa region. See Roman Catholic Archdiocese of Toronto, *Walking the Less Travelled Road: A History of the Religious Communities within the Archdiocese of Toronto, 1841–1991* (Toronto: Mission Press, 1993), 21, 54–5; Sister Maryan, "The Work of the congregation of the Good Shepherd in Toronto, 1875–1973," *York Pioneer*, 1974, 38–48; "The Home of the Good Shepherd," *Catholic Register*, 4 December 1924; Archives of Ontario (AO), Department of Public Welfare Papers, "Annual Report of the Minister of Public Welfare," 1936, 7, 41–2.
5 Michel Foucault, *Discipline and Punish: The Birth of the Prison*, translated by Alan Sheridan (New York: Vintage Books, 1979). Disciplinary

practices were not specific to the modern prison system and had long before been adopted in monasteries and armies.

6 Margaret Reeves, *Training Schools for Delinquent Girls* (New York: Russell Sage Foundation, 1929), 337–8; Foucault, *Discipline and Punish*, 177–84; David Garland, *Punishment and Welfare: A History of Penal Strategies* (Aldershot: Gower Publishing Company, 1985), 131–56; Adrian Howe, *Punish and Critique: Towards a Feminist Analysis of Penalty* (London: Routledge, 1994), 82–122.

7 The report of the Brown Commission in 1849 was the first government report calling for separate facilities for juvenile delinquents. Previously, young offenders were detained in adult prisons and gaols. The 1857 Prison Inspection Act allowed for the building of reformatories. The first one, Îsle aux Noir, was opened in 1858 on the Richelieu River, and in 1859 the Penetanguishene Reformatory for boys was built on Georgian Bay. The Andrew Mercer Reformatory for women in Ontario was constructed in 1874.

8 Andrew Jones, "Closing Penetanguishene Reformatory: An Attempt to Deinstitutionalize Treatment of Juvenile Offenders in Early Twentieth Century Ontario," *Ontario History* 70 (December 1979): 227–44.

9 Paul W. Bennett, "Turning 'Bad Boys' into 'Good Citizens': The Reforming Impulse of Toronto's Industrial School Movement, 1883 to the 1920s," *Ontario History* 78 (1986): 210.

10 Garland, *Punishment and Welfare*, 136.

11 Foucault, *Discipline and Punish*, 170.

12 Susan E. Houston, "Victorian Origins of Juvenile Delinquency: A Canadian Experience," *History of Education Quarterly* 12 (1972): 273, 257. See also her article "'The Waifs and Strays' of a Late Victorian City: Juvenile Delinquents in Toronto," in Joy Parr, ed., *Childhood and Family in Canadian History* (Toronto: McClelland and Stewart, 1983), 129–42.

13 D. Owen Carrigan, *Crime and Punishment in Canada: A History* (Toronto: McClelland and Stewart, 1991), 408.

14 AO, Ontario Department of Public Welfare, RG 29–138–0–18, "An Historical Review of Ontario Legislation on Child Welfare," 1957, 31.

15 Dorothy E. Chunn, *From Punishment to Doing Good: Family Courts and Socialized Justice in Ontario, 1880–1940* (Toronto: University of Toronto Press, 1992), 20–1; David Garland, *Punishment and Modern Society: A Study in Social Theory* (Chicago: University of Chicago Press, 1990), 134; David J. Rothman, *Conscience and Convenience: The Asylum and Its Alternatives in Progressive America* (Glenview, Ill.: Scott, Foresman, 1980), 252–3; Steven Schlossman, "Delinquent Children: The Juvenile Reform

16 Houston, "Victorian Origins of Juvenile Delinquency"; Jones,"Closing Penetanguishene Reformatory"; Bennett, "Turning 'Bad Boys' into 'Good Citizens,'" 210.
17 Michael B. Katz, Michael J. Doucet, and Mark J. Stern, *The Social Organization of Early Industrial Capitalism* (Cambridge: Harvard University Press, 1982); Gordon Darroch and Michael D. Ornstein, "Ethnicity and Occupational Structure in Canada in 1971: The Vertical Mosaic in Historical Perspective," *Canadian Historical Review* 61 (September 1980): 305–33.
18 Gordon Darroch, "Domestic Revolution and Cultural Formation in Nineteenth-Century Ontario, Canada," *Family History: An International Quarterly*, forthcoming. For aspects of the argument and differing interpretations, see Bruce Curtis, "Policing Pedagogical Space: 'Voluntary' School Reform and Moral Regulation," *Canadian Journal of Sociology* 13 (1988): 283–304; Chad Gaffield, "Children, Schooling, and Family Reproduction in Nineteenth-Century Ontario," *Canadian Historical Review* 72 (1991), 157–91.
19 Darroch, "Domestic Revolution and Cultural Formation," 18.
20 Ibid.
21 In 1939, when industrial schools were no longer popular and training schools were promoted as the innovation in juvenile corrections, both schools took on the designation of training schools for juvenile delinquents. See Paul W. Bennett, "Taming 'Bad Boys' of the 'Dangerous Class': Child Rescue and Restraint at the Victoria Industrial School 1887–1935," *Social History* 21 (May 1988): 86; Curt T. Griffiths and Simon N. Verdun-Jones, *Canadian Criminal Justice* (Toronto: Harcourt Brace, 1994), 600–1; AO, Ministry of Correctional Service, RG 20, J 2, vol. 22, "Report of the Committee Appointed to Investigate the Present Juvenile Reformatory School System of Ontario," 1935, 37.
22 Archives of the Roman Catholic Archdiocese of Toronto (ARCAT), Archbishop James McGuigan Papers, Catholic Adjustment Bureau memo, October 1936; Archbishop Neil McNeil Papers, Memo on the number of Catholic delinquents by nationality, 1934; Rothman, *Conscience and Convenience*, 253. For a discussion of class and ethnic biases in the Toronto Police Court, see Gene Howard Homel, "Denison's Law: Criminal Justice and the Police Court in Toronto, 1877–1921," *Ontario History* 73 (September 1981): 174–7.

23 Figures for the girls sent to the Good Shepherd Refuge and the few Catholic boys who were placed in Protestant institutions do not exist, and thus the numbers are only approximate.
24 AO, "Report of the Committee Appointed to Investigate the Present Juvenile Reformatory Schools System of Ontario"; Carolyn Strange, *Toronto's Girl Problem: The Perils and Pleasures of the City, 1880–1930* (Toronto: University of Toronto Press, 1995).
25 AO, Department of the Provincial Secretary, St Mary's Industrial School Papers, RG 8, J.J. Kelso, superintendent, neglected and dependent children, to Hon. W.D. McPherson, provincial secretary, 7 February 1917, 18 November 1918, 19 February 1919.
26 Reeves, *Training Schools for Delinquent Girls*, 337–38.
27 "Proper Function of Correctional Institutions," *Catholic Register*, 6 December 1929; Rothman, *Conscience and Convenience*, 264; Schlossman, "Delinquent Children," 330–1; Mariana Valverde, "Building Anti-Delinquent Communities: Morality, Gender, and Generation in the City," in Joy Parr, ed., *A Diversity of Women: Ontario, 1945–1980* (Toronto: University of Toronto Press, 1995), 32–4.
28 AO, Department of Public Welfare, "Annual Report of the Minister of Public Welfare," 1932–33, 8; 1933–34, 23; 1934–35, 12–13; 1936–37, 29.
29 Ibid., 1936–37, 28.
30 Ibid., 1936–37, 27; Valverde, "Building Anti-Delinquent Communities," 32.
31 AO, "Annual Report of the Minister of Public Welfare," 1936–37, 26.
32 Ibid., 1933–34, 31.
33 Ibid., 1934–35, 17.
34 Kelly Hannah-Moffat, "From Christian Maternalism to Risk Technologies: Penal Powers and Women's Knowledges in the Governance of Female Prisoners" (PhD dissertation, University of Toronto, 1997), 122.
35 Foucault, *Discipline and Punish*; Jacques Donzelot, *The Policing of Families* (New York: Random House, 1979); Nikolas Rose, *The Psychological Complex: Psychology, Politics and Society in England, 1869–1939* (London: Routledge and Kegan Paul, 1985); Chunn, *From Punishment to Doing Good*.
36 AO, Children and Youth Corrections Records, Training School Advisory Board, St Mary's Training School Ward Files, RG 60-11, MS1124-7; St John's Training School Ward Files, RG 60-9, MS1090-7, "Inspection of Home for Parole Reports," "School Attendance Reports," "Committal Reports," "Authority for Parole Reports," "Magistrate's Court Reports," 1919–39, passim.

37 AO, St Mary's Training School Ward Files, RG 60–11, MS1124–7; St John's Training School Ward Files, RG 60–9, MS1090–7, "Committal Reports," "School Attendance Reports," 1919–39, passim.
38 Ibid.
39 Ibid.
40 AO, "Annual Report of the Minister of Public Welfare," 1931–32, 39.
41 AO, St Mary's Training School Ward Files, RG 60–11, MS1125, Mental Health Director's Report, 8 March 1937.
42 AO, "Annual Report of the Minister of Public Welfare," 1933–34, 33.
43 Ibid.
44 Bennett, "Taming 'Bad Boys,'" 82.
45 AO, "Annual Report of the Minister of Public Welfare", 1932–33, 38. Similar issues are discussed in Bennett, "Taming 'Bad Boys,'" 82; Rothman, *Conscience and Convenience*, 245, 275; Reeves, *Training Schools for Delinquent Girls*, 248–9; Chunn, *From Punishment to Doing Good*, 19; Valverde, "Building Anti-Delinquent Communities," 32–3.
46 Franca Iacovetta and Wendy Mitchinson, "Social History and Case Files Research," in Iacovetta and Mitchinson, eds., *On the Case: Explorations in Social History* (Toronto: University of Toronto Press, forthcoming), 8, 21.
47 AO, "Report of the Committee Appointed to Investigate the Present Juvenile Reformatory School System of Ontario."
48 For similar arguments in the post-World War II era, see Franca Iacovetta, "The Making of a Delinquent Girl: 'Truth," Fiction, and 'Expert "Opinion in Family Court Cases, 1940s-1960s" (Paper presented at the Canadian Historical Association annual meeting, Brock University, June 1996).
49 AO, St Mary's Training School Ward Files, RG 60–11, MS1124–7; St John's Training School Ward Files, RG 60–9, MS1090–7, "School Attendance Reports," "Placement Officer's Reports," "Inspection of Home for Parole," 1919–39, passim.
50 AO, St Mary's Training School Ward Files, RG 60–11, MS1124–7; St John's Training School Ward Files, RG 60–9, MS1090–7, "Placement Officer's Reports," 1919–39, passim.
51 Andrew Jones and Leonard Rutman, *In the Children's Aid: J.J. Kelso and Child Welfare in Ontario* (Toronto: University of Toronto Press, 1981), 114–19; John Bullen, "J.J. Kelso and the 'New' Child-Savers: The Genesis of the Children's Aid Movement in Ontario," *Ontario History* 82 (June 1990): 115–17; Peter Oliver and Michael D. Whittingham, "Elitism, Localism and the Emergence of Adult Probation Services in Ontario, 1893–1972," *Canadian Historical Review* 38 (1987): 225–58.

52 Bullen, "J.J. Kelso and the 'New' Child-Savers," 115–17; Chunn, *From Punishment to Doing Good*, 46.
53 Carrigan, *Crime and Punishment*, 415–16.
54 Children from other religious groups, including Jewish children, were provided for by Protestant workers.
55 Griffiths and Verdun-Jones, *Canadian Criminal Justice*, 604; Curt T. Griffiths, John F. Klein, and Simon N. Verdun-Jones, *Criminal Justice in Canada: An Introductory Text* (Toronto: Butterworths, 1980), 287; D.W.F. Coughlan, "The History and Function of Probation," in R.C. Macleod, ed., *Lawful Authority: Readings on the History of Criminal Justice in Canada* (Toronto: Copp Clark Pitman, 1988), 265–270.
56 Neil Sutherland, *Children in English-Canadian Society: Framing the Twentieth-Century Consensus* (Toronto: University of Toronto Press, 1979), 126–34.
57 Ibid., 127–8.
58 Rosemary Howorth, *For the Love of Children: A History of the Catholic Children's Aid Society of Metropolitan Toronto, 1894–1994* (Toronto: The Catholic Children's Aid Society of Metropolitan Toronto, 1994), 9–10.
59 "Catholic Charities," *Catholic Register*, 26 December 1918.
60 Catholic Welfare Bureau, "The Prevention of Delinquency: Boy Guidance – The New Profession," *Catholic Register*, 12 February 1925.
61 ARCAT, McNeil Papers, file MN WL04.214, "Charity Bulletin," 26 September 1925.
62 *Globe*, April 1905; cited in Jones and Rutman, *In the Children's Aid*, 116.
63 Catholic Big Brothers, "Habits," *Catholic Register*, 25 December 1930.
64 Mariana Valverde, "Governing Out of Habit" (unpublished manuscript).
65 Catholic Big Brothers, "Habits."
66 Catholic Welfare Bureau, "When Children Find Good Behaviour as Interesting as Bad," *Catholic Register*, 5 April 1928; Catholic Big Brothers, "Better Books for Boys," *Catholic Register*, 7 November 1929; Catholic Welfare Bureau, "Responsibility to Be Placed on Parents for Juvenile Crime," *Catholic Register*, 14 November 1929; Catholic Big Brothers, "How to Keep Our Children Happy during the Long Vacation," *Catholic Register*, 12 June 1932.
67 Catholic Big Brothers, "The Parent," *Catholic Register*, 19 March 1931.
68 Catholic Big Brothers, "The Thoughtless and Untidy Child," *Catholic Register*, 5 June 1930.
69 Catholic Big Brothers, "Protecting The Mind of Childhood," *Catholic Register*, 3 June 1930.

70 The Catholic Big Brothers, "Habits."
71 "Joint Meeting of the Big Sisters and Girls' Activity Chapter," *Catholic Register*, 6 June 1935.
72 Garland, *Punishment and Welfare*, 124–5.
73 Ibid., 46, 238–43; Mariana Valverde, *The Age of Light, Soap and Water: Moral Reform in English Canada, 1885–1925* (Toronto: McClelland and Stewart, 1991), 147–54.
74 Garland, *Punishment and Welfare*, 249.

CONCLUSION

1 Archives of the Roman Catholic Archdiocese of Toronto (ARCAT), Catholic Charities Papers, file OC 11 RE05, "75 Year Annual Report."
2 ARCAT, Catholic Charities Papers, file OC 06 CH07, "Staff Report to the Board of Directors Council of Catholic Charities," 27 August 1973.
3 ARCAT, Catholic Charities Papers, file OC 11 RE05, "Catholic Children's Aid Society Annual Report," 1975.
4 ARCAT, Catholic Charities Papers, file OC 06 SU01, "Catholic Charities: The First 75 Years," 1988.
5 Josephine Rekart, *Public Funds, Private Provision: The Role of the Voluntary Sector* (Vancouver: University of British Columbia Press, 1993), 7.
6 Cathy Majtenyi, "Who Will Protect Society's Have-Nots?" *Catholic Register*, 6 November 1995, 9; Michael Valpy, "The Corporate Philanthropists," *Globe and Mail*, 19 June 1997, A19.
7 Ministry of Community and Social Services, Ontario, "Welfare Fraud Control Report 2000–2001" (www.gov.on.ca: 80/CSS/page/brochure/fraud01.html).

Index

Act for the Prevention of Cruelty to, and Better Protection of Children (1893), 116, 118–19
Ames, Herbert B., 37, 47
Archdiocese of Toronto: anti-communist activities, 82–3, 85, 86–90; boundaries, 132, 166n15; creation of centralized structures to monitor financing, 31–2; Cold War anti-communist activities, 97–102; credit unions, 52; Depression-era anti-communist campaign, 90–4; failure to condemn fascism, 93–4; fundraising and accounting administration, 24; hard hit by Depression, 68–9; industrial schools established by, 103–4, 105; labour schools established by, 101–2; opposition to birth control and sterilization for families on relief, 80; police cooperation with, 86, 90; population, 18, 19, 131–2, 161n8; post-war expansion of charitable services in, 127–8; private policing and surveillance activities by, 82–3, 86–90; receives diocesan status, 18; rehabilitation of young offenders, 103–24; and rumours of communist infiltration, 99–100; social welfare survey commissioned by Archbishop McNeil, 57–8; use of social work practices, 9–10, 38, 45–7

"back-to-the-land" movement, as Catholic social action program, 52–3
Ballantyne, Murray (editor of *Beacon* newspaper), 93
Barnabas, Brother (director of Catholic Charities), 55
Basilian Fathers, 22; social activism of, 51–2
"boyology" courses, sponsored by Knights of Columbus, 56, 120
British North America Act (1867), 119; entrenchment of separate school education in, 20–1, 108
Bureau of Municipal Research (Toronto), 41

Canadian Federation of Newman Clubs (Catholic university organization), 100
casework, social. *See* social casework
Cassidy, Harry, 47, 66, 73
Catholic Big Brothers and Catholic Big Sisters, 13, 43, 56, 134, 152n28; assisted by other organizations, 123; expansion of services by, 120–1; formation of, 120; on moral behaviour, as formed by habits, 121–3
Catholic charities: in Canada, 12, 145n19; government grants to, 25, 136, 137. *See also* Toronto, Catholic charities in

Catholic Charities (centralized management organization), 31, 54–5, 57, 134; directors of, as educated in U.S., 54–5; early membership of, 152n28; formation of, 40–1; recommended restructuring of, 58. *See also* Catholic Welfare Bureau

Catholic Children's Aid Society, 7, 127; begins hiring professionally trained workers, 55; hires first probation officer, 120; use of standardized reports on young offenders, 113

Catholic Church, in Canada: as advocate of workers' rights, 26–7, 50; concept of charity, as contrasted with Protestant philanthropy, 27–9; early tensions with Protestants, 19–20; later cooperation with Protestant churches on social reform, 26–7, 50; ultramontanism, 20–1, 148n25. *See also* Archdiocese of Toronto

Catholic immigrants. *See* immigrants, Catholic

Catholic Madonna Apostolic, and food bank initiative, 128

Catholic newspapers: *Beacon* (Montreal), 93; *Catholic Worker*, 91; *Social Forum*, 91. *See also Catholic Register*

Catholic Register, 50, 61, 93; anti-communist stance of, 87, 91, 101; defence of CCF, 93; weekly social action columns by Henry Somerville, 50–1, 156n33

Catholic schools, funding for, 20–1; as leading to Catholic charity infrastructure, 21–2

Catholics in Toronto. *See* Toronto, Catholic population of

Catholic social action, 46, 49–53; activities at St Michael's College, 51–2; "back-to-the-land" projects, 52–3; credit unions, 52; Henry Somerville, as champion of, 50–1, 156n33. *See also* Catholic social work; Friendship House; social gospel (Protestant); social reform

Catholic social work, 53–9; academic programs in Quebec, 53; and de-emphasis on institutionalization, 64–5; non-sectarian recognition of, 56–7; as practised in U.S., 54; recognition of, in non-sectarian circles, 56–7; schools of, in Canada, 157–8n55; and training of Catholic aid workers, 9–10, 38, 45, 53, 54–5

Catholic Welfare Bureau, 7, 13, 40, 64, 69, 123, 134, 135; appeals for help to Department of Public Welfare during Depression, 77; as casework agency, 43, 57; casework assessments conducted during Depression, 67, 70; Child Caring Division, 59, 60, 65; directors of, as educated in U.S., 54–5; on family and social problems, 60; Family Welfare Division, 59, 60; formation of, as response to archdiocesan survey, 58–9; lobbies for legitimization of casework, 70; Michael Jo McGrath (superintendent), anti-communist activities of, 95–6; partnership with city of Toronto during Depression, 66–7; regulation and casework assessment of "social problem" families, 78–80, 140–1; transfer of families to Social Welfare Division during Depression, 72, 77, 94–5. *See also* McGrath, Rev. Michael Jo

Catholic Women's League, 12, 100

Catholic Women's League Hostel, 74–5

CCF (Co-operative Commonwealth Federation), 92; allegations of communist infiltration into, 92–3; confusion over Catholic Church position on, 92–3; defence of, by Henry Somerville and Murray Ballantyne, 93; modification of platform by, 93, 169–70n53

Central Bureau for Unemployment Relief (Toronto), 73–5

centralized self-management by charities, 39–41; Catholic Charities, 40–1; Neighbourhood Workers Association (Protestant), 40; parallel developments in the U.S., 41

Charbonnel, Armand-François-Marie de (bishop of Toronto, 1850–60), 18, 20–3; banking and accounting initiatives of, 24; establishes Catholic charity infrastructure, 21–2; lobbies government for financial support, 25; and separate schools debate, 20–1; steps down as bishop of Toronto, 23; ultramontane principles of, 20–1

charities, Canadian: bureaucratization of, 30–2, 36–44; Catholic-Protestant rivalries, as affecting government grants, 25; centralized fundraising by, in Toronto charities, 41–4; centralized self-management by, 39–41; government regulation and funding of, 5–7, 30–1; partnerships with governments, 4, 12, 66, 71–2; religious charities, as used to convert aid recipients, 19; scientific management of, 31, 36–8. *See also* government and charities, link between; government regulation of charities

charities, Catholic, 12, 145n19; government grants to, 25, 136, 137. *See also* Toronto, Catholic charities in

charities, Protestant: attempts to convert aid recipients, 19; formation of Neighbourhood Workers Association, 40; later cooperation with Catholic Church on social reform, 26–7, 50; membership in Federation for Community Services, 41; outdoor relief programs, as favoured by government funding, 35–6; philanthropy of, as contrasted with Catholic charity, 27–9, 54; used by unemployed Catholic men during Depression, 74

charity, Catholic concept of, as contrasted with Protestant philanthropy, 27–9, 54

Charity Aid Act (1874), 31, 34–6; opposed by Orange Order, 35

children: "boyology" courses, 56, 120; Child Savers Movement, as pioneering probation of, 103, 118–19; communist work among, 87–8, 89; girls in industrial schools, taught only traditional women's skills, 111–12; illegitimacy and institutionalization of, impact of social work on, 64–5; illiteracy of, as considered mental deficiency, 115; legislation regulating, 116, 118–19; medical and psychiatric examination of, in industrial schools, 114–15; "normalization" of, through casework assessment, 113–15; taught moral value of good habits, 121–3. *See also* Catholic Big Brothers and Catholic Big Sisters; children's aid societies; families; industrial schools; orphanages; young offenders

children's aid societies, 7; Catholic Children's Aid Society, 7, 55, 113, 120, 127; formation of, 119; responsibility of, for children on parole and probation, 116–17, 118–20; St Vincent de Paul Children's Aid Society, 59, 116, 119, 120, 133

Children's Aid Society (non-denominational), 7, 119, 120

Child Savers Movement, 103, 118–19

Chrétien, Jean, 3–4

Christian Brothers, 22, 105, 108

Civic Unemployment Relief Committee (Toronto), 72, 73, 74, 75

Coady, Moses, 51, 52

Cold War, 98–9; anti-communist activities by Catholic Church during, 97–102; Catholic anti-communism, as benefiting national security strategy, 98; as mixed social economy, 98

communism: activities against, by Catholic Church, 82–3, 85, 86–90, 111; activities against, by Catholic Welfare Bureau, 95–6; activities against, by Toronto Red Squad, 82, 86–8; Cold War–era activities against, by Catholic Church, 97–102; as denounced by papal encyclicals, 92–3, 168n37, 169n47; Depression-era campaign against, by Catholic Church, 90–4; fear of infiltration by, among central and eastern European immigrants, 85; labour schools in Toronto, as way of combating, 101–2; political organization of, in Canada, 85–6, 165n4; rumours of infiltration by, into Archdiocese of Toronto, 99–100; scope of activities in Toronto, as reported by Catherine de Hueck, 89; surveillance of, on university campuses, 100; use of social mapping to track, 89–90; viewed

with hope by advocates of social reform, 86; vulnerability of specific immigrant groups to, 87–8; work with youth and children, 87–8, 89
Communist Party of Canada, 85–6, 165n4; as targeting Catholic relief recipients, 95–6; *The Worker* (newspaper), 88, 91
Co-operative Commonwealth Federation. *See* CCF

Daily Bread Food Bank, 128
de Hueck, Catherine, 52; as administrator of Friendship House, 96–7; commissioned to investigate communist activities in Toronto, 88–9, 97; controversies surrounding, 96–7; as favouring work projects over direct social relief, 92; founds Madonna House apostolate, 97; speaking engagements, 91–2
Department of Public Welfare (Toronto), 75–6, 94; Charlotte Whitton, as opponent of, 76; families on relief as either "unemployed" or "social problem" cases, 78–81; funding application procedure, as problematic, 76–7; increased home investigations by, 77; Social Welfare Division, 69–70, 72; sweeping controls over relief, as exercised by, 77–8; transfer of families to, from Catholic Welfare Bureau, 72, 77, 94–5; voucher system established for outdoor relief, 77
Draper, Brig.-Gen. Denis C. (head of Toronto Red Squad), 86–7
Drew, George, 98–9, 171n79

Emigrant Temporary Asylum, 6, 16
encyclicals, papal, 92–3, 101, 168n37, 169n47; confusion over Catholic Church interpretation of, 92–3; *Quadragesimo anno* (1931), 49, 92, 168n37; *Rerum novarum* (1891), 26–7, 49, 92, 168n37

families: birth control and sterilization, as advocated for relief recipients, 80; casework assessment of young offenders, as method of investigating problems in, 112, 113–14; as either "unemployed" or "social problem" cases, 78–81; as focus of welfare practices, 60–1, 65; illegitimacy and institutionalization of children, impact of social work on, 64–5; parole and probation systems, as exerting control over, 117, 118; regulation and casework assessment of "social problem" families, 78–80, 140–1; as relief applicants, 75; removal of children from, to industrial schools, 106–7, 109–10, 117; social casework, as method of investigating problems in, 61–3, 65, 75; as source of and solution to social problems, 60–1, 118, 120
fascism: failure of Archdiocese of Toronto to condemn, 93–4; support for, in Toronto, 86, 94
Federation for Community Services, 31, 41–4; expulsion of Catholic charities from, 43; as predecessor of United Way, 41. *See also* United Welfare Fund
Federation of Catholic Charities, 31–2, 45, 55; formation of, 43; government funding for family casework, 75
Foucault, Michel, theories of: discipline, 102, 105, 106, 112; governance, 8, 9, 11, 44, 144n14; inspectors as panopticon, 32; security and welfarism, 59
French Catholics: "anti-popish" sentiments towards, 20, 22–3; "Canadian" identity as distancing English Catholics from, 26; Irish Catholic hostility towards, 23
Freudian psychology: Catholic Church attitudes towards, 53; as influence on casework, 71
Friendship House, 13, 52, 135; as administered by Catherine de Hueck, 96–7; founded to counteract communism, 96; services offered by, 96. *See also* de Hueck, Catherine
Fullerton, Rev. John G., 55
fundraising, for Catholic charities, 23–5; banking and accounting initiatives, 24; centralized management, as ensuring accountability, 41; Charity Aid Act (1874), as benefit to, 31, 34–6; and government grants, 25, 136, 137

Furfey, Paul Hanley: on hereditary nature of anti-social behaviour, 61

Gallagher, Rev. F. Hugh, 55, 57
Gauthier, Georges (archbishop of Montreal, 1923–40): and anti-CCF pastoral letter, 93
Good Shepherd Female Refuge for Fallen Women, 105, 133
"governance": concept of, 8, 11; techniques of, 8–9, 11
government and charities, link between, 3–4; historical studies of, 10; as mutually beneficial, 12; partnerships, as formed during Depression, 66, 71–2
government regulation of charities, 5–7, 30–1; bureaucratization techniques, 30–2, 36–8; collection of statistical data, 33, 34, 35, 71; inspections, 32–3; numerical computations, 33; scientific management, 36–8; Social Service Commission, as extending, 39

Haley, Rev. Joseph, 55, 56–7, 62
Harris, Mike, 3; government of, cuts social programs, 128, 143n4; workfare program introduced by, 4, 129, 143n4
Hepburn, Mitchell: elected on platform of unemployment relief, 78, 163n45
homeless, in Toronto: early treatment of, 16; Out of the Cold program, 4, 128; St Vincent de Paul Hostel, 74, 135
House of Industry (Protestant), 6, 16, 19, 39, 42, 94; casework assessments, as used to determine eligibility of applicants, 70; government grants to, 34–5, 136; increase in applicants to, during Depression, 69; labour test for aid recipients, 27; outdoor relief programs, as funded by government, 36, 69; transferral of outdoor relief to Department of Public Welfare, 77
House of Industry Act (1837), 17
House of Providence, 22, 42, 69, 96, 133, 152n28; as beneficiary of Charity Aid Act (1874), 34–5; bombing attempt on, 23; government grants to, 25, 136, 151n12; outdoor relief programs not funded by government, 36

immigrants, Catholic: fear of communist infiltration among, 85; post-war influx of, 127; from specific regions, as vulnerable to communist organization, 87–8
industrial schools, 103–4, 105–8, 173n4, 175n21; activities and curriculum of, 110–12; as administered by charitable organizations, 107; ages of children in, 110; as distinguished from reformatories, 105–6, 174n7; as educational rather than penal in nature, 107, 108, 110, 124; as emphasizing moral discipline over corporal punishment, 105–6; explanations for rise of, 107–8; increased regulatory powers of, as enabled by legislation, 107; medical and psychiatric examinations of children by, 114–15; percentage of Catholic children in, 109; placement of working-class children in, 106–7, 109, 117; Protestant-run, industrial schools, objections by Archdiocese of Toronto to, 108; release of children from, on parole, 116–17; reasons for placement of children in, 109–10; social casework, as used in, 112–16; standardized reports, as used by, 113–14
Industrial Schools Advisory Board, 116–17
Inspector of Asylums, Prisons and Public Charities, Office of (Ontario), 31, 33, 34, 151n7
Irish Catholics, in Toronto, 15, 17, 19; adoption of "Canadian" identity by, 26; anti-French sentiment among, 23; attempts by Protestant charities to convert, 19; dominance of, under Bishop Lynch, 23; as fleeing Irish potato famine, 15, 18; increasing social mobility of, 26; in religious orders, as empathetic to aid recipients, 28

juvenile delinquents. *See* young offenders

Kelso, J.J., 118, 119; on need to rehabilitate families, 121

Kingston Penitentiary, 104
Kirkconnell, Watson, 97, 101
Knights of Columbus: "boyology" courses sponsored by, 56, 120; recreational camps, 123

labour schools: as established by Archdiocese of Toronto, 101–2
Lamb, Marjorie (director of Toronto Alert Service), 100
Langmuir, John Woodburn (inspector), 33; reform of government funding criteria by, 34, 35
Laver, Albert W. (commissioner of public welfare), 76–8; as advocate of birth control and sterilization for families on relief, 80. *See also* Department of Public Welfare (Toronto)
lay communities, in Toronto, 22, 24, 133–5; as examples of Catholic concept of charity, 28–9; participation in social work, 56; reduced autonomy of, as caused by centralized management, 40. *See also* religious orders, in Toronto; *see also names of individual religious orders and lay communities*
Lynch, John Joseph (bishop of Toronto, 1860–88), 23, 26

MacDonnell, Rev. Angus (Catholic prison chaplain), 104, 105
McGoey, Rev. Francis, 52–3
McGrath, Rev. Michael Jo (superintendent of Catholic Welfare Bureau), 95–6 ; advocates work projects for unemployed to combat communism, 95; anti-communist intelligence gathered by, 95
McGuigan, James (archbishop of Toronto, 1934–71), 57, 85, 101; appointed cardinal, 166n14; association with Toronto Alert Service, 100; failure to condemn fascism, 94; promotes anti-communist surveillance on university campuses, 100; reproached by communist newspaper, 98; on Vatican fear of communism, 82

McGuire, Rev. Charles E. (administrator of Toronto labour schools), 101–2
McNeil, Neil (archbishop of Toronto, 1912–34), 43, 74, 76, 93; as advocate of social work practices, 45; anti-communist activities under, 85, 87, 88–90; anti-communist campaign launched by, 90–1; commissions Catherine de Hueck to investigate communist activities, 88–9; commissions social welfare survey, 57–8; contributes to anti-communist brochure, 90–1; and restructuring of Catholic charities, 57–9
Madonna House, 97; and food bank initiative, 128. *See also* de Hueck, Catherine
Marshall, Douglas (police inspector for Toronto Red Squad), 87–8
"mixed social economy," concept of, 9, 10–11; as applied to policing and surveillance activities, 83; parole system for young offenders, as example of, 116
Moran, Sister Susan, 4, 128
Mount St Francis Colony, 52, 135
Mulroney, Brian, 3, 128
Municipal Institutions Act (1866), 17
municipalities, Ontario: partnerships with charities during Depression, 66; subsidization of homeless shelters by, 4; use of property taxes to support social programs, 17, 128, 143n4
Mussolini, Benito, 86, 94

National Conference of Catholic Charities (U.S. organization), 54, 57
National Conference of Social Work (U.S. secular organization), 54
Neighbourhood Workers Association (Protestant centralized management organization), 40, 69, 70, 72, 158n29; appeals for help to Department of Public Welfare during Depression, 77; lobbies for legitimization of casework, 70; membership in Federation for Community Services, 41; partnership with city of Toronto during Depression, 66

newspapers, Catholic: *Beacon* (Montreal), 93; *Catholic Worker*, 91; *Social Forum*, 91. See also *Catholic Register*

Ontario, 17–18; anti-communist concerns of George Drew, 98–9, 171n79; government intervention in charitable relief, 6–7, 17–18, 30; Mike Harris government cuts to social programs, 3, 128, 143n4; Mitchell Hepburn elected premier, 78, 163n45; rise of private health care agencies, 11. *See also* municipalities, Ontario

Orange Order, 18, 20; dominance of, as adversely affecting Toronto Catholics, 68; hostility towards Catholic charities and religious orders, 22–3; opposition to Charity Aid Act, (1874), 35

orphanages: Charity Aid Act (1874), as benefiting Catholic orphanages, 34–5; foster care as alternative to, 39, 64; government grants to, 137; impact of social work on placements in, 64–5; Protestant Orphans Home and Female Aid Society, government grants to, 34–5, 137; transferral of older children from, to industrial schools, 110

Out of the Cold program, 4, 128

papal encyclicals, 92–3, 101, 168n37, 169n47; confusion over Catholic Church interpretation of, 92–3; *Quadragesimo anno* (1931), 49, 92, 168n37; *Rerum novarum* (1891), 26–7, 49, 92, 168n37

philanthropy, Protestant concept of, as contrasted with Catholic charity, 27–9, 54

Pius XI: call for social reform by, 49–50

policing. *See* private policing and surveillance

poverty, in Toronto, 16, 19; bureaucratization of, by classification of poor, 79–81; during Depression, 66, 68–9, 74; during 1920s, 57; as social rather than economic problem, 80–1

Power, Michael (bishop of Toronto, 1842–47), 18, 24; arrival of, as impetus to growth of Catholic charities, 18–19; collaboration with public school system, 21

Principles of Scientific Management, The (Taylor), 37

prison chaplains: Catholic clergymen as, 104; as established by legislation, 104; as instrumental in separating young offenders from adults, 104–5

private policing and surveillance: of Catholics, by Archdiocese of Toronto, 82–3, 86–90; definitions of, 83, 165n7; and Foucault's theory of discipline, 102; by philanthropic institutions, 83–4

Protestant charities: attempts to convert aid recipients, 19; formation of Neighbourhood Workers Association, 40; later cooperation with Catholic Church on social reform, 26–7, 50; membership in Federation for Community Services, 41; outdoor relief programs, as favoured by government funding, 35–6; philanthropy of, as contrasted with Catholic charity, 27–9, 54; used by unemployed Catholic men during Depression, 74

Protestant churches: anti-French sentiments, 20, 23; clergymen, as prison chaplains, 104; industrial schools established by, 108; and Orange Order in Toronto, 18, 20, 22–3, 68; reaction to ultramontanism, 20; significant role of, in social services, 47–8; and social gospel, 46, 49; tensions with Catholics, 19–20, 22–3

Protestant Orphans Home and Female Aid Society: government grants to, 34–5, 137

Public Welfare, Department of. *See* Department of Public Welfare (Toronto)

Quadragesimo anno (papal encyclical of Pius XI, 1931), 49–50, 92, 101; confusion over Catholic Church interpretation of, 92–3; as denouncing communism, 168n37; as supporting right to private property, 169n47

Red Squad. *See* Toronto Red Squad
reformatories, 105–6, 174n7; opposition to, by Child Savers Movement, 118. *See also* industrial schools; young offenders
religious orders, in Toronto, 22, 49, 133–5; French origin of, as causing hostility among Irish Catholic hostility, 23; members of, as university-educated, 54–5, 56; as playing leading role in welfare work, 55–6; reduced autonomy of, as caused by centralized management, 40; voluntary service of, as financial advantage for charities, 22, 24–5, 130. *See also* lay communities, in Toronto; *see also names of individual orders and lay communities*
Rerum novarum (papal encyclical of Leo XIII, 1891), 26–7, 92, 101; Catholic social action, as response to, 49; as denouncing communism, 168n37; as supporting right to private property, 169n47
Richmond, Mary E., 62–3, 71
Roman Catholic Archdiocese of Toronto. *See* Archdiocese of Toronto
Roman Catholic Orphanage Asylum, 42, 133; as beneficiary of Charity Aid Act (1874), 34–5; government grants to, 25, 151n12, 137; Protestant raids on, 23
Royal Canadian Mounted Police (RCMP), 82, 94, 100; Catholic Church defence of, 167n24; surveillance of communist activity by, 87
Ryerson, Egerton, 20–1

St Francis Catholic Friendship House, 13, 52, 135; as administered by Catherine de Hueck, 96-7; founded to counteract communism, 96; services offered by, 96. *See also* de Hueck, Catherine
St John's Industrial School, 22, 103–4, 105, 108, 109, 134; activities and curriculum of, 110–11; importance of recreational pastimes, 111; "opportunity classes," as offering remedial instruction, 110–11, 115; religious education in, 111

St Laurent, Louis: as exploiting Catholic anti-communism, 98
St Mary's Industrial School, 104, 105, 108, 109, 134; activities and curriculum of, as limited to traditional women's skills, 111–12
St Michael's College (University of Toronto): social activism at, 51–2, 91; St Michael's Social Guild, 51–2
St Vincent de Paul Children's Aid Society, 59, 116, 119, 120, 133–4
St Vincent de Paul Hostel, 74, 135
St Vincent de Paul Society, 12, 22, 43, 69, 133; as example of Catholic concept of charity, 28–9; and women's confraternities, 22, 133–5
scientific management, concept of, 37; as applied to charities, 31, 36–8; centralized self-management by charities, 39–41; as origin of professional social work, 47; origins of, in Victorian England, 37; Social Service Commission, as model of, 38–9; as way of monitoring aid recipients, 38
scientific theories: Catholic Church attitudes towards, 53
secularization thesis, challenge of, 47–9
self-management by charities, 39–41; Catholic Charities, 40–1; Neighbourhood Workers Association (Protestant), 40; parallel developments in the U.S., 41
separate schools, funding for, 20–1; as leading to Catholic charity infrastructure, 21–2
ShareLife (Catholic fundraising organization), 44
Sisters of St Joseph, 22, 23; increasing Irish component of, 23; as subsisting solely on charity, 149n34; as targeted by Social Service Commission, 39
Sisters of Service, 74–5
Sisters of the Good Shepherd, 105, 108
"social, the," concept of, 16–17, 59
social casework, 9, 61–3; as conducted during Depression, 66–8, 69–71, 78–80, 140–1; differential and diagnostic models of, 63, 71, 162n20; as enabling collec-

tion of data on aid recipients, 71; as enabling multi-tiered welfare system, 67–8; legitimization of, as public policy, 69–71; Mary E. Richmond, as pioneer of field, 62–3, 71; methods of, as adapted to Catholic Church teachings, 63; "normalization" of children through, 113–15; questioned in academic circles, 71; as used in industrial schools, 112–16. *See also* Catholic Welfare Bureau

social Darwinism, 47, 53; as part of Protestant philanthropy, 27

social gospel (Protestant), 46, 49. *See also* Catholic social action; Catholic social work; social reform; social work

social mapping: as used to track communist activities in Toronto, 89–90

"social problem" cases, classification and stigmatization of relief recipients as, 78–81

social problems: categorization of, 9; family, as source of and solution to, 60–1, 118; as mutual concern of church and state, 11, 49; social governance, as way of dealing with, 16–17; study of, through social work, 47–8; substance addiction, resources to combat, 127; unemployment, as economic rather than moral problem, 72, 80–1; unemployment in Toronto, as managed during Depression, 71–5; welfarism, as response to, 7–8, 59–61. *See also* homeless, in Toronto; poverty, in Toronto; unemployment relief, in Toronto during Depression

social programs: as advocated by Catholic social action, 49–53; as linked to national growth, 7–8; recent government cuts to, 3–5, 13–14, 127–9, 143n4

social reform: as advocated by Catholic social action, 49–53; and Catholic approach to charity, 27–9; cooperation of Catholic and Protestant groups on, 26–7, 50; Henry Somerville, as champion of, 50–1, 156n33; importance of *Rerum novarum* (papal encyclical), 26–7; in the U.S., 50; workers' rights, advocacy of, 26–7, 50

social sciences, rise of, 7, 9; adaptation of churches to, 9–10, 45, 53

Social Service Commission: management of charities by, 31, 38–9

social services, professionalization of, 9, 46; origins of, in scientific management theory, 47

Social Welfare Division, Department of Public Health (Toronto), 69, 72, 94; study of poverty, as legitimizing casework, 69–70

social welfare system: casework, as enabling multi-tiered system, 67–8; development of, in Canada, 16–18; as favouring men over women, 75; postwar expansion of, 127–9

social work: Catholic schools of, in Canada, 157–8n55; as distinguished from voluntary religious charity work, 45–6; as mechanism for governing social programs, 9, 59; professionalization of, 9, 46; rise of, as element of welfarism, 59–60; secularization theory of, as flawed, 47–9; training of Catholic aid workers in, 9–10, 38, 45, 53, 54–5; as way of monitoring aid recipients, 46–7. *See also* Catholic social work

Somerville, Henry (editor of *Catholic Register*): anti-communist editorials, 91; defence of CCF, 93; weekly social action columns, 50–1, 156n33

Superintendent of Neglected and Dependent Children, Office of (Ontario), 33, 119

Taylor, Frederick W., *The Principles of Scientific Management*, 37

Toronto: anti-communist activities by police, 82, 86–8; cholera epidemics in, 16; direct involvement in public relief by, during Depression, 69–71; fiscal crisis in, as leading to scientific management of charities, 36; formation of Department of Public Welfare, 75–7; homeless shelters in, 4, 74; social reform movements in, 16. *See also* poverty, in Toronto; unemployment relief, in Toronto during Depression

Toronto, Catholic charities in: arrival of Bishop Power as impetus to growth, 18–19; Charity Aid Act (1874), as benefit to, 31, 34–6; cooperation with Protestant social agencies, 15–16; and Federation for Community Services, 41–4; formation of Catholic Charities organization, 40–1; formation of Federation of Catholic Charities, 43; formation of ShareLife organization, 44; fundraising for, 23–5; government grants to, 25, 136, 137; and Irish hostility to French clerics and religious orders, 23; list of (1849–1930s), 133–5; as lobbying for legitimization of casework, 70; as modelled on French charities, 22; post-war expansion of services, 4, 127–8; and recent cuts to government funding, 128–9; restructuring of, 57–9; rise of infrastructure, 15, 18–25; transfer of families to Social Welfare Division during Depression, 72, 77, 94–5; and United Welfare Fund, 43–4; use of social work practices, 9–10, 38, 45–7. *See also* Catholic Welfare Bureau; lay communities, in Toronto; religious orders, in Toronto

Toronto, Catholic population of, 18, 19, 131–2, 161n8; discriminatory employment practices against, 68, 69, 85; fear of communist infiltration among European immigrants, 85; as hard hit by Depression, 68–9; as increased by post-war immigration, 127; support for fascism in, 86, 94

Toronto Alert Service (secular anti-communist organization), 97, 100

Toronto Red Squad (anti-communist branch of police department), 82, 86–8, 102; intelligence gathered by, 87–8; successor organization maintained by Ontario government, 171n79

trade unions. *See* unions

ultramontanism, 20–1, 148n20

unemployment, as economic rather than moral problem, 72, 80–1; recognition of, as leading to Canadian unemployment insurance legislation, 81

unemployment relief, in Toronto during Depression, 71–5; "back-to-the-land" projects, 52–3; Catholics, as seeking relief from Protestant agencies, 74; Catholic Welfare Bureau work with single unemployed men, 73, 138; Central Bureau for Unemployment Relief, 73–5; Civic Unemployment Relief Committee, 72, 73, 74; eligibility requirements for aid applicants, 73; government attitudes towards single unemployed, 72, 73; lack of services for single women, 74; monitoring of unemployed, 73–4; used to suppress political dissent, 73

unions: Catholic union movement in Quebec, 101; labour schools, as alternative, 101–2; Vatican view of, 101

United Way, 41; Federation for Community Services and other predecessor organizations, 41–4

United Welfare Fund, 43–4 ; membership of Catholic charities in, 43–4; successor organizations, 44

University of Toronto: Department of Social Service, 46, 55, 57, 71; Newman Club, as financed by archdiocese to combat communism, 100; St Michael's College, social activism at, 51–2, 91; School of Social Work, 46, 47

Valverde, Mariana, 10–11, 83, 121
Vatican: anti-communism of, 82, 90, 168n37; dealings with Mussolini government, 86, 94, 170n57; and unions, 101. *See also* papal encyclicals
voluntarism, 3–4

welfarism, 59–65; casework, as enabling multi-tiered welfare system, 67–8; family, as principal target of, 60–1; as favouring men over women, 75; as response to social problems, 7–8, 59–61; rise of social work, as element of, 59–60

Whitton, Charlotte, 47, 57; leads opposition to Department of Public Welfare, 76

women, as aid recipients: care of, at Catholic Women's League Hostel, 74–5; as constituting high percentage of "special problem" cases, 79; lack of services for unemployed, 74; as largely ignored by government, 75; mothers of young offenders, investigation of, 114; as placed in domestic service by YWCA, 74; unmarried mothers, care of, 64–5

women, involvement of, in Catholic charities, 22, 24, 56, 133–5; as affected by centralized management, 40; as relegated to casework rather than administration, 55–6

Woodsworth, J.S., 37

workers' rights: as advocated by Catholic Church, 26–7, 50; as championed by Henry Somerville, 50–1

workfare (Ontario government program), 4, 129, 143n4

young offenders, 103–24; industrial schools for, 103–4, 105–12; legislation regulating, 119; medical and psychiatric examination of, 114–15; "normalization" of, through casework assessment, 113–15; and parole system, 116–17; and probation system, 118–23; separated from adult prisoners, 104–5, 174n7; social casework, as method of investigating behavioral problems, 112–16; standardized reports, as used to monitor, 113–14